Mahaffy
A biography of an Anglo-Irishman

The portrait of Mahaffy by Sir William Orpen
(reproduced by permission of the trustees of the
Municipal Gallery Dublin)

Mahaffy
A biography of
an Anglo-Irishman

W. B. Stanford &
R. B. McDowell

London
Routledge & Kegan Paul

First published in 1971
by Routledge & Kegan Paul Ltd
Broadway House, 68–74 Carter Lane,
London E.C.4.
Printed in Great Britain by The Camelot Press Ltd,
London and Southampton
© W. B. Stanford and R. B. McDowell 1971
No part of this book may be reproduced
in any form without permission from the
publisher except for the quotation of brief passages
in criticism
ISBN 0 7100 6880 8

Contents

List of illustrations

Preface

We are indebted to Mr Rupert Mahaffy for placing at our disposal all of his grandfather's papers in his possession. We are also most grateful to Sir Shane Leslie for generously letting us have a considerable quantity of material relating to Mahaffy, including his own reminiscences and typescript copies of letters no longer available. Our colleagues R. B. D. French and D. A. Webb have read our work and made many helpful and critical suggestions. Mrs W. B. Stanford has assisted us in reading the proofs. We are grateful to the staffs of the libraries in which we have worked for their ready co-operation and to the following for assistance and information: E. J. F. Arnould, John Bithrey, Mrs A. F. Brett, H. M. T. Cobbe, R. Ellmann, T. M. Farmiloe, C. Franklin, Mrs Synolda French, G. E. Gill, G. H. P. Hewson, V. Holland, R. T. Hunter, Mrs Ruth Jameson, Miss Bay Jellett, D. Jenkins, J. Johnston, T. J. Johnston, J. Kerr, A. A. Luce, J. V. Luce, Mrs Amy McKay, Sir Henry Mack, Mrs Elizabeth Martin, Mrs Michael O'Regan, H. W. Parke, A. C. C. Peebles, Miss Olive Purser, J. Quin, L. J. D. Richardson, M. Russell, J. H. Shaw, W. F. Starkie, J. H. A. Sparrow, W. A. C. Stanford, Brigadier W. N. Stokes, Mrs Margot Vernon, G. and Mrs Waterhouse, J. H. Grove White, T. de V. White, M. Wilkins, T. C. Wilson, D. E. W. Wormell and also B. P. Boydell, E. J. Furlong and F. La T. Godfrey. Some others are thanked in the footnotes.

Unless otherwise stated, autobiographical material is drawn from the 'Brief summary of the principal stages of my life' which Mahaffy wrote shortly before his death. A list of the abbreviations used in the references is given on page xiv.

Introduction

The story of John Pentland Mahaffy's life moves through contrasting regions of the nineteenth-century world – Bavaria under that romantic classicist Ludwig I, the bleak countryside of famine-stricken Monaghan, the cosy domesticity of a protestant clerical family, Greece while still a land of brigands and bedbugs, Dublin in peacetime and in war, Irish country houses before the decline and fall of the Irish landed gentry, drowsy board-rooms, vituperative conference halls, and the courts of Europe during the last decades of their regal and imperial splendour. Historian and philosopher, man of letters and musician, conversationalist and controversialist, sportsman, publicist, diner-out and don – even among so versatile a race as the Irish and in an epoch so favourable as the Victorian, Mahaffy was outstanding. He was much admired and much disliked. Descriptions by friends and enemies range from near idolatry to sheer venom. 'The last of the Olympians', they called him, 'an out-and-out snob', 'a singularly lovable and sympathetic person', 'an arrant humbug', 'an unclerical cleric', 'the man who missed the tide', 'a grandee', 'a born comedian', 'the old sybarite', 'a great Irish character', 'perverse and fascinating, warm-hearted and repellent, learned and careless in turn'.

These widely divergent opinions can partly be explained by conflicting elements in his character and career. Primarily a scholar, he published so rapidly and profusely that for many years he incurred scathing criticism for lapses in accuracy and judgement; but in the end he won international acclaim. Living and working almost entirely in Ireland, and recognizably an

Irishman as soon as he opened his mouth, he was execrated by many of his countrymen as an enemy of the Irish nation. The most celebrated don of Trinity College, Dublin, at a time when it was at the height of its wealth and fame, he was by no means a popular member of that conservative community, and he suffered his severest disappointment when he lost the provostship in competition with a much less eminent rival. Though by ordination a Christian clergyman, and by nature a kindly man (except towards his rivals and critics), he acquired a reputation for scepticism and arrogance. When he intervened in matters of high policy – and he was sometimes prophetically in the right – his candour and freedom of speech frustrated his proposals for innovation and reform. In fact long before his death Mahaffy had become a legendary figure, the subject of many anecdotes, believable and unbelievable. The purpose of the present biography is to explore this contradictory and often extravagant legend.

It is strange that a full account of Mahaffy's life and work has not already appeared, considering how often he is mentioned in other people's memoirs. But autobiography seems to suit the Irish temperament better than biography. Perhaps, too, the wide range of Mahaffy's interests may have deterred any single biographer.

Mahaffy himself refused to publish any memoirs. For this uncharacteristic display of reticence he gave a characteristically blunt reason. Approached by a publisher, he replied: 'I write no memoirs. I'm a gentleman. I cannot bring myself to write nastily about persons whose hospitality I have enjoyed.' When the publisher suggested that this would not preclude him from writing nice things about them, Mahaffy answered, 'I'm not a liar.'

In the last few months of his life he did, however, write a short matter-of-fact account of his life, which fills sixty pages of a quarto-sized notebook. He begins: 'This brief summary of my life is intended for my children and grand-children – but there is no secrecy about it. No one will think it worth publishing. My record is my work and my public acts.' He ends – and here his writing, up to this point remarkably clear for a man of eighty, becomes thinner and frailer – with the words, 'I sign this bald and jejune document this 26 February 1919, on which I enter my

81st year. It is a day I hate for on this day 11 years ago I lost my beloved wife.' Behind his stern attempt at objectivity and his efforts – not always successful – to avoid such references to personal acquaintances as 'would represent human nature in so unpleasant a light . . . that to put them on record would be a lasting act of unkindness', his 'brief summary' is a very revealing document, and we have drawn freely on it. Besides this, we have been able to use a number of Mahaffy's letters, as well as the many autobiographical passages in his academic works. Memoirs by his contemporaries have provided a large quantity of scattered anecdotes and *aperçus*, and information has been generously supplied by several who knew Mahaffy personally.

A warning should perhaps be added to those diminishing few who were brought up on the golden legend of Mahaffy as a man of effortless brilliance and success (except when envious inferiors conspired to deprive him of his rights). As the present writers have come to see it, that urbanely magnificent figure belonged to Mahaffy's later years when he was provost of Trinity, the friend of kings, the patron of gifted youths, and the Alcibiades of Irish politics. Behind it lay many years of bitter rivalries, quarrels and disappointments, and a constant struggle against faults of personal temperament. Those who would prefer to see only the glittering top of Olympus and not the dusty plains and rough foothills on the way to the summit will not find their ideal here. At any rate one can be quite sure that Mahaffy himself would not have commended a biography that showed only the final victory and not the hard-fought battles that won it.

List of abbreviations

Ac.   The Academy
Ath.   The Athenaeum
Cont.R.   The Contemporary Review
CR   The Classical Review
H.   Hermathena (listed by numbers, not vols.)
JHS   Journal of Hellenic Studies
MM   Macmillan's Magazine
NC   Nineteenth Century
Proc. R.I.A.   Proceedings of the Royal Irish Academy
REG   Revue des Études Grecques

chapter one

The early years

Though both his parents were Irish, Mahaffy's earliest memories were of Switzerland and Germany. Vevay, where he was born on 26 February 1839, and later Lucerne, with their vistas of fierce mountains and placid lakes, gave him an affection for dramatic landscapes – he never felt the same about the sea – which prompted many purple patches in his future writings. When he was four his parents moved again, this time to Kissingen, a small town in central Germany, pleasantly placed on a swift-flowing river amongst rolling woodlands. It had recently become celebrated in England as a result of the work of Dr Augustus Bozzi Granville, a well-known medical pioneer and popularizer, and a specialist in 'mineral hydrology'. In his *Spas of Germany*, published in 1837, he highly praised Kissingen, which had had a local reputation since the sixteenth century when a bishop of Würzburg had been persuaded to drink its waters. Ludwig I, the enterprising King of Bavaria, helped to develop the Spa, placing over the baths a 'highly tasteful, light, dégagé pavilion of cast iron bronzed, resembling a gothic arcade' and imposing strict dietary rules on the hotels and lodging houses.[1] Soon visitors were flocking there during the season, when 'the general mingling of crowned heads and other illustrious personages with the ordinary mass of invalids' tended to give the spa 'that tone of high bearing and respect which is not to be met with at all watering places' – and which also, it was hinted, had beneficial effects on the health. A sedate but not uninteresting routine kept the visitors occupied. Early to rise – a brass band

sounded the reveille at six in the morning – and early to bed, was
the rule. At fixed hours visitors took baths or drank the waters.
At set times there was music and promenading in the gardens
and twice a week, dancing. Many of the visitors were English,
and Granville, when he visited Kissingen in 1846, noted that for
some seasons past a Church of England service had been conducted every Sunday 'with exemplary zeal by the Rev. N. B.
Mahaffy from Ireland who has settled permanently with his
family at Kissingen'. It was to be hoped, Granville added, that
'every Christian and wealthy English visitor' would subscribe
generously towards the chaplain's support.[2]

Granville also noticed the number of children to be seen at the
promenade 'decked out in some of those manifold, fantastical yet
becoming *tournures* which distinguish the modern infantile age
from all that went before'. Amongst the children running through
the fashionable crowd John Mahaffy, a healthy, happy boy,
could have been conspicuous. Kissingen, he considered, marked
the first stage in his education. There he effortlessly learned to
speak German. And there he first began to meet people. Two
foreign acquaintances stood out in his memory. The Tsarevitch –
the future Alexander II – wanting to practise his English took
Mahaffy out for a walk. The Tsarevitch was most amiable but
'his rude barbarous suite' treated the boy with contempt.
Mahaffy also met Ludwig, the King of Bavaria, a great patron of
architects and archaeologists, who was often to be seen in
Kissingen, walking fast, talking earnestly and gesticulating
furiously. Ludwig not only chatted to Mahaffy but introduced
him to a fellow countrywoman, the Limerick-born Lola Montez,
the king's notorious mistress, for a while the most powerful
woman in Bavaria. Mahaffy soon discovered that his parents did
not approve of this introduction, but it was a long time before he
realized why.

In the Proustian world of Bad Kissingen, gossipy, hypochon-
driac, and acutely aware of social variations, the Mahaffy home
was a stronghold of evangelical protestantism. The parents
usually spoke English, Nathaniel Mahaffy, proud of his classical
attainments, disdaining to learn German. Mrs Mahaffy, who
seems to have quietly dominated the little household, took her
children carefully through the Bible with the aid of Thomas
Scott's commentary, a formidable work in three large quartos,

containing the old and new testaments in the authorized version surrounded by a complex accumulation of marginalia, cross-references, footnotes and practical observations reflecting evangelical scholarship and piety. But if the Mahaffy home was characterized by serious piety, it was not dull. Nathaniel Mahaffy and his wife were both good talkers and enjoyed social life. There was a constant stream of visitors, German, English and Irish, to their house. The Irish visitors whom Mahaffy met included Whiteside, later chief justice of Ireland, and a flamboyant rhetorician, O'Brien, bishop of Ossory, author of a work on justification by faith, for many years an evangelical classic, Lloyd, son of a provost of Trinity, Dublin (who was twenty years later to become provost himself), and Mahaffy's cousin, Nathaniel Hone, then 'quite poor, but presently Hone of Saint Dolough's' (the Hone house on the outskirts of Dublin).

This happy time at Kissingen was ended by a catastrophe. In the autumn of 1845 the potato crop in Ireland was found to be infected; during the next few years crop after crop failed; famine was succeeded by disease and over large stretches of Ireland the agrarian economy almost collapsed. The Mahaffy income, derived from rents of their Monaghan estate, fell disastrously. Then in 1848 revolution swept over central Europe. Mahaffy's acquaintance, the King of Bavaria, regarded in England as 'a doting old man',[3] was forced to abdicate, and there was rioting in many German cities. With the future so menacing, at the end of the autumn the Mahaffys decided to go back to Ireland.

For a small boy the journey was very exciting. As their carriage passed through Frankfurt, where a national assembly, threatened by mobs, was striving to draw up a constitution for Germany, they saw troops patrolling the streets and blood on the pavement. As they passed through hilly country near the Rhine they heard hungry wolves howling. However, they reached the Rhine safely, managed to catch a Rhine steamer, and reached Rotterdam, and after a stormy passage landed at Hull where John saw with astonishment for the first time in his life that symbol of nineteenth-century England – a sirloin of beef. The Mahaffy family crossed England and travelling via Liverpool on the 'Iron Duke' arrived at Kingstown. For the rest of his life John had a vivid picture of his first sight of Ireland – 'of landing on the pier with a coat of snow on the ground and being packed into

a vehicle, which . . . went off sideways – the old Irish covered
car'. After staying some time in Blackrock Mr and Mrs Mahaffy
took their family down to Newbliss, near their estate in County
Monaghan, and started to cope with the problems presented by a
badly managed estate in a famine-stricken country.

There were ancestral reasons for their return to Ireland and
to that bleak out-of-the-way county of Monaghan. The name
Mahaffy is of Scottish Gaelic origin, being an anglicized form of
MacCaffey, meaning 'son of the servant of Saint Cathobad', which
occurs both in Scotland and in Ulster.[4] John Pentland Mahaffy,
the subject of this book, when he came to draw up an account of
his family history did not try to discover its Gaelic ancestry, but
began by stating bluntly 'as to the origin or advent of the first
Mahaffys to south Donegal I have no information. Tradition
asserted the first of the name to have been a Cromwellian trooper
who acquired lands under that occupation. He may just as
well have been a Jacobean settler. But the family has now
no history reaching back beyond about 1750.' Thirty years
later, in 1780, Mahaffy's great-grandfather, Ninian Mahaffy, is
described in the Trinity College Dublin entrance book as 'agri-
cola'. He must have been a fairly substantial farmer, because he
placed two sons in learned professions, the elder, also named
Ninian, in the law and his younger brother Robert, in the church.
Ninian graduated at Trinity, was called to the Irish bar and had
a moderately successful legal career, culminating in his appointment to a commissionership in bankruptcy. Robert's ecclesiastical career was undistinguished. He held curacies in the dioceses
of Ossory and Raphoe and was for a short time beneficed as
perpetual curate of Kilteevogue, a poor Donegal living. Both
brothers were matrimonially fortunate. In 1791 Ninian married
Maria Hone, the daughter of Brindley Hone, a Dublin merchant,
and four years later Ninian's brother Robert married her sister,
Sarah. The Hones, a family which for two centuries played a
notable part in Irish life as bankers and cricketers, were already
well established. Brindley Hone was a very successful merchant,
and his son was to become Lord Mayor of Dublin. Moreover, no
fewer than five or six of the Hone family were to attain varying
degrees of celebrity as artists, and it was probably from the
Hone strain in his ancestry that Mahaffy derived his keen awareness of aesthetic values which was both to help and hinder his

career as a scholar. What is certain is that both sisters were reasonably dowered, Robert Mahaffy obtaining through his wife some land in Donegal.

Robert had several children, including a son, Nathaniel Brindley, who entered Trinity in the year after Waterloo. In 1821 Nathaniel was elected a scholar of the college and in the following year he graduated. He had the reputation all his life as being 'an agreeable and persuasive talker' and one episode in his college career suggests that this reputation was not undeserved. He persuaded Barrett, the erudite and eccentric vice-provost, in whom miserliness attained an heroic level, to lend him money. After graduating, Nathaniel Mahaffy was ordained as a curate in the parish of Monkstown just south of Dublin, a parish which covered 'one of the most luscious and lively portions of the south coast of County Dublin and which contained gay hamlets, clusters of villas and the gardens'.[5] The rector of Monkstown was Charles Lindsay, archdeacon of Kildare (his father was bishop of that diocese) and also rector of Saint Mary's, Dublin. Lindsay might have been a pluralist, but he was energetic and hard working, and at the time Nathaniel Mahaffy arrived a new parish church had just been built for the members of the established church. In Moorish gothic, with turrets and minarets, it was a startling sight, but it could seat twelve hundred people.

In 1827, while working in Monkstown, Nathaniel Mahaffy married Elizabeth Pentland, the only child of John Pentland, a leading Dublin medical man who had been master of the Rotunda, Dublin's great maternity hospital. Like his father, Nathaniel Mahaffy in the worldly sense married well, for his wife was an heiress. Her father was both a successful professional man and a landowner in two counties. His Meath estate entailed on heirs male went to his brother, but Elizabeth Mahaffy inherited a small estate near Newbliss in County Monaghan. She was not only a woman of property; she also possessed charm, accomplishments and goodness. A keen musician, she was a fine pianist and, according to her son, 'so sympathetic and clever as an accompanist, that Tommy Moore, who was often at her father's house and warbled his Irish melodies with very little voice and no knowledge of time, would not sing them at all or with any other pianist, if my mother was present'. Mahaffy was to inherit his mother's love of music (his colleague Salmon sardonically remarked that Mahaffy would have done nothing but sing if he had had a better voice).[6] But what was much more significant was that Mrs Mahaffy was a fervent evangelical who shortly before her marriage had undergone that religious experience which formed the watershed in so many lives. Evangelicals profoundly believed that the individual should have a deep, intimate relationship with God. They were convinced that in the Bible they had an inexhaustible store of wisdom and precept. And, living under the shadow of eternity, always aware of man's unworthiness, Heaven, Hell and the inevitability of judgement, they had an intense sense of responsibility. Elizabeth Pentland, after her conversion, 'turned her energies, which were very great, to practical piety and to charity'. So it was not surprising that she should meet and marry an able, hardworking young clergyman. What followed, however, was somewhat unusual. The young couple went off on 'a long wedding tour' of the continent which stretched over two and a half years.

When they returned from this prolonged holiday they settled down in an elegant terrace near the sea in Blackrock. By 1834 they had a family of four small children and were taking a very active part in parochial work. Then 'a great disaster befell them'. Virulent scarlatina shattered the family. The three eldest children died in three days; the youngest and his nurse were only saved with the greatest difficulty. Mahaffy and his wife decided to leave Dublin. With their surviving son, Philip, they made back to the continent, first to Vevay on the Lake of Geneva, then further east to Lucerne, and eventually over the frontier of Germany into Kissingen. While they were still at Vevay their two youngest sons were born, Robert in 1837 and John Pentland two years later.

Now in 1848 the family was back again in Ireland. Monaghan is in a double sense a frontier county, lying as it does on the southern fringe of protestant Ulster and placed between the rich lands of the pale and the poorer west of Ireland. It is a county of small lakes and low undistinguished hills, of many badly drained fields and untidy hedges. Newbliss itself was a small Irish town (with a population of over five hundred, by English standards hardly more than a village). It was regarded by contemporaries as a 'neat pleasant place' with its comfortable inn and recently built, much-pinnacled protestant church. The most prominent feature in the little town was the Mahaffy house, a solid Georgian block, flush with the street, facing a small country road which trailed over the hills to Clones, the principal market town of the district.

For the Mahaffy parents it must have been a depressing existence after the lively company and innocent gaiety of Kissingen. Years afterwards Mahaffy explained that 'with the grandees of the county (beyond the Kerrs of Newbliss House) none of whom lived within easy reach of Newbliss, we had no intercourse, but with a large society of local squires and country rectors with incomes of £2,000 a year down to £500 we had constant social intercourse and none at all with any "business people" who were therefore to me strangers'. It should be added at once that the Kerrs, though an old Monaghan family, were scarcely county magnates. They had a relatively modest acreage and their great distinction was that in the middle of the eighteenth century they had introduced the 'seceders' – evangelical presbyterians – into Monaghan. As for the clergy, few incumbents in the diocese of Clogher had incomes of over £500 per annum.

But to schoolboys – or to boys who under usual circumstances would have been schoolboys – Monaghan had much to offer. 'We were,' Mahaffy wrote, 'shown the field sports of the district – excellent trout lakes and rivers, which the pike had not yet destroyed and snipe shooting (along with ducks, woodcocks etc.) in the countless small bogs with which the country is studded between its little hills.' Naturally he became a keen shot and an ardent fisherman. Mahaffy also enjoyed visiting the cottages of his mother's tenancy, a mixture of Catholics and 'sturdy' Protestants. Most of the tenants were Catholics, 'delightful, sympathetic Roman catholic peasants (as yet undefiled by politics)', but others might have commented that it was Mahaffy himself who was still undefiled by politics then. The Protestants, Mahaffy found, were 'the richest . . . most respectable and the least agreeable'. So he learned early to distinguish between social charm and economic vitality. In the cottages the boys met with the same welcome, tea and hot oaten cakes and an invitation 'to make a cayley of it' ('cayley' being Mahaffy's phonetic version of the Irish word for a party). It was a society in which conversation was one of the great sources of entertainment, family history providing a staple of talk, and stories about local heroes, reshaped in repetition, becoming legend. It was also a society in which life was passed in close dependence on the workings and whims of nature; and in which skill in the sports of the field was prized and won respect. Sixty years later Mahaffy remarked that the rural Ireland of his youth was the Ireland of Maria Edgeworth. It also, it might be said, was in many ways reminiscent of Hesiodic Greece.

After coping for a few years with the trials of an Irish landlord the restless Mahaffy parents moved back to Dublin, partly for the sake of their children's education and partly, paradoxically enough, to economize because 'the keeping . . . of open house for tenants and dependants, who were always in the kitchen and about the place' had become too expensive. They settled on the north side of the city, an area summed up as being an 'epitome of all that is hot, arid and empty'. There could be seen 'tall brick houses browbeating each other in gloomy respectability across the white streets, broad pavements promenaded mainly by the nomadic cat, stifling squares where the infant of unfashionable parentage is taken' and grimmest of all 'the unvarying dark of the window panes and the almost forgotten type of ugliness of the window curtains'.[7] The north side was already in decline, and, worse still, the Mahaffys lived on the wrong side of Dorset Street, a street of eighteenth-century houses already invaded by small shopkeepers. In contrast with the taller houses across the way, their house was low and cramped. Long afterwards John Mahaffy wrote 'the observer of today will indeed wonder that such a house could harbour a family of gentry however poor'. One hopes the family were spared the final ignominy of knowing that they appeared in the Dublin Directory under the name Maheefy.

During the years immediately preceding his entrance to the university Mahaffy discovered how limited and exasperating existence could be for a family living on a small unearned income. Mahaffy does not explain why his father, who at the time of his marriage was a keen and able clergyman, ceased to pursue his professional career. Nathaniel seems to have been an easy-going man, not perhaps in the best of health. His wife's income, not large but adequate enough, was available, and probably without making a conscious decision at any point he drifted along without looking for a benefice or taking a curacy. And it is almost certainly safe to say that John Mahaffy, though very fond of his father, at an early age was vividly impressed with the disadvantages of an aimless and underemployed existence.

Mr and Mrs Mahaffy had lost touch with Dublin social life and were not in a position to take energetic steps to revive their contacts with it. A few old friends did entertain them, and Mahaffy remembered gratefully in later life the hospitality of his father's old rector Lindsay, 'a very rich man', of Colonel Pratt who had fought at Corunna, and of the Mahaffy's cousin Nathaniel Hone who had just finished building his suburban seat.

But on the whole the boys lived solitary lives. Their main recreation was going out for long walks into the countryside round Dublin, fishing for trout in the Tolka or the Dodder or shooting woodcock at Leopardstown – with one gun, a muzzleloader, between the three of them. Salmon, a rising younger fellow in Trinity who was a friend of their father, secured permission for the boys to play cricket in the College park. They threw themselves into the game with enthusiasm, and this brought them into touch with their contemporaries. They were asked to come up and play at St Columba's college, a school on English public school lines 'open to the sons of the nobility and gentry generally' which had recently been established on the foothills near Rathfarnham. In fact, as Mahaffy wrote in later years, they were 'thought respectable enough to be received and played against at Saint Columba's'. Mahaffy was duly presented to the warden, Dr Williams, a fellow of King's College, Cambridge. At first Mahaffy felt awed at his 'awful dignity', but he quickly realized that he had often at Kissingen spoken to 'men far grander than he was'. In fact just about the time Mahaffy met him the unfortunate warden was being pressed to resign by the school's great patron, John Beresford, Archbishop of Armagh, who was afraid that Williams' avowed sympathies for the Eastern Orthodox churches might frighten Irish protestants.[8]

It is remarkable that the Mahaffy boys were never sent to school – even after their parents had settled in Dublin. From Kissingen days they were educated at home, Mr Mahaffy, a good classic, teaching them Latin and Greek, tutors being called in from time to time to supplement his work by giving lessons in Euclid, algebra and arithmetic. The problem of education was

simplified for Mr and Mrs Mahaffy by their decision that two of
their sons were not academically gifted. The eldest had a bent
towards farming and had already as a boy showed himself to be
a shrewd judge of cattle, so, after a short unsuccessful period in
Trinity he was apprenticed to a farmer in Sligo. The second, since
he had no special talent, was prepared for emigration by being
taught practical arts such as carpentry and horse-shoeing. It was
the third son, John Pentland, who showed intellectual promise.
The family nicknamed him 'the learned gentleman'. His mother
was soon convinced that he would become a fellow of Trinity.

Nathaniel Mahaffy seems to have been a good teacher. He
laid the foundations for his son's successful undergraduate career
and must be given credit for the fact that when the boy went up
to college he had read much more widely, and had thought much
more profoundly, than the average freshman. His father's system
was effective, if unusual. The Mahaffy boys had no set holiday
periods. They were kept working regularly all the year round
'with a liberal supply of single holidays when a good occasion
for sport or other recreation turned up'. Book learning and field
sports – Nathaniel Mahaffy was a keen fisherman – were interspersed, and Mahaffy unconsciously discovered that for him
learning and life were inseparable. But John Mahaffy was not
subjected to the disciplined drive of a good sixth form master,
nor did he meet his contemporaries in class-room competition.
In later life, indeed, he was to refer contemptuously to 'some of
those . . . competitions in schools, which sap all the vigour and
originality of our children and waste them on the most vain and
useless imitations of learning'. Throughout his life his writings
were to be marked by vigour of expression rather than polish,
and he always lacked those built-in protective devices against
inaccuracy that are so necessary to a scholar.

His unusual education profoundly influenced him in another
way. It is well known that schoolboys can combine a sophisticated
skill in detecting human faults and failings with a head-hunter's
savagery in attacking them. Once they find a weakness in a
contemporary or a master they are capable of exposing and
exploiting it to the full. An intelligent boy soon discovers that a
protective reserve and reticence are requisites for social survival
in life. But John Mahaffy, growing up in an admiring and encouraging small family circle, never learned the dangers inherent

in reckless self-exposure. All his life he was happily candid and outspoken. Moreover, unlike many boys privately educated, he grew up a robust youth abounding in physical energy, leaving his social exuberance unchecked by the timidity and uncertainty which accompany an awareness of physical frailty.

Of course he had his quota of childish illnesses. At Kissingen he fell and broke his arm and as a result was bled – this traditional remedy being still in vogue even at that fashionable spa. Later, shortly after his family returned to Ireland, he was seriously ill, suffering from 'first an inflammation of the lungs and then the liver', and again he was subjected to traditional treatment, being copiously leeched and cupped. The first sign that he had turned the corner was his answer to what he would like to eat. The future bon vivant replied, 'Lobster salad'. Then, according to himself, a two-year diet of that great Victorian specific cod liver oil finally built him up to enter college in good shape.

In one respect John Mahaffy was unusually fortunate. From an early age he had easy access to books and was encouraged to read widely. Soon after his family settled in Dorset Street he secured a ticket of admission to the Royal Dublin Society's library, a good general collection. There he stumbled on Grote's *History of Greece*, of which the first ten volumes had been published in 1852. For a boy studying the classics, reading Grote was an illuminating experience and one which many of his contemporaries enjoying a more orthodox education would be likely to miss. Grote was a master of swift, lucid narrative, and his whole work is pervaded by a living interest in great general themes – the virtues of pan-Hellenism, the development of Greek democracy, and the contrast between Athenian freedom and Spartan organization. One theme, to judge from Mahaffy's early work in Greek history, particularly impressed this young Irishman, the tensions caused in the development of Greek thought by a struggle between 'a firm belief in the reality of the mythical world and an inability to accept its details'.

About the time John Mahaffy was working through Grote, his father gave him a copy of Whately's *Elements of Logic* (a new edition of which had just appeared in a series of cheap reprints, the *Encyclopaedia Metropolitana or a system of universal knowledge*). Whately's slim volume is an excellent exposition of what is often regarded as a dry subject. He appreciates the difficulties of the beginner but encourages him by assuming he is prepared to make an effort to master the technicalities involved. The whole book is inspired by the conviction that logic, 'the science and art of reasoning', is closely related to practical affairs. It is typical of Whately to see the pun as evidently a mock argument founded on a palpable equivocation of the middle term, and to remind his readers that a fallacy, 'which when stated briefly in a few sentences would not deceive a child, may deceive half the world if diluted in a quarto volume'. But though Whately's *Logic* is a first-class text book, lucid and as lively as the subject permits, a boy of fourteen must have found it stiff going. However, Mahaffy got to grips with it and developed a penchant for abstract thought, which he never lost – in old age he could declare that he found the works of Bergson (a far cry from Whately) more fascinating than a novel.

It would almost certainly be a mistake to assume that Whately influenced Mahaffy only through his text book on logic. During Mahaffy's boyhood and youth, Whately, who was the most distinguished Victorian to live for any length of time in Dublin, was both Archbishop of Dublin and a prolific author much in the public eye. A whig and a latitudinarian in a country where whiggery was weak and strong opinions prevalent, he had a powerful intellect and a careless disregard of the conventional. Respectable Dublin was startled to see him smoking a long clay pipe while swinging on the chains in front of his palace on Saint Stephen's Green, or scrambling up a tree while playing with his dogs. He was renowned for his puns, conundrums, hard-hitting retorts and pungent conversation. What he said about the works of Paley might well apply to his own writings. Paley's works were, Whately wrote, 'characterized by a remarkably clear and forcible style, very simple with an air of earnestness, generally devoid of ornament, and often homely but occasionally rising into a manly and powerful eloquence'.[9] And Whately contrasted Paley very favourably with those writers who 'affect a sort of mystical, dim, half intelligible kind of sublimity'. To Lecky, Mahaffy's exact contemporary, Whately's outstanding characteristic was 'the love of truth for its own sake',[10] and though Lecky perceived Whately's limitations, especially his complete inability to comprehend or sympathize with men of a different cast of mind, he emphasized how greatly his intellectual independence and integrity impressed the Trinity undergraduate world of the fifties.[10] In a Dublin which carried the Georgian architectural tradition far into the Victorian age, Whately lived on as a spirited representative of eighteenth-century robust common-sense. His predilection for quick, hard-hitting, if amiable, conversational pugnacity had a lasting effect on Dublin manners. Mahaffy deplored Whately's deliberate ruggedness, but he was undoubtedly influenced by his methods and manner as a teacher and conversationalist.

Whately and Grote influenced Mahaffy from a distance. His parents influenced his intellectual development much more intimately and directly. His father's gifts as a teacher of the classics have already been noticed. His mother's abilities as a teacher are no less striking. By fourteen Mahaffy had been taken through the Bible ('omitting of course a few chapters not fit for family reading') six times, without becoming wearied or losing sympathy for the Christian tradition. And in Dublin the close study of the Bible was supplemented by listening to sermons. Evangelicals in general attached immense importance to the ministry of the word, and Irish evangelicals in particular prided themselves on possessing a number of powerful preachers, including Krause, Mathias' successor at Bethesda Chapel, who had served as an officer at Waterloo, Gregg, downright and energetic, who became bishop of Cork, and Day, later bishop of Cashel. Mahaffy, who shared to the full the Victorian interest in preaching as an art in itself as well as a strengthening experience for the hearer, heard all these men. He also went to hear Maturin of All Saints, Grangegorman, one of the few representatives amongst the Irish clergy of the Oxford movement. A high churchman of the early tractarian school, and a ritualist with solid dislike of popery, he managed to shock extreme protestant opinion by what an admirer called 'the modest ecclesiastical decencies of his church'.[11] And when he was an undergraduate Mahaffy with many of his Trinity contemporaries went to hear Newman, then rector of the Catholic University, preach.

But it was the Irish evangelicals whom Mahaffy in his youth heard repeatedly and regularly. Half a century later he was still conscious of their power, though by then fully aware of their limitations. Men of learning and breeding, gentlemen, as he emphasizes, loyal to their Church and its liturgy, they treated

the sermon as a vital force and preached with tremendous vigour
and emotional earnestness. The Bible was their absolute and
infallible rule of faith. Mahaffy says that he himself 'actually
heard a clergyman on a platform assert the verbal inspiration
of the English Bible on the grounds that the same influence
which guided the pens of the original writers could not have
failed to guide in the same way the translators who were to
make known to the English nation the message of the gospel'.
'They boldly preached that while man was free to do evil, and
therefore responsible for it, he was unable owing to Adam's
transgression to do anything good of himself. And yet they never
doubted the benevolence of the Deity though they called every
conversion a miracle. They lived saintly and charitable lives, they
inveighed against the value of good works. They controlled their
congregations as spiritual autocrats, though they denied all
efficacy in apostolic succession.'[12]

Given Mahaffy's bookish tastes and family background, that
he should become an undergraduate at Trinity Dublin was almost
inevitable. The word 'almost' is justified because so great was
his enthusiasm for music that the idea of becoming a professional
musician crossed his mind. What sort of musician, is doubtful.
He, himself, in old age talking to a lively-minded undergraduate,
remarked, 'A sense of purpose is necessary for all achievement.
At one time I had thoughts of becoming a violinist but when I
realized I could not become a great violinist, I decided to remain
a musician, just a musician.'[13] On the other hand his mother,
though she loved music, was very thankful that her son 'had not
a tenor voice (a great snare) but only a bass voice, fit to sing in
quartets'. But whether as a vocalist or an instrumentalist, to
have become a professional musician would have been – unless
he had been exceptionally successful – a form of social suicide,
which he would find titillating to dwell on when he was provost.
So in June 1855, at the age of sixteen he entered Trinity College,
the college of his father and grandfather.

'Entrance' marked for Mahaffy not only the beginning of a new
era in his life but the complete and saddening end of his boyhood
world. The year he entered college his father died; about the
same time the younger of his two brothers emigrated to Australia
and shortly afterwards the elder brother was killed in a shooting
accident. For the remainder of her long life Mahaffy was to

remain in constant touch with his beloved, his 'sainted' mother. But the happy, united, kindly family circle in which he had come to maturity was gone. Fortunately, it might be said, he had a new home. Trinity, where he was destined to spend over sixty strenuous years as student and don, was truly his *alma mater* – though in Mahaffy's considered opinion a Spartan mother.

Trinity college when Mahaffy entered was one of the most conspicuous and influential institutions in Ireland. Conspicuous because with its buildings, 'studious temples' pillared and pedimented, squares, park and 'wildernesses', it spread over almost forty acres in the very centre of Dublin; influential because it was the university of what were still the ruling classes of Ireland. Until 1850 indeed it had been the only Irish university but in that year the Queen's University of Ireland had been constituted as a federated university with colleges in Belfast, Cork and Galway, and in 1854 the Catholic university was established by the hierarchy and Newman invited over to be rector. But neither the Queen's University with its colleges scattered over Ireland, nor the Catholic University unchartered and poor, could seriously rival the University of Dublin or Trinity College (the terms were practically synonymous), with its massive buildings, large endowments, and two and a half centuries of history.

'Trinity' or 'old Trinity' as it was often affectionately called, was a unique and in many ways a strange institution in Ireland. In its constitution and terminology – it had a provost, fellows and scholars, freshmen and sophisters, fellow-commoners and sizars – in its buildings, quadrangles, chapel, dining hall, library, and in its routine, punctuated by the sounding of the great college bell, recently lodged in its new classical campanile, and in its close alliance with the establishment in church and state, it resembled an Oxford or Cambridge college. But as a university it was much smaller than either Oxford or Cambridge.

When Mahaffy entered, Trinity had an undergraduate population of about nine hundred – numbers having fallen, it was said, owing to the Crimean War and the aftermath of the famine. About one hundred and twenty of the undergraduates 'lived in', a small proportion by Oxford and Cambridge standards, but large enough to give vitality, cohesion and colour to the undergraduate world. At the other extreme a substantial number of the undergraduates only appeared in college to take examinations, a feature reminiscent of the university of London, an institution with which nineteenth-century Trinity men would not wish to establish comparisons. The academic staff numbered approximately fifty-five, including thirty-five fellows, and twenty non-fellow professors. The fellows, senior and junior, constituted the core of the academic staff. They were responsible for all the teaching in the ordinary B.A. course, and much of the honour teaching. A number of them held chairs, tutorships, or other offices, and they monopolized administrative power within the university. There were in 1855 seven senior and twenty-eight junior fellows within the university. The seven senior fellows with the provost formed the board, the governing body of the college, which exercised a plentitude of legislative, executive and judicial power. The senior fellows also divided among themselves the major and more lucrative college offices and a substantial share of the college revenues. Indeed at the time when Mahaffy was an undergraduate the excessive incomes enjoyed by the senior fellows were arousing angry criticism. However, it was generally agreed that from the beginning of the nineteenth century the board had shown itself to be reasonably responsive to current educational trends.

Mahaffy at entrance was an outstanding and unusual young man. Tall and big-boned, according to himself 'an ugly, serious looking boy with a broad head but no other external sign of ability', he was uncertain how he stood in comparison with his contemporaries and inclined, as often happens with men who have been isolated in boyhood, to talk over-freely when his reserve melted. Well ahead of his contemporaries in reading and in awareness of the world, he had one important asset which was to be of some value to him as an undergraduate and of enormous importance in his later career, his easily acquired knowledge of French and German. A few years after he entered Trinity a report on the teaching in Irish schools revealed a lamentable state of affairs. While the standard in classics was reasonably high and mathematical teaching was improving, English and history were very badly taught (many undergraduates on arrival were unable to spell correctly), and few of the candidates for university entrance had even a smattering of French. In England the position, as far as modern languages was concerned, was not much better. Consequently in an age when German was the key to advanced work in almost every sphere of learning, Mahaffy's grasp of foreign languages was to be of immense advantage to him. Indeed in later days he frequently emphasized with marked, and some might feel offensive, complacency the value to a scholar, especially to one functioning within an insular tradition, of a wide European background.

However, at the time he entered Trinity his self-assurance was sustained not by dwelling on his linguistic acquirements but by his conception of his social status. As later he put it bluntly, 'we that lived from land however poor had then an absurd contempt for trade which did not rank as a gentleman's profession. The church, the law and the army were the only professions worthy of a gentleman.' The barriers were not as rigid as Mahaffy implies and were placed subjectively at different points in social life. Undoubtedly, however, the possession, maintenance or loss of gentility loomed large in the Victorian mind. This preoccupation with status could result in arrogance, social brutality, narrowness and an excessive, and at times obsessive, concern with the *minutiae* of manners, dress and speech. A remark attributed to Mahaffy expresses this in a simple and rather silly form: 'The man can't be a gentleman,' he said. 'He gets his wine from his grocer.' But there was another side to the matter. By assuming he was a gentleman, a man implicitly bound himself to observe exacting standards of conduct and bearing. A gentleman was expected to be courteous, tell the truth, keep his word, have a scrupulous sense of honour, and preserve his dignity by displaying, when circumstances demanded it, a courageous independence. As the *obiter dicta* scattered through his writings imply, Mahaffy not only was conscious – some would say too much conscious – of being a gentleman by birth and breeding but also submitted to the demands of a severe code. Gentility for him had its duties as well as its rights.

Compared with many of his contemporaries Mahaffy had not the qualities that go to make an expert examinee. He lacked an adequate grounding. His father, kind and eager to help, could not supply the disciplined drive of a first-class sixth-form master, and years later Mahaffy confessed that when he arrived at Trinity he could write in German better than in English. Moreover, he had not been compelled to pay attention to examination

technique. As a result, in the first two terms of his junior freshman year he secured only second class honours. But native
intelligence and sturdy perseverance enabled him to remedy his
shortcomings very quickly. By the end of his first year, and
always from then on, he was in the first rank. In his third year
he won a foundation scholarship and finally in 1859 he graduated
with a senior moderatorship (a first class degree) in two subjects,
classics and logic (philosophy). It was undoubtedly a satisfactory
undergraduate career but, significantly, he was not always 'first
of the firsts'. In a second-year honour examination he was
defeated by Gerald Fitzgibbon, 'a tall, handsome but very raw
boy, also home bred', who was to become a friend of Mahaffy's
and a lord justice of appeal. And in the moderatorship examination he was second both in classics and in philosophy. But he
was decidedly the best all round man of his year.

As his record shows, Mahaffy worked hard, but he does not
seem to have been exhilarated by the teaching he received as an
undergraduate. 'Many of the fellows,' he wrote long afterwards,
'whose business it was either to make new researches into science
and letters or at least to teach the undergraduates with zeal,
and stimulate their intellects, many of them, I repeat, were fit
to do neither. . . . They merely gave perfunctory lectures, took
perfunctory care of their College pupils as Tutors, examined
more or less carefully in the subjects they had been obliged to
master in order to obtain fellowships,' and yet he added, 'they
belong to so great a corporation, so wealthy and renowned in
former days, that they gave themselves airs of superiority, to
which the Irish public willingly submitted'. In fact, Mahaffy
seems to have felt in an acute form the intelligent young man's
disappointment at meeting the human instruments of higher
education. His disappointment was intensified by the fact that
the Trinity teaching body had a strongly mathematical bias.
For example, the head of the classical school, Thomas Stack, the
Regius Professor of Greek, before being elected to fellowship,
had been a mathematical prizeman. Later, he had, in the words
of his obituarist 'mastered the collateral Greek and Latin
literature requisite for proficiency in the classical text books in
Trinity College'[14] – a qualified eulogy which does not suggest
inspired teaching. Nor had Stack a very attractive personality.
'A short, pale-faced man', in clerical black with an eye glass,

wearing a tie which, 'according to popular legend', had once been white, and a large expanse of grubby shirt front, his ferocity as an examiner had earned him the soubriquet of 'Stick, Stack, Stuck'.[15] While Mahaffy was an undergraduate, seven junior fellows acted as honour lecturers in classics. Three of them may have merited his disapproval – at least they have left no published work on which they can be judged – but the other four were sound, hard-working scholars who between them fill four and a half columns of the British Museum catalogue. Unfortunately one of them was an economist and the other three, though linguists, were not primarily interested in classical literature. But Mahaffy gratefully acknowledged the help he received from one of the fellows, Toleken, 'the quiet and gentle old Dr Toleken'. Toleken is now almost completely forgotten. But he, in his day, exercised considerable influence over the shaping of the curriculum. He devised the first course in modern history and, first by slipping questions into examinations, he quietly introduced German idealism into the philosophy course hitherto dominated by the Scottish metaphysicians and by Mill.[16] In contrast with their utilitarianism, Toleken's emphasis on Kant with his powerful arguments for obeying the demands of duty was bound to have a strong appeal to an intelligent, serious young man brought up in the Irish evangelical tradition.

It is not possible to paint a completely rounded picture of Mahaffy as an undergraduate. Too many of the details are missing, and we are reminded by two descriptions which survive that very different patterns of student life could co-exist in Trinity at this and any other time. William Hartpole Lecky, the historian, entered college in the same term as Mahaffy. Living in bright, booklined rooms in Botany Bay, Lecky usually breakfasted by the fire with a book, attended lectures in the morning, often in the afternoon went down to Kingstown for a solitary walk on the west pier, and after commons (which was at the old-fashioned and inconvenient hour of five o'clock) would entertain friends in his room to wine. After wine Lecky 'insisted on having tea and bread and butter, which was the signal for the fiercer spirits to retire', but the conversation would go on uninterrupted 'even by the simmering of a kettle'. Talk would range over literature, politics and religion. In poetry, Lecky recalled years afterwards, 'Tennyson and Longfellow reigned

Cm

supreme'; in politics it was the heyday of Victorian liberalism and John Stuart Mill was at 'the zenith of his fame and influence'. But the ideas of the classical economists which dominated social thinking were being stridently challenged by Carlyle, while Buckle and Comte provided bold and broad interpretations of the historic process. Though 'Darwin and Herbert Spencer had not yet risen above the horizon', Lecky and his friends discussed not only the perennial Roman controversy but the bearing of recent geological discoveries on the Mosaic cosmogony.[17]

There was another set of rooms in the Bay where intellectual life was less strenuous. There in the sitting room a visitor found 'the furniture consisted of an old table on three legs and an uneasy chair which belonged to the last proprietor, two cracked tea cups and one saucer, a large array of tumblers and wine glasses, all more or less in a damaged state. In one corner of the room lay a heap of prawn shells in another a heap of oyster ditto, while a rough Scottish terrier and a half empty cask of pale ale occupied the remaining two; a black bottle supported on either side by a long clay pipe and a seal-skin tobacco pouch formed the characteristic ornaments of the chimney-piece.' The occupant of such a set had a routine distinct from Lecky's. Rising late after being up all night at an oyster party, he went for a walk, drifted on to commons and then after a game of billiards, 'drinks and smokes until night-roll, to escape which he goes to the theatre at half-price or joins a small supper party. And such is a day.'[18]

Mahaffy was too serious and hard-working an undergraduate to be able to enjoy the life of sustained relaxation which had a strong appeal to many of his college contemporaries. On the other hand, significantly enough, he was not one of the group of lively and able young men (which included his friend Fitzgibbon) who drifted in and out of Lecky's rooms. Mahaffy himself admits that as a young man, while talkative to a fault he lacked 'any faculty for fun or making jokes'. Indeed it is highly probable that as a conversationalist he already displayed many of the qualities of a keen lecturer, and may have seemed to his contemporaries rather heavy intellectually. In any event Mahaffy was too busy to feel left out. He was reading for two honour degrees, he seems to have kept up his cricket, and he was a member of the two major college societies, the University Philosophical Society, and the College Historical Society. Each of these societies was small with a dozen to a score of active members, met weekly and had its distinctive procedure; the Philosophical to hear and debate a paper and to have tea and barmbrack, the Historical, an older society with a distinguished and stormy history – it had twice been expelled from college – to debate a motion. The Philosophical was didactic, the Historical rhetorical.

Mahaffy did not play a leading part in the Historical Society, though he spoke twice in debate, in 1858 opposing a motion which enunciated that 'the Act of Union cannot be defended on grounds of moral or political rectitude', and in 1859 opposing the motion that 'Pitt's policy towards Ireland was partial and corrupt'. He had a more distinguished career in the Philosophical Society. Though he was blackballed on his first attempt to join,[19] he ultimately became a member and was elected president for the session 1858–9. At the opening meeting he delivered a presidential address, the first of his published works. This address shows him to have been a high-minded, level-headed, hard-working young man, quite prepared to try to improve his contemporaries. On educational issues he was a moderate conservative. He regarded the college course as 'eminently fitted to lay the foundation of a truly useful and elegant education'. He expressed shocked surprise that a fellow of an Oxford college (Congreve, the well known Positivist) should have challenged 'the dominant theory which looks on all really high education as having necessarily for its basis the languages of Greece and Rome'. (Congreve had accentuated the force of his challenge by issuing it in the preface to his edition of Aristotle's *Politics*.) Mahaffy felt no doubts about the place to be assigned to the classics in a liberal and intelligent educational system. 'The skeleton of an education,' he asserted, should be 'formed by mathematical and metaphysical studies, covered with muscles and flesh by the classics and clothed in a becoming garb by a good knowledge of English.' But though he was not anxious 'in any way to encourage the spirit of blind iconoclasm', Mahaffy clearly hankered after intellectual distinction, and he stressed that one of the important benefits of steady reading was 'the supply which we gain of hints for original trains of thought'. Later during the meeting, Jellett, the future provost, then a junior fellow, dryly remarked that it was unlikely that young men would underrate originality, though they might be inclined to overrate their own ideas.[20]

Mahaffy was fortunate in the year of his graduation, being one of the first beneficiaries of a reforming wave of moderate dimensions which followed the Royal Commission's report. In 1858 the board created fourteen studentships, each worth £100 per annum and tenable for seven years. Studentships were to be awarded on the basis of moderatorship and had no duties attached to them. They were in fact, as Mahaffy was to explain half a century later, the equivalent of the Oxford and Cambridge prize fellowships, which were 'regarded as a pecuniary help either to fellowship candidates or to young men going to the professions'.[21] The first two studentships were offered in 1859 and Mahaffy by a narrow margin – fortunately for him, the man who had beaten him in classics secured only a second in ethics and logic – was awarded the classical studentship. One hundred pounds per annum was a very respectable income for a young man at this time. Possibly, indeed, the board when fixing the value of studentship may have been unconsciously influenced by its own income level. And since he also held his scholarship until 1862, Mahaffy was, in his own words, 'a student who need not help himself by teaching, except for luxuries'.

With his economic future temporarily secured Mahaffy had time to look around and decide on a career. At first he considered the target so many able Trinity men were aiming at – the Indian civil service, which besides providing a career open to administrative talent and a large pension offered a great opening for the exercise of the imperial virtues. However, owing to the upper age limit for candidates, Mahaffy had only one opportunity after he graduated of taking the examination and in his own words he 'was only prevented by an accident from doing so'.[22]

There was another possibility. Sir William Stokes, the great Dublin doctor (one of the men who introduced the use of the stethoscope), and also an enthusiastic archaeologist and musician, pressed Mahaffy hard to take up medicine. When Mahaffy told him he was going to try for fellowship in Trinity, Stokes remarked, 'There is Mahaffy, he'll get fellowship and then he'll marry and then he'll die.' Mahaffy protested, pointing out that a fellow of the college whom he named had written a book since he married. 'Old Dr Stokes took a fresh pinch of snuff and answered oracularly, "My dear fellow, he was never married. He has a thing he calls his wife and things he calls children, but he was never married." '

If Stokes thought that Trinity dons tended to be emotionally stunted, Mahaffy himself seems to have condemned many of the fellows for being deficient in intellectual drive. Nevertheless, he decided to compete for fellowship which after all had considerable attractions. Once elected, a fellow could hold his fellowship for life; he was no longer (since 1840) obliged to remain celibate, he enjoyed a reasonable salary, and as vacancies occurred above him he moved up the list until he at last became one of the senior fellows, with a seat on the board and a large income. Whenever there was a vacancy amongst the fellows it was filled by competitive examination. Until the middle of the nineteenth century in the fellowship examination one subject, mathematics, outweighed all the others. But fortunately for Mahaffy in 1855 the examination was widened to include papers and vivas not only in mathematics but in classics, philosophy, Hebrew and experimental science, candidates usually taking one or other of the two main subjects, mathematics and classics. The examination, which was held shortly after Easter, aroused intense interest and, it was said, widespread betting, and the result was announced ceremonially by the provost on Trinity Monday to a large audience.

Mahaffy first presented himself in 1862, this being the first occasion on which there was an examination for fellowship since he had graduated. He was runner-up, being beaten by Thomas Thompson Gray, a young mathematician who was four years his senior. The following year there was again a vacancy and again Mahaffy was first out, being on this occasion defeated by an unusual candidate, Thomas Ebenezer Webb, a man of over forty. Webb, Professor of Moral Philosophy and later Regius Professor of Laws, was a versatile scholar in his time. He composed Latin orations, translated *Faust*, published philosophical works which showed that 'his literary gifts were greater than his philosophical powers', and wrote on the Shakespearian problem. A brilliant talker and an eloquent speaker, Webb after a few years resigned fellowship and concentrated on his practice at the bar. Mahaffy may well have resented Webb's belated emergence as a competitor for fellowship and his careless if

belated rejection of the prize. At least this would explain why
Webb was the victim on one occasion of a bludgeon witticism.
Webb, a guest on commons when discussing his prospects of
securing a law officership, remarked 'They all know I am not for
sale.' 'Well' said Mahaffy, 'you have been a long time in the shop
window.'[23]

Samuel Madden, an eighteenth-century benefactor of the
college, had founded a prize to be awarded to the candidate who
was first out in the fellowship examination. In the eighteen
sixties this was worth well over £300 – considerably more in
fact than the first year's income of fellowship. Mahaffy, who won
the prize twice running, spent the money on two long continental
tours, journeys which 'gave me an enlarged view of Europe'.
On the first trip, accompanied by Edmund Bewley, later a high
court judge and a well known genealogist, he travelled from
Dresden to Cracow, 'a most barbaric place', and then through the
Carpathians to Budapest 'then also very barbarous'. On the
second tour with Brougham Leech as a companion, he went
down to Trieste by way of Vienna, and then up through Trent
and Munich home. Having enjoyed the fruits of defeat in two
successive years he finally, in 1864, secured the long desired
fellowship. According to himself he had to 'disguise' his knowledge, since Stack, the examiner in Greek composition, set a
piece translated from Thucydides which Mahaffy could repeat by
memory in the original Greek. It was the last time on record that
Mahaffy disguised his knowledge.

chapter two

A fellow of Trinity

Shortly after he became a fellow in 1864, at the fairly early age of twenty-five, Mahaffy made three important decisions. He decided to publish as soon as possible a really challenging book; he took holy orders; and he married. He gives his main motive for the first decision in his autobiographical essay: 'My earliest work was . . . , so to speak, thrown at the heads of the idle Fellow critics of the College who no doubt despised their new colleague as a mere talker . . . no doubt I did talk too much and was apt to overrate to them the virtue of my foreign life and use of languages.' He was determined, too, that the title given to Trinity College, Dublin, in Oxford and Cambridge, 'the silent sister', should become invalid. Eventually he published over thirty books on classical, historical and philosophical subjects, and a huge corpus of contributions to learned journals and popular magazines – not without controversies and disappointments, as later chapters will describe.

His decision to be ordained was less unusual in 1864 than it would have been a decade later. The fellows of T.C.D. (with five exceptions) were still bound by statute to be in holy orders, and in fact when Mahaffy was elected out of the thirty-two fellows twenty-four were clergymen. Public opinion, though changing rapidly, still believed that education, especially in the grammar schools, the public schools and the universities, was to a great extent a form of pastoral work which ought to be entrusted to the clergy of the Established Church. And to Mahaffy personally, as the son and grandson of clergymen, a convinced Christian, interested in many aspects of ecclesiastical life, it must have appeared natural enough that on becoming a fellow he should seek ordination. At the same time the fact that he lived amongst devout members of the Church of Ireland who both strongly disapproved of sacerdotalism and continually dwelt on the responsibilities of the Christian layman, lessened the significance without diminishing the seriousness of taking orders. But, though he could not have realized it at the time, Mahaffy's ordination marks the end of a long epoch in college history. After his ordination twenty years were to elapse before another fellow sought orders. The climate of opinion was bound to make some men uncertain of their orthodoxy. And the disestablishment of the Church of Ireland in 1869, in the words of Arthur Palmer, a young junior fellow, took away from the fellows 'the chief object for becoming clergymen'.[1] It would be unfair to accuse Palmer of cynicism. Disestablishment meant not only the disappearance of the better endowed benefices but was bound to lessen the status and influence of the Church of Ireland clergyman.

Mahaffy was not only the last of a long line of fellows who took orders under the old conditions, he was also one of the last fellows to contemplate going out on a college living. In 1867 the college living of Drumragh in the diocese of Derry fell vacant and was offered, as was customary, to the clerical fellows in order of seniority. It was declined by all of them who were senior to Mahaffy, but when it came to his turn he seems to have considered taking it. However, before finally making up his mind to do so he consulted G. S. Smith, the Professor of Biblical Greek, a sometime fellow who years before had resigned fellowship for the living of Aghalurcher. According to Mahaffy, Smith 'proved by documents' that Drumragh was not worth more than £720 per annum and that in addition it was subject to a building charge which would cut down the income to £620. On learning these facts Mahaffy refused Drumragh, a decision which he may have regretted when some years later at disestablishment, it was shown that the income was £1,098. The then incumbent was Smith who, on Mahaffy's refusal, had accepted it.[2]

In 1865 Mahaffy married Frances Letitia MacDougall, the daughter of William MacDougall, a wealthy Dublin solicitor who lived at Drumleck House, Howth. The MacDougall family always thought that Mahaffy, socially speaking, married well.

And in fact through his marriage he came closely connected with a great Irish academic and intellectual dynasty, the Stokes family. In 1787 Whitley Stokes was elected fellow of Trinity College, Dublin. Stokes, who was a warm-hearted man with original views on many subjects, arranged the college mineralogical museum, wrote on Irish economics, opposed Malthus on the population question and Paine on religion, drafted a plan of parliamentary reform for the Dublin society of United Irishmen, and concerned himself with the sick poor and the conversion of the Irish catholics to protestantism – characteristically expressing the hope that his fellow countrymen would appreciate his motives and not be offended. Whitley Stokes had a son William, the eminent physican, who has already been mentioned as Mahaffy's early friend and adviser. William had three sons, Whitley, William and Henry and a daughter Margaret. The first two sons and their sister are all noted in the Dictionary of National Biography along with their father and grandfather. Margaret was a distinguished archaeologist. Whitley attained distinction in two spheres. As a jurist he published works on Indian law, as a philologist he helped to lay the foundations of modern Celtic studies. William was a notable physician. Henry, an Indian civil servant who in 1866 married Mary MacDougall, the sister of Mrs Mahaffy, was the father of Adrian Stokes, a pioneer in pathology and preventive medicine.

Mahaffy may have been fortunate in his wife's background and relations, but what is far more important, he made a supremely happy marriage. In the eyes of the world robust, self-assured and even arrogant, he always needed the sympathetic support of an able woman, and this, he thankfully recorded at the close of his life, he successively received from his mother, his wife and his daughter Rachel. His wife was kind, highly intelligent, interested in literature, and a good housekeeper – tradition says that taking advantage of a fall in prices towards the close of the century she steadily saved from her housekeeping money until she was able to present her unobservant husband with a seaside house. She had, too, an unusual trait which might have handicapped her husband but which in practice seems to have turned into a social advantage. Though an admirable hostess, Mrs Mahaffy did not enjoy dining out or visiting other people's houses. This might have kept Mahaffy at home, but, defying Victorian convention, the Mahaffys managed to establish that he – one of nature's guests – should visit and be entertained unaccompanied by his wife. So Mahaffy was able to combine something of the social freedom and flexibility of a bachelor with a secure home base.

After his marriage Mahaffy and his wife set up house at 38 North Great George's Street, which remained his Dublin home for nearly forty years. On the north side of the river, in an area of dignified Georgian houses which during Mahaffy's lifetime slowly declined (in the early nineties a few houses in the street slumped into tenements), North Great George's Street, when the Mahaffys arrived, was a respectable street of private houses and solicitors' offices. No. 20 was the home of (Sir) Samuel Ferguson, the poet and antiquary, who became a close friend of the Mahaffys. Later, John Dillon, the nationalist leader (with whom, however, Mahaffy was not acquainted), lived in No. 2. No. 38, a fine red-brick house, four storeys high with a basement, certainly had plenty of room for Mahaffy and his family – he had two sons and two daughters, all born between 1866 and 1874 – and it provided an adequate background for a hospitable don with a liking for spacious living.

Mahaffy could afford to live comfortably enough. In the early seventies a maidservant in Dublin was paid about £7 a year, and coal cost about 21*s.* a ton. By then Mahaffy's college income was verging on £700 per annum. Later when he became one of the senior junior fellows it must have risen to between £800 and £900, and when he was a senior fellow and senior lecturer he enjoyed an academic income of £1,500 per annum. He also must have earned over the years a fair amount from his literary work. He himself states that his British and American royalties on his *Old Greek Life*, a small primer, amount to £750, and he was always ready with genial determination to badger his publisher for better terms. 'To please a sentimental author and keep him in good humour,' he pointed out to Macmillan, 'was only shrewd business management.' On one occasion he told his publisher he was writing to him 'in the presence of a wife and four starving children'. On another, he declared 'After careful deliberation I have chosen this most vulgar day (Easter Monday) to write to you upon a vulgar subject' – royalties.[3]

It was fortunate for Mahaffy that he was free from intense financial worry and had an affectionate, smooth-running home, because from the time he became a fellow he was a very busy man, driving himself hard at work and play. To begin with, college duties, lecturing, examining and looking after his tutorial chamber occupied, during term at least, a substantial part of his time. As a lecturer he seems to have been competent but not outstanding. Pass lecturing, which meant teaching at fairly simple level, he found pleasant and unexacting. Honour lecturing, however, meant teaching small groups of classical honour men, and Mahaffy's published lectures suggest that he was at his happiest when launched on broad themes before a large and appreciative audience. Consequently it is probable that Trinity honour men found his younger colleagues, Tyrrell, Palmer, Bury, and Purser, devoted adherents of accuracy and delighting in the finer points of scholarship, more satisfying than Mahaffy with his bold generalizations.

By chance an undergraduate's impression of what he was like in the examination hall survives. Shortly after Mahaffy was elected to fellowship, Swift MacNeill, later a nationalist M.P. and an expert in constitutional law, entered Trinity. He was finishing an examination paper when Mahaffy, 'an athletic looking, splendidly built man, with a wealth of brown hair and with a marked individuality of manner', arrived to pick up the examinees' answers. MacNeill, who wanted to add something to his script, in his own words 'held on to it, but he pulled it from me, saying with the kindest of smiles, "No, no, this won't do at all. You must learn to economise your time." '[4]

Mahaffy's friendliness must have stood him in good stead as a tutor. The Trinity tutor did not, *qua* tutor, teach his pupils; he was an adviser in the intricacies of academic life and if necessary an advocate. Tutorial efficiency varied. A tutor could be protected from being overworked by a reputation for testiness or simple inaccessibility. Mahaffy's approachability – he always enjoyed conversational contacts – must have pleased his pupils, and in later years he boasted that 'they used to say of me when I was a tutor that you could drop me anywhere in Ireland and I should not be more than three miles from my dinner. I had so many followers and relations and friends of pupils that I was known everywhere and made at home all over the country.'[5]

In one respect he was fortunate compared to the modern don. Committees, those octopuses of university life, did not occupy

much place in nineteenth-century Trinity. One committee, the
board, tended to monopolize power. And Mahaffy, who it is
clear was not one of nature's academic politicians, was from the
time of his election vigorously engaged in literary work. He had
many other interests and distractions. His childhood had inspired him with an intense love of travel which as the years
went on he gratified to the full. He toured Germany and the
Low Countries, he thoroughly explored Italy, he worked in the
Nubian valleys of the Lower Nile.

Early in 1875 he was sent with his friend Atkinson, the
Professor of Sanskrit (later to become the source of his quarrels
with the Gaelic League), to represent the University of Dublin at
the tercentenary of the University of Leyden. There was snow
and ice on the ground. Years afterwards Mahaffy dwelt on the
incredible cold in the church where the rector of the university
delivered his state address, and he was annoyed by the inter-
minable speech-making which stifled conversation at the banquets he attended. But he thoroughly enjoyed exuberant evenings
with the students, whose 'eager young faces warmed his heart'
and who had good wine and cigars for their friends. And he was
delighted to meet learned men from all over Europe – 'Oriental-
ists, Hellenists, Latinists, Historians, Philosophers, Physiologists,
Jurists, Theologians . . . all jabbering away in a number of
languages, so that it was profanely remarked that but for the
absence of one important personage, it seemed a veritable day of
Pentecost.' Mahaffy was especially impressed by Cobet, the
great Leyden classicist who spoke in Ciceronian periods, a man
who obviously was thinking in Latin. Characteristically as soon
as he returned from the festivities Mahaffy stated emphatically in
a widely read periodical that the leadership in classical studies
had passed from England to Holland. 'Oxford and Cambridge,'
he wrote, 'might well ask themselves what were they doing for
the thought of Europe? who among their scholars was a real
leader of men?'[6]

Within a few weeks of his return to Dublin he was off further
afield. Having written with such enthusiasm about Greece,
Mahaffy naturally wanted to get there, and in the spring of
1875 he was offered an opportunity of doing so in leisurely and
comparatively luxurious style. William Goulding, the founder of a
famous Irish firm, was anxious that his eldest son William, a

Cambridge undergraduate of nineteen, should make a grand tour
of the classical world with Mahaffy as his companion and guide.
So Mahaffy found himself provided with a vigorous young travelling companion – the younger Goulding was to become an able
man of affairs – and adequate funds. Leaving Dublin early in
April Mahaffy and Goulding travelled down to Rome. John
Richard Green wrote to his fellow-historian Freeman:

> *My* Hellenism, however, pales before that of Mahaffy,
> whom we found here in Rome, refusing with scorn to look
> at any 'Roman thing'. He was on his way to Athens, and
> simply picking up stray bits of Hellenism, sculptures and
> what not by the road. One of his aims is to verify Greek
> busts; he doubts, 'Pericles', and a little doubts Alexander –
> whereat I wept and fled. Likewise he is seeking to know how
> Hellenic young women kept their clothes on, a question
> wrapt in the deepest mystery, and insoluble by the Highest
> Germany. Perhaps it was too insoluble for the Hellenic
> women themselves, as to judge from the later sculptures
> they seem to have dropt the effort to keep their clothes on.
> Perhaps that is why Mahaffy calls the Periclean age the age
> of Decadence.[7]

However, Mahaffy and Goulding did not make directly for
Greece because about the middle of June they met Oscar Wilde
in Florence and with him paid a short visit to some towns in
north Italy. At Venice on the first day the party visited San
Marco, the Doge's palace and the Lido, ending the day by
gazing at San Marco bathed in moonlight. The next day they
spent 'in gondolas and markets'. Wilde thought San Marco
glorious and 'most gorgeous'.[8] Mahaffy later compared it disparagingly with the Parthenon and instanced Saint Mark's portal
as an example of 'the tawdriness which affects the decadence of
a great style'.[9]

After visiting Venice the party broke up, Wilde making back
towards home, Mahaffy and Goulding pushing down to Naples
where they boarded a French steamer for Athens. Their fellow
passengers were a friendly polyglot collection – Russians, Greeks,
Turks, French and English – and Mahaffy thoroughly enjoyed
their conversation. But having heard that they would first sight
Greece in the early hours of the morning, 'eager to get the earliest

possible sight of the land which still occupies so large a place in
our thoughts', he 'started up at half past three in the morning'
and stood on deck in a soft, damp, grey dawn watching the long
serrated ridges with snow-clad peaks emerge through the mist.
Alone, without a guide or map, he recited to himself the name of
each mountain and promontory, 'filling out the outline of many
books with reality itself'. And with his predilection for parallels,
he soon found himself comparing Greece with its purple coloured
mountains, innumerable inlets and rocky shores, to the west coast
of Ireland.[10]

Piraeus, the port of Athens which they reached a day or so
later in the evening, 'differed little alas from vulgar harbours,
in the noise and confusion of disembarking, in the absurdity of
its custom house, in the extortion and insolence of its boatmen'.
Mahaffy as he struggled to get himself and luggage ashore
recalled Plato's phrase, 'the haunt of sailors where good manners
are unknown'. When he and Goulding finally went wearily to
bed in Athens they soon found that 'the stillness of the night
was a phenomenon hardly known in the city'. No sooner did
pedestrian and horse traffic cease than the dogs began to bark,
'ably seconded by the cats as well as by an occasional wakeful
donkey'. 'How is a man to admire art and revere antiquity,'
Mahaffy exclaimed, 'if he is robbed of his repose?' But at dawn
when, half slept and bad tempered, they got up and looked out,
they saw right opposite 'the rock which of all rocks in the world's
history has done most for literature and art – the rock about
which poets and orators, and architects and historians have ever
spoken without exhausting themselves, which is ever new and
ever old, ever fresh in its decay, ever perfect in its ruin, ever
living in its death – the Acropolis of Athens'.

For the rest of his life Mahaffy never ceased to be fascinated
by the Acropolis. Aesthetically and historically it enthralled
him. He came back to it again and again and he was convinced
that 'a proper honest study of the Acropolis is an epoch in the
art training of any man, and so far as the aesthetic side of man
influences his morals, a progress in piety and in toleration'.[11]
His toleration was soon put to a severe strain. When standing
on the precipice of the Acropolis he was enraged to see down
below in the Theatre of Dionysus, a young Greek who was
practising with his pistol, using as a target a fine piece of carved

marble. Having appealed in vain to a custodian, Mahaffy and Goulding 'adopted the tactics of Apollo at Delphi': hurling stones at 'the wretched barbarian' below they quickly drove him out of the theatre. This was not the only time that Mahaffy took energetic action in Athens. Years later an Athenian cabbie was ill-treating his miserable horse. Two English women remonstrated. The cabbie told them to mind their own business. Mahaffy, then a man of seventy, bore down on the group, seized the cabbie round the waist, flung him on the ground and held him down until he apologized.

On his first visit to Greece Mahaffy was also exasperated by the condition of the museums in Athens. He held strong views on museum organization. It was, he thought, a mistake to concentrate everything in the great national museums. The British Museum was so enormous and overwhelming that it was of little use to anyone 'except the trained specialist who goes in with his eyes shut and will not open them until he has arrived at the special class of objects he intends to examine'. Mahaffy therefore highly approved of the arrangements in Athens where there were at least four museums devoted to classical antiquities. But when he visited them he was shocked to find masses of fragments heaped up in uncatalogued disorder, statues lying on the floor and no attempt being made to follow the Italian practice of restoring broken statuary by adding new limbs and noses (a practice which now would receive severe condemnation). Also the Greek archaeologists, being vain and quarrelsome, recorded their discoveries in different and competing journals and newspapers – to the confused bafflement of an ardent foreign inquirer.

On this tour of Greece there was much to be seen in addition to Athens. Mounted on mules, Mahaffy and Goulding covered wide stretches of Attica, Thebes, and the Peloponnese. Mahaffy, who had both a good eye for natural beauty and a countryman's interest in the use of the terrain, enjoyed the constant changes of scene and was delighted by frequent glimpses of fairyland scenery. The lightness and clearness of the air exhilarated him and the weather was so uniformly good that they ceased to notice it – whereas in Ireland it provided one of the main topics of conversation. Above all Mahaffy constantly enjoyed the simple and satisfactory pleasure and stimulus of living in the environment which had inspired the literature that meant so much to him. At Marathon when they plunged into the shallow blue water he 'could not but think of the scene when Cynaegeirus and his companions rushed in armed to stop the embarkation of the Persians', and when he wandered in the woods of Cephissus where the nightingales sang all day in the deep shade and solitude as if it were a prolonged twilight, he was reminded of Aristophanes' line; 'hearing the plane tree whispering to the elm'. Thebes brought to mind Pindar and Epaminondas and at Chaeronea he gazed with reverence at the little open-air theatre cut into the hillside rock, 'the only spot in Chaeronea where we can say with certainty that here Plutarch sat'.

Travel in Greece had its hazards. Bandits were still a threat – the Dilessi tragedy had occurred only five years before Mahaffy's visit and he was not reassured when a famous Athenian professor having told him that no country in Europe was as safe as Greece gave as a decisive reason that '*for two full years* no bandits had been seen or heard'. There were bedbugs to be coped with and the risk of starvation, 'both for want of food and for want of eatable food'. One incident combined bandits and bugs. When staying at Levadia Mahaffy and Goulding rode out into the country towards the ranges of Helicon and Parnassos. As evening closed in nothing could be heard in this vast wilderness 'save the metallic pipe of a water ouzel by the river and the scream of hawks about their nests, far up on the face of the cliffs'. While Mahaffy and Goulding rode back towards the town they saw at several points scarlet caps and swarthy faces peering down on them. They rode on but soon were surrounded. However, the suspicious figures turned out to be policemen sent to search for the English travellers, and they returned to the town escorted by a large crowd of idlers and officials. They were entertained to a rich dinner by the medical officer of the district, and, Mahaffy wrote, 'the entertainment would have been as excellent as even the intentions of our host, had not our attention been foolishly distracted by bugs walking up the table cloth'. But Mahaffy emphasized that all the discomforts of Greek travel could easily be borne: they reminded the traveller of life in the classical past (did not Dionysus in Aristophanes' *Frogs* ask for inns where the bugs would be fewest?), and when the tour was finished 'they form a pleasant feature in the recollections of a glorious time'.

It was probably during his stay in Athens that Mahaffy had an experience which he used to recall in later life. As he was sitting with a friend from the British embassy in an Athenian restaurant, a stout, elderly woman, dowdily dressed in total black, and obviously of unimpeachable bourgeois respectability, came in. His friend nudged him excitedly and whispered 'Look! Look!' 'Why should I look at her?' Mahaffy asked. 'She is plain and *unprepossessing*.' 'She is Byron's Zoë,' was the reply.

Mahaffy was clearly conquered by both Greece and its people. He realized that the Greeks had many faults – that they were vain, jealous of one another, greedy of gain and politically immature. During the summer of 1875 the country was in the middle of one of its recurrent political crises, the conservative prime minister, M. Boulgaris, having been dismissed and replaced by the radical M. Trikoupis. M. Boulgaris was being prosecuted by his opponents for violating the constitution and sentenced to hard labour along with the confiscation of his property. Mahaffy, 'by way of amusement', used to plead Boulgaris' case earnestly with hot-headed radicals, asking them would they have expected Mr Disraeli to have Mr Gladstone sentenced to hard labour for having disestablished the Irish church? 'I asked them,' Mahaffy wrote, 'were they not afraid that if M. Boulgaris were persecuted in so violent a way, he might, instead of occupying the opposition benches betake himself to occupy the mountain passes, and by robbing a few English travellers, so discredit the new government as to be worse and more dangerous in opposition than in power. No, they said, he will not do that; he is *too rich*. But, said I, if you confiscate his property he will be poor. True, they replied, but still he will not be able to do it, he is *too old*. It seemed as if the idea he might be too respectable never crossed their minds.'

Mahaffy need not have worried about the future prospects of M. Boulgaris. M. Trikoupis, being certain he would win the general election, did not use the military to control the polling booths. He lost the election and M. Boulgaris returned to power. In Mahaffy's opinion what Greece clearly needed was a wise dictatorship. It was, he asserted, a ridiculous blunder to offer the British constitution to scarcely emancipated slaves. And if he offended the Greeks by saying this, he could only add, 'That I hold my own nation – the Irish – to be equally unfit for an

advanced constitution'. But with all their faults Mahaffy liked
the Greeks. They were clever, they were spirited, they were good
talkers, they were friendly and hospitable. If Mahaffy's remark
about the King of Greece, 'Quite the nicest king I know', is
ben trovato, it reflects his affection for Greece. Shortly after his
return from his first visit to Greece he expressed his regret that
England 'in the days of her naval greatness', instead of merely
annexing Malta and the Ionian Islands, had not seized Sicily
and Southern Greece. Then, Mahaffy wrote, 'our invalids and
sybarites would have spread wealth and refinement through the
beautiful uplands of Sicily, our route to India would have
lain through Greece, and years ago every curious traveller might
have gone by rail to Athens as he now goes to Brindisi. Greek art
and antiquities would have become the household property of
good society, instead of being seen only by a few privileged
people, to the great disgust of their envious neighbours.'

While Mahaffy was enjoying Greece and appreciating its art
and antiquities an academic storm was gathering in Dublin. The
pleasantest season of the year for touring south-east Europe
coincided with Trinity term in Dublin, lectures beginning on
10 May. And just before leaving Dublin Mahaffy had taken
inadequate steps to provide for the performance of his college
duties by writing to the secretary of the tutorial committee,
Tarleton, a precise and conscientious mathematician. His letter
is short enough to be quoted in full:

> My dear Tarleton,
>   Will you be kind enough to present to the Bursar a
> list of the lectures delivered for me last term during my
> absence in Leyden on my public mission, that he may
> send Dr Longfield the amount to be paid to my deputies.
> I also desire to give you notice that I have obtained from
> the provost leave of absence for the next term and that
> you will arrange accordingly.

Before Tarleton could reply to this curt and casual communica-
tion Mahaffy was off. When the tutorial committee met on
4 May, the very day on which Green described his meeting with
Mahaffy in Rome, and were officially informed of his absence, its
members were unsympathetic to a sulphurous degree.

'Some members of the committee,' Tarleton wrote, 'had heard of Mr Mahaffy's intended departure before it took place but they were under the impression that he was going at considerable personal expense to study the remains of Greek art at Athens with a view to the production of a course of lectures and ultimately of a book upon the subject. Laudable as this design would have been and useful as its fulfilment might possibly have been to the college, the committee think that he ought not to have been allowed to have set out, even for such a purpose, until it was ascertained that satisfactory arrangements had been made for the performance during his absence of his duties as tutor, lecturer and examiner. If, on the other hand, as is generally and apparently on good ground believed, he has accepted an engagement for pecuniary considerations the committee think that the proposal to absent himself from his college work in order to fulfil such an engagement ought to have met with an immediate and decided negative, and, if, as is also alleged, whilst really entertaining this latter purpose he did not disclose it in seeking leave of absence, such a proceeding appears to the committee to be deserving of grave censure.'

The committee placed the matter before the board, emphasizing that 'if it were supposed outside the walls that a fellow could depart, for whatever reason without making proper arrangements for the discharge of the duties for which he is responsible, still more if it were believed that he could practically at his own will desert his official work for any end of private gain, the college would seriously and justly suffer in private and in public estimation, and if this the first instance of the kind which has come under the notice of the committee were allowed to pass without animadversion on their part, they might be taken as acquiescing in such irregularities, and other members of the college might heretofore consider themselves free to follow the example which has been set'. The board replied to the committee by promising 'to make full enquiry into all the circumstances of Mr Mahaffy's absence, as soon as they have an opportunity of communicating with him on the subject'. One member of the board, Carson, that most meticulous of examiners, was not satisfied with this decision. He unsuccessfully tried to get the board to rule that no pupils be assigned to Mahaffy until he had answered the charges made against him by the tutorial committee.

Trinity term ended with Mahaffy still away and it was not until the beginning of Michaelmas term that the board was able to tackle this college *cause célèbre*. It acted carefully and judiciously. The tutors' complaints were forwarded to Mahaffy, his answer was transmitted to them, and Mahaffy appeared before the board and made a full statement. Finally the board resolved that, 'The provost and senior fellows . . . are of opinion that Mr Mahaffy did not state with candour the purpose of his absence . . . nor did he sufficiently provide for his tutorial work, and that his conduct in both respects is deserving of grave censure.' This, one of the severest censures passed on a fellow of Trinity during the whole of the century, probably seemed to Mahaffy to be a further proof of his assertion that 'now-a-days boards and parliaments have neither conscience or human feeling'. Certainly it showed that exuberant originality, however much enjoyed by the outside world, was not appreciated by Mahaffy's colleagues in Trinity. Mahaffy knew what it was like to have one's Hellenic ideals and enthusiasms douched with very cold water by *alma mater*.

Forty-three years later Mahaffy recorded his still indignant recollections of this incident. Having explained that his motive for visiting Greece had been to obtain 'that living knowledge of the land, which older Greek historians, even Grote and Thirlwall, had not thought worth adding to their learning', he continues:

> . . . my departure was received with something like indignation by the stick-in-the-muds, who desired that I should be mulcted my pound of flesh in lectures, and do nothing to produce a contrast to their sleepy life. Everything was done to bring me back, to fine me, and clip my income, in fact to baulk and worry my endeavour to rise out of the ordinary ruck of 'Fellow and Tutor'.

But though the stick-in-the-muds could clip his salary, they failed to clip his wings. In 1877 Mahaffy made another visit to Greece, accompanied by the young man who was to become his most famous literary pupil, Oscar Wilde.

Wilde had entered T.C.D. in 1871 with Mahaffy as his tutor. During his first two years in the college he had done very well in classics, better in fact than Mahaffy himself had done, being twice 'first of the first' in a year that included a future Disney Professor of Archaeology in Cambridge (William Ridgeway) and a future Professor of Latin in T.C.D. (L. C. Purser). He also won two of the highest honours open to an undergraduate, a foundation scholarship and the Berkeley medal for special proficiency in Greek. If he had continued in that style, he would have been fairly sure of a fellowship – in fact seven of the Berkeley medallists in the following years became fellows in classics, among them being five scholars of some distinction, Bury, Starkie, Mooney, Smyly and Alton. But in his third year Wilde began to lose ground. He decided to go to Oxford. According to tradition Mahaffy had said to him, 'Go to Oxford, my dear Oscar: we are all much too clever for you over here.'

No details survive of Mahaffy's relations with Wilde during his three years at T.C.D. As there were only fifteen and a half years between them, Mahaffy must have seemed more like an elder brother than a father. In later life Wilde asserted that Mahaffy's Hellenism and conversational talents had impressed him strongly. Perhaps, too, his admiration for aristocratic society – his *superstition nobiliaire*, as a French biographer of Wilde has put it – and his humanistic and artistic, rather than scientific and scholastic, approach to the classics, influenced Wilde, too. And, according to Mahaffy's classical colleague Tyrrell, Wilde got most of his superciliousness from trying to imitate Mahaffy.

Clearly Wilde's departure to Oxford caused no estrangement between him and Mahaffy, for Mahaffy in the preface to the first edition of his *Social life in Greece* (dated 4 November 1874) thanked 'Mr Oscar Wilde of Magdalen College, Oxford' for 'having made improvements and corrections all through the book'. This was the book that contained a notably frank discussion of Greek homosexuality, as will be described in a later chapter.

In 1875, as already mentioned, Wilde had spent a few days in North Italy with Mahaffy, and Mahaffy had taken the opportunity of fostering his former pupil's interest in classical studies by bringing him to see the famous manuscripts in the Ambrosian Library at Milan. But Wilde did not continue with him to Greece on this occasion.

In August 1876 Wilde wrote from Dublin to his friend William Ward:

> I am with that dear Mahaffy every day. He has a charming
> house by the sea here, on a place called the Hill of Howth
> (one of the crescent horns that shuts in the Bay of Dublin),
> the only place near town with fields of yellow gorse, and
> stretches of wild myrtle, red heather and ferns. . . . I
> arrived just too late to go on a charming party to the North
> of Ireland – Mahaffy, Seyss [Sayce] of Queen's Appleton the
> editor of the *Academy* and my brother. . . . Mahaffy's book,
> of Travels in Greece will soon be out. I have been correcting
> his proofs and like it immensely.

On this occasion Mahaffy made no acknowledgement of Wilde's help with his proofs: perhaps he did not find Wilde's efforts worth recording. (Sometimes a friend thinks that he is 'correcting' proofs when the author believes that the friend is merely being given the benefit of reading an advance copy of his work.) At all events, Mahaffy a few weeks later promised to look over a review which Wilde had just written.[12]

It was in the spring of the next year that Wilde accompanied Mahaffy on what was to be for him a fateful journey to Greece. By that time Wilde had become strongly attracted to Roman Catholicism. At the same time he felt that he was wasting his life as a classical student at Oxford. He had a feeling, as his despondent letters show, that a decisive moment was approaching – 'This is an era in my life, a crisis. I wish I could look into the seeds of time and see what is coming.'

Actually one of the things that he would have seen, if he could, was the looming figure of Mahaffy, for when Wilde set out for Rome at the end of March 1877 Mahaffy went with him. Mahaffy was accompanied by George Macmillan (soon to be a founder of the Hellenic Society) and young William Goulding. Wilde's intention was to leave them at Genoa. But fate and Mahaffy decided otherwise, as Wilde's postcard, 2 April 1877, from Corfu describes:

> I never went to Rome at all! What a changeable fellow
> you must think me, but Mahaffy my old tutor carried me off
> to Greece with him to see Mykenae and Athens. I am

awfully ashamed of myself but I could not help it and will take Rome on my way back. We went to Genoa, then to Ravenna and left Brindisi last night, catching sight of Greece at 5.30 this morning. We go tomorrow to Zante and land near Olympia and then ride through Arcadia to Mykenae. . . .

On the same day he wrote an explanatory (and, as it happened, ineffectual) letter to his tutor in Magdalen:

My old tutor Mr. Mahaffy, Fellow of Trinity College Dublin, met me on my way to Rome and insisted on my going with him to Mykenae and Athens. The chance of seeing such great places – and in such good company was too great for me and I find myself now in Corfu, I am afraid I will not be able to be back at the beginning of term. I hope you will not mind if I miss ten days at the beginning: seeing Greece is really a great education for anyone and will I think benefit me greatly, and Mr. Mahaffy is such a clever man that it is quite as good as going to lectures to be in his society.[13]

Why had Mahaffy imposed this change of plan on Wilde? Presumably during the journey to Genoa he had found out about Wilde's failure in his attempt to win the Ireland Scholarship and had sensed his feeling of futility and waste during his recent months at Oxford. No doubt he had also observed Wilde's inclination towards Roman Catholicism. If Wilde could be brought to drink at the Greek fountainheads of classical civilization he might regain the academic steadiness that he had shown in T.C.D., forget his Pateresque aestheticism, and abandon his advances towards Rome.

The only extant piece of evidence about Mahaffy's intention emphasizes the last motive. Mahaffy wrote home to his wife on the same day as Wilde was writing his two letters:

We have taken Oscar Wilde with us, who has of course come round under the influence of the moment from Popery to Paganism, but what his Jesuit friends will say, who supplied the money to land him at Rome, it is not hard to guess. I think it is a fair case of cheating the Devil.

The methods adopted for the general reformation were not, it seems, entirely velvet-gloved:

> He has a lot of swagger about him which William Goulding vows he will knock out of him as soon as he gets him on horseback in Arcadia. We call him Snooks on account of this – to his much disgust.[14]

Gogarty, however, suggests that the lessons he learnt were not entirely chastening: it 'did little good for any humility a youth should have' to hear Mahaffy correct the King of Greece:

> I am afraid Your Majesty is labouring under a misapprehension. These tunnels are not catacombs. The Greeks were never so barbarous. They are entrances to silver mines.
> Plato, for all we know, may be a profiteer.

However, it seems that the King was well disposed towards Mahaffy, for on 15 February in that same year (1877) he had conferred on him the gold cross of the Order of the Redeemer 'for his philhellenic feelings'.

Wilde on his late return to Oxford was punished by 'rustication' for the rest of the term – 'I was sent down from Oxford for being the first undergraduate to visit Olympia' he remarked late in life, and by a fine of half his salary as a Demy (which was repaid in the following year). He wrote from Dublin to Oxford in May '. . . Mahaffy is raging! I never saw him so indignantly angry: he looks on it almost as an insult to himself.'[15] For some years after that Mahaffy and Wilde went on separate paths.

The acrimonious appendix to Mahaffy's earlier journey to Greece – presumably on the second he made more satisfactory arrangements for his second absence – suggests that, though so thoroughly successful and happy in so many spheres, he was not always at ease with his colleagues in Trinity. Unfortunately there are only too many other indications that this was so. Shortly before he left for Leyden Mahaffy clashed violently with McIvor, the professor of Moral Philosophy, who in 1874 complained to the board that Mahaffy would neither withdraw nor prove the charges he had made against him in connection with the recent moderatorship examination. The board having investigated the matter resolved that Mahaffy should apologize and Mahaffy wrote a letter which the board transmitted to McIvor withdrawing his charges 'on all points except the examining in subjects not indicated in the published course'. Years later Mahaffy himself appeared before the board as a plaintiff when he complained that the senior lecturer had called on Selss, the professor of German, to examine in French, 'while he, though a fellow and competent to examine was passed over'. The board decided that the senior lecturer had acted with fairness to all parties. At least once Mahaffy clashed with an even higher college authority than the senior lecturer. According to himself, when he was acting as an examiner for fellowship, 'my free speaking about the stupidity of one of the candidates was assumed to imply that I had treated him unfairly. Provost Salmon actually demanded to see the papers I had marked, and had them tested by two other fellows – an insult never before or since offered to any examiner here. When my results were justified the provost and board never even offered me an apology! Of course I knew that Salmon, though a great and good man was no gentleman, but had I had even a small independent income to support my family, the college would never have seen me again.'

Salmon's comment was Mahaffy 'owes his trouble to his own indiscreet way of talking which led men to think he was a partisan and his habit of overstating any case in which he is interested'.[16]

Mahaffy's outside interests, combined with unrestrained individuality and impetuosity, made it hard for him to 'fit in'. His autobiography makes it quite clear that some of his older colleagues, probably the majority in fact, did not impress him very favourably. They were, after all, mostly commonplace dons immersed in college teaching and administration and in the quiet social round of the Dublin professional classes. But by the 1870s the younger members of the Trinity classical school could scarcely be dismissed as dull or routine-ridden. Three years after Mahaffy became a fellow Arthur Palmer was elected to fellowship and in the following year, 1868, Robert Yelverton Tyrrell was elected. Tyrrell, who was to be one of the foundation members of the British Academy (a body to which Mahaffy never belonged) was one of the most gifted scholars of his time. A good editor of classical texts and an unsurpassed writer of Greek and Latin prose and verse, witty, urbane and charming, he encouraged undergraduates both by setting high standards –

he would wince at a false quantity – and by always endeavouring, even during a *viva*, to find true worth.

Arthur Palmer, one of the first Cheltonians to come to Trinity, developed into a remarkable scholar with an aptitude for emendation. Indeed emendation 'was a passion with Palmer'. Housman ranked him second only to Bentley in emending Ovid's *Heroides* and equal to Baehrens in Propertius, adding 'Palmer was a man more singularly and eminently gifted by nature than any scholar since Badham and than any English Latinist since Markland'. He had other talents. A fair cricketer, he was good at racquets and golf. And his range of interests is shown by two articles he contributed in the middle eighties to the *Quarterly Review*. The first is a critical study of the plays of Aristophanes, which contains incidentally, as might be expected in the *Quarterly*, some shrewd hits at Gladstonian liberalism; in the second, which is a balanced survey of horse-racing in England, Palmer displays a keen and well-informed interest in the Turf.

Tyrrell and Palmer were largely responsible for the journal called *Kottabos*, a famous source of original composition in Latin and Greek in its day. Its name taken from the Greek after-dinner wine-game suggests its purposes, or cheerful disavowal of any purpose. It published translations, parodies (in which Tyrrell excelled), lyrics and light verse. What was sought was verbal facility, easy transition from language to language, sentimental charm and a quick sense of the absurd. A number of the contributors – A. P. Graves, Edward Dowden, Thomas Rolleston, Oscar Wilde, John Bagnall Bury and Standish O'Grady – have niches in literary history. Mahaffy contributed only two short poems. The erudite frivolity which *Kottabos* cultivated could not have appealed to him. He was now engaged in the steady production of a series of works on classical literature and history intended both for the serious attention of his fellow scholars and for a wider public.

In addition he had sport, sociability, hospitality, travel and controversy to keep him fully occupied. Basil Gildersleeve, who will reappear in a later chapter as one of his severest critics, has left a lively picture of him at the beginning of the eighties. 'I called on Mahaffy in his rooms in Trinity,' he wrote, 'but I was informed by his servitress that Mr Mahaffy was umpiring a cricket game. . . .

[next day] as I was sitting in a rather forlorn mood at dinner
in the Shelbourne Hotel, a waiter handed me a note from
Mahaffy with an invitation to dinner that very evening. The
note had been belated in its delivery, and, immediately after
I had finished my meal, I mounted a jaunting-car, and
hastened to Mahaffy's house in order to make due apologies.
The hearty anathemas pronounced on the remissness of the
hotel people warmed my heart and set me at my ease. 'The
great feature of the dinner,' he said, 'was a salmon of my own
catch.' He was sitting in his dining-room when I arrived,
and pointed with pride to a row of silver cups which he had
won at various shooting matches. He had previously expressed
his disappointment at my failure to receive his note in due
time because he had wished me to hear his performance
as precentor in Trinity Chapel. The next day, as we
were walking along the arcade of Trinity, he was stopped
by a collegian who consulted him as to a difficult question
of counterpoint, and, a few steps further, he was held up
by one of the dons, who said that they were in great trouble
about the setting of an examination in Italian. 'Oh well,'
said Mr Mahaffy, 'I can manage it for you. . . .' As we
parted, he said with a sly smile: 'I will not give you a
letter to Jebb'. Jebb and he were engaged in a bitter quarrel
at the time, and Jebb knew how to hate.[17]

A few months after Gildersleeve's visit Mahaffy himself gave
an equally breathless account of his activities in a letter to a
friend:

I will tell you what I am doing. I am printing my big book
on Gk Lit & have only got through the first vol in four
months. I am engaged to write a work on Descartes by
Blackwood, who upon my refusing said he would give special
terms to the Master of Balliol, the Archbp of York & myself
if we wrote in the series (rather a swagger thing). I am
likewise engaged to write on Greek Education in a series of
Kegan Paul's, & do stray things at times in the——— I won't
tell you the names. I am lecturing and examining in Trin
Coll till I am black in the face, & last July I was appointed
Inspector of Schools under the Royal Commission now
sitting & go travelling about all over Ireland. Besides this

there is the correspondence with 120 pupils & their papas
& mamas, the care & nurture of a 'large small family',
as they say in Ireland, & besides my poor soul to be saved –
Is it any wonder I am a bad correspondent, when the
correspondence is mere pleasure? . . . You do me a great
kindness recommending me good books, though I don't know
whether one of them can be so called. Most seductions are
consummated, therefore that part of it seems hardly original;
as for an unconsummated marriage, it has been done *ad
nauseam* in *Mlle Giraud ma femme.* (By the way the Venus
de Gordes by the same Belot is a far stronger & better
book.) So that from neither point of view your author hit
on a new idea. If you are plotting a similar work yourself,
as I suspect, let me suggest a baby got by spontaneous
generation (?) – that might be a new idea, provided you
made perfectly sure in the story that the bottle was her-
metically sealed, & that it was the internal combustion
which produced it. This was the account I heard of Tyndall
from a very clever old orthodox schoolmaster in the country:
'Do you know what he says he is investigating, and so
busily that he can't appear any more in public?' 'No,'
said I. 'Well, he says he is inquiring *whether certain
maggots* would come out of a bottle, if you kept the cork in.'
This is not a bad account of the theory. But it would do well
for a society novel, for it would completely avoid any
obscenity of detail. My wife says Miss O'Brien's *Light &
Shade* is a good & clever book written about Ireland by a
woman of good breeding who knows it. . . . If Henry
Y[ates] T[hompson] comes over here & goes in for Home
Rule, I will have lots of dead cats ready, and men to throw
them at him – and it's well if he gets away with his life.
Liberals of all people ought to stand firm against these
dishonest knaves. But don't give up your liberal principles
because Gladstone has made some mistakes. After all, he is
worth the whole of them.[18]

Mahaffy it should be said was not easily labelled politically.
His profession debarred him from an active political career, and
temperamentally he found it hard to accept the restraints which
party loyalty imposes. At a general election which occurred

shortly after he was elected to fellowship, he played a conspicuous and inconsistent part in the university contest. He joined the committee of an ultra-conservative candidate and on the hustings seconded the liberal candidate.[19] Fourteen years later, in spite of his admiration for Gladstone, Mahaffy was a leading member of a majority in the University Senate which, when voting an address of condolence to the viceroy on the Phoenix Park murders, insisted on emphasizing that there was a widespread disorder in Ireland. In his speech Mahaffy declared that 'as a loyal body', the Senate 'should let it go forward that these murders were only the climax of many others'. After an acrimonious debate, in which Mahaffy's grammar was sharply criticized, his views prevailed.[20]

Mahaffy's feelings at this meeting of the Senate were probably intensified by awareness that he himself might have shared the fate of Burke and Cavendish. On 6 May he was to have been introduced to the new chief secretary. Just as Mahaffy was about to leave college for the Castle, he was detained by a pupil, looking for a loan. Having dealt with his pupil, Mahaffy started for the Castle, missed the chief secretary, followed him as far as the Park gate and then turned back. Mahaffy, it is said, 'used to tell the story in awestruck tones which left the listener feeling how much more terrible the crime might have been if there had been a third victim'.

At the close of the seventies Mahaffy was entrusted with a task which gave him an opportunity to travel widely in Ireland, to display his gifts as an observer, and to indulge in his penchant for controversy. In August 1879 the Endowed School commissioners asked him to make an inspection of the Irish grammar schools and during the next twelve months Mahaffy travelled all over Ireland, inspected a number of schools, visited seven well known English schools for the purpose of comparison, and produced a long, idiosyncratic, racily written report. School life always interested him. It had for Mahaffy the fascination of the often observed but never experienced. And his school tour gave him plenty to comment on and a good opportunity for the production of *obiter dicta* on a wide range of educational topics. In one school he was surprised to find the senior boys reading late in bed with paraffin lamps, a habit he thought extremely dangerous. In another he was annoyed to find the boys forbidden to talk during dinner, 'a practice', he declared, 'unsocial and unwholesome'. He was dismayed when visiting Saint Columba's College to find an excellent racquet-court and two Eton fives-courts unused. 'It does not seem natural,' he wrote, 'that boys should prefer walking about the country to playing good games.' He thoroughly disapproved of flogging, being sure that to treat boys with lenity and kindness was 'the right extreme if any extreme be right'. Yet he saw that there was 'an ingrained idleness in many boys not to be encountered by moral suasion' and he noted that in one school where the headmaster was 'an apostle' of the theory of treating boys with lenity and generous confidence, discipline was not good. Mahaffy also disapproved of the cubicle system for dormitories. When a headmaster told him it encouraged prayer, Mahaffy retorted, 'There are other things promoted by privacy besides prayer.'

In his report he made a number of sensible suggestions. Small schools should be amalgamated. Buildings should be improved and kept clean and well ventilated. Good school libraries should be provided and elderly masters pensioned off. As an example of what could happen in the absence of a retirement scheme, Mahaffy told how, when visiting an isolated school in the Midlands, he had met an aged master, perhaps a centenarian, quite incapable of teaching, who according to tradition had once 'pulled an ear off a boy'. Mahaffy also urged that the members of governing bodies should be 'practical educators and men young enough to keep the pace with the changing fancies and theories of this age. For these are the real conservatives in such matters. No one is so likely to be led away by novelties as the elderly amateur in education who knows nothing of its practical working and legislates on specious theories.'[21]

Mahaffy himself was extremely critical of contemporary educational trends.[22] He strongly attacked what he considered to be a fundamental mistake, 'that with the proper desire of giving boys general information and teaching them useful and practical knowledge, there is come in the stupid notion that this is to be done effectually by pouring these subjects directly into the mind'. The result was that both in England and Ireland boys were overworked and '*addled by the multiplicity of their subjects*'. In Ireland, Mahaffy emphatically pointed out, the recently established Intermediate Education Board by its systems of monetary rewards, based on examination results, was supplying a false stimulus to education. Boys were getting merely a smattering of a number of subjects and 'the present boa constrictor system of competitive examination is strangling our youth in its fatal embrace'. Mahaffy suggested one immediate reform of the intermediate system, the exclusion of 'music, Irish language, natural science and all the other lesser subjects from the competition'. He strongly criticized the principles on which, he believed, contemporary educational policy was based. He did not agree with the philosophic radicals, who 'insisted with Plato (though they had probably never read a line of his dialogues) that vice is ignorance' and that with the spread of education most social evils would vanish. Instead, Mahaffy suggested, with the spread of education 'the forms and types of lawlessness may change, the vices of the fashionable world – and they are not a few – may replace those of the slums, there will be at times a perceptible cheering improvement; but then will come some fatal moment when some disaster, the sword, pestilence or the famine, may break down barriers solicitously constructed against wrong and show us schemes of injustice, violence and cruelty in the most civilized countries of the world'. Sceptical about the inevitability of progress, Mahaffy was convinced that for the bulk of mankind education was bound to be limited. 'Inequality,' he wrote, 'is and must be the first condition of every society.' Therefore, the aim of education generally speaking, should be to fit a man for the station in life he was almost bound to occupy. 'What we want,' Mahaffy wrote, 'is not an additional crowd of shoddy graduates, but a large number of earnest farmers, artisans and shopkeepers.' Primary education he thought, should be restricted to 'something clear, definite, and almost universally attainable', supplemented for many by vocational and technical education. And since the spread of literacy had led to the widespread reading of 'the lowest and worst forms of ephemeral literature', he wanted the free library service to be greatly extended.

But what, it may be asked, about the poor boy of outstanding abilities? Mahaffy was ready with an answer. If a youth had outstanding ability the road to the top had long been open to him. 'We can point with pride,' Mahaffy declared, 'to some of the greatest Irishmen who have begun life as sizars of Trinity College,

Dublin.' But 'is it a splendid thing,' he went on to ask, for the poor boy 'of average smartness and ambition . . . to leave his sphere and become an ordinary member of the professional class? . . . Is he likely to be happier and more content? Is he likely to do more good? Or are we not raising up a large body of malcontents, who will distract society and seek to destroy those more refined classes who refuse to take them at their own estimation?'

He was outspokenly contemptuous about extension schemes and 'sham universities', which were primarily examining bodies. 'The B.A.,' he remarked, 'is like the commission in the army which used to mark the officer and the gentleman, and which is therefore very attractive to those whose claim to the latter is doubtful.' True education, best exemplified in the ancient universities, was essentially 'the prolonged teaching of the great subjects of knowledge, currently to pupils under moral discipline, leading a common life and having their characters moulded by subtle forces which operate perpetually upon the common life'. And this sort of education, he bluntly pointed out, would not be cheap. The great subjects were of course classics, mathematics and philosophy. Reluctantly he admitted that the pressure of modern science 'may compel us to extend somewhat the old curriculum'. But in the early nineties he doubted if modern languages should be university subjects. 'We learned the classics far more thoroughly,' he remarked, 'before the faddists inflicted on us papers on comparative philology.' He condemned 'the modern fallacy of infecting the study of history with that of political economy' – which probably marred 'the great qualities for the historian'. And it may be added that as late as 1913 he was prepared to assert that a man who had secured a degree in classics or philosophy could 'read his history and his English literature for himself'.[23]

Though temperamentally an optimist – 'I always find things turn out better than one expects', he wrote to a friend in 1885 – Mahaffy could not help being pessimistic when he contemplated educational trends. But at least he must have been conscious that he himself had been educated on sound principles, and the early nineties, the very time when he was publishing his jeremiads, was a buoyant epoch in his career. His publication of the Flinders Petrie papyri in 1891–3 made his reputation as a serious

scholar. And just at the time when he was adding to that reputation Trinity embarked on a series of ceremonies and festivities
which gave scope to his social gifts. In 1891 it was decided that
in the following year the tercentenary of the College should be
celebrated. The choice of this year in preference to 1891, 1893
or 1894, all possible dates, could be justified on sound historical
grounds. But it can now also be said that placing the Trinity
College Commemoration midway between the two jubilees
unconsciously emphasized that for Trinity the Victorian age
had been a great era of peace, prosperity and solid achievement,
and that amongst the fellows and professors of Trinity there were
a goodly number of Victorian worthies.[24]

The first step was to appoint a planning committee, and this
committee appointed no fewer than ten sub-committees. Mahaffy
was a member of the main committee and of six of the
sub-committees – the dinner committee, the commencements
committee, the house committee, the concert committee, the
reception committee and, perhaps most important of all, the
invitations committee. Invitations were sent out world wide to
many learned bodies and distinguished people, including the
Queen, who expressed regret that she could not bear the fatigue
of the journey. Two most eminent Victorians, Tennyson and
Gladstone, were also regretfully unable to come. Gladstone at the
close of 1891 wrote, 'it would be very daring on the part of a
man now on the stroke of 82 to enter into any engagement for the
coming July – but if I do not profit at the proper time by this
gracious summons, it will not be my fault but my misfortune'.
In fact when the time came he was campaigning vigorously in a
general election. However, in addition to a galaxy of scholars
representing universities and colleges at home and abroad,
a number of well known figures accepted invitations, including
Lord Acton, Lord Dufferin and Ava, Wolseley, Lecky, Alma-
Tadema, Frederick Pollock, Aubrey de Vere, Creighton and
Henry Irving, who was chaired by the undergraduates. Most of
the guests arrived on 4 July by the Holyhead–Kingstown mail-
boat, and the editor of the Tercentenary Records with extraordinary enthusiasm emphasized that though those who would
be present at the next centenary would 'no doubt boast that they
are living better than their ancestors in most things . . . it is very
doubtful whether they will, even in a hundred years, have

EM

surpassed the splendid boats of the City of Dublin Steam Packet Company'. From the morning of 4 July the guests in academic robes, headed by the band of the Sussex regiment, went in procession to Saint Patrick's Cathedral. Then there were garden parties, a great commencements at which seventy-one degrees were conferred, banquets, a cricket match, a performance at the Gaiety of the *Rivals* 'very well acted' by a student cast, a smoking concert, a visit to Birr to see the great telescope, and a ball. Trinity was delighted, in Tyrrell's words, 'to see the hearty hand of good fellowship stretched out to us by all the world'. Or, as Mahaffy said in one of the two speeches he delivered during the celebrations, the tercentenary made Trinity men feel 'they were members of one great family of men of letters and learning which tends to make human nature larger, and loftier, and purer throughout the world'.

A brief description of Mahaffy's appearance just at that time has survived in a Dublin gossip-journal: 'a tall, heavily built man, with reddish hair, sanguine complexion, over-hanging brows and grey eyes [others thought them blue], like a brace of surgeon's knives. He has large hands, thick wrists and a habit of occasionally pinching his lower lip during concentrated meditation.'[25]

But he had little time for meditation during the tercentenary celebrations. He was largely responsible for the historical section of the *Book of Trinity College* which was produced for the occasion. He proposed the health of the universities of the world at a college dinner in a speech which probably sounded better after dinner than it reads in cold print. (It rather tactlessly confined its special eulogies to the universities of Holland, Germany, Austria and Italy, as 'those to whom I for one feel very special obligation'.) Every day, as precentor, he conducted a full choral service in the college chapel. Most important of all, he took the lead amongst the fellows in promoting a scheme suggested by a number of graduates, that the tercentenary should be marked by the erection of a new building in college. (Mahaffy, as his contribution to the *Book of Trinity College* shows, was already deeply interested in the architectural history of the college: to him building was a great sign of collegiate vitality.) At a meeting held during the celebrations he was able to report that over £6,000 had already been subscribed – remarking that at a previous meeting many who 'came to scoff, remained to pay'. And he pointed out that as the board had promised a site in college the new building would have to be of 'the most solid and handsome kind'. The site given by the college was the strip on the north side of Library Square occupied by a Queen Anne terrace, known from its condition as Rotten Row. The Graduates Memorial Building, completed in 1902, which replaced it, is certainly solid. Useful in so far as it provides chambers for undergraduates and rooms for college societies, it is a plain, rather graceless building, vaguely French Renaissance in style but remarkably devoid of ornament out of deference to the austere eighteenth-century library which faces it across the square. When, shortly afterwards, Mahaffy began to admire the Georgian style particularly and became the first president of the Dublin Georgian Society, he may have regretted his committee's choice of architecture. But at least his enthusiastic efforts had produced a liberal response. As he watched the plans approaching fulfilment his mind perhaps turned to the completion of his own college career – the provostship.

chapter three

The sociable man

'Take me all round, I am the best man in Trinity'

During these years of steady advancement in academic influence and scholastic reputation, another side of Mahaffy's life had given him deep satisfaction, though it also provoked the most malicious criticism that he had to endure. This was his enjoyment of what he called 'high society'. At times it almost seems as if he valued it even more than his academic achievements. In his autobiographical *Summary* he turns at one point from a critical commentary on the state of T.C.D. in the past to consider his own 'psychological history'. He attributes what he modestly calls his 'limited success' in life first to 'moderate abilities, promoted by a general education far wider and more stimulating than that of most boys', together with diligence and quickness. Next, and more emphatically, he mentions his social advantages – musicianship, fluency in French and German, familiarity with foreign countries, and skill in shooting, fishing, and cricket ('which was a useful introduction to good society').

Unfortunately for his biographers, after less than five hundred words Mahaffy abandoned this inquiry. Enough is said to convey the apparently unconscious implication that when he thought of 'success' (a word which occurs frequently in his *Summary*), what was foremost in his mind was social success. Then, tantalizingly, instead of examining his motives further he sheers off the topic, like this:

... the psychological history of any man who has gone

through a long life, and who has been obliged by his profession to teach, is a difficult and delicate enquiry, which only the man himself can write, and on which he may readily appear to the reader a suspect witness. On the whole then I think it wiser to postpone this side of my life to another essay . . .

'Obliged by his profession to teach' is a curious phrase when used by a man celebrated as a singularly zestful and enthusiastic teacher. Does it, in the light of the accompanying emphasis on social success, imply that looking back over his life Mahaffy regretted the long hours of academic toil which had kept him from fuller enjoyment of society? Were the happiest hours of his life those spent 'among the *élite* at a banquet, in the shade of a family tree' (as his young disciple Gogarty, expressed it in a mild lampoon, to be quoted in a later chapter)? In fact unfriendly critics bluntly accused him of being a social climber and a snob. Others, who knew him better, denied or at any rate qualified these hurtful accusations. Before trying to decide which view was nearer the truth it may be well first to glance at some of the personal talents which Mahaffy regarded as his chief social assets.

Music remained Mahaffy's favourite art until in his later years he turned to the special study of architecture. He had once thought of becoming a professional musician himself. Indeed his musical gifts as a child had caused his mother some anxiety, for 'in the semi-Puritan society of those days, no professional artist could aspire to a good social position'. So in the hope that he 'might attain to a higher walk in life' she had discouraged his professional ambition. Eventually, when it had become certain that her son would never have a good singing voice – a 'weird, cracked voice' a friend called it in later life – she 'used to thank God from her heart' for that deliverance. Perhaps, then, one may detect a slight tone of regret, as well as modesty, in Mahaffy's remark:

The only thing for which I had any exceptional gifts was for music. From very early days I had an accurate sense of pitch, and could give on my voice any note required, and my memory for the things I heard was very quick and very retentive.

On the other hand, though music was not ranked as a gentle-man's profession, the puritan tradition, even in its stricter forms, encouraged amateur music in the home, and Dublin had been a city of good music since the eighteenth century, when Handel had come over for the first performance of his *Messiah*. Well-bred people were expected to cultivate their musical gifts. Mahaffy's mother had in fact been an accomplished pianist in her day, having taken lessons from as eminent a teacher as Moscheles. So Mahaffy was taught violin, piano, and singing, and, besides, he was taken regularly to the musical services in the two Church of Ireland cathedrals in Dublin and to concerts. In later life he remembered particularly a performance of Mendelssohn's *Elijah* at which John Stanford, father of the Dublin-born composer C. V. Stanford, sang the bass solo. Later in life Mahaffy had some controversy with C. V. Stanford on musical matters, and once when he had the worse of an argument he was heard to mutter, 'I don't like the stamp of genius on my toes'.[1]

Music, besides being a source of constant enjoyment, extended his social scope, as he notes in a repetitive passage of his *Summary*:

> . . . for music I had considerable gifts, and a very great and accurate memory; yet . . . I could never create an original melody which withstood my criticism when it was a week old. On the other hand, playing the violin moderately, but accurately, and transposing my accompts [*sic* for accompaniments] on the piano, brought me into interesting society. I need only mention that I often played in a trio or quartet when the 'cello was in the hands of Sir Thomas Staples, who had been Irish M.P. in 1800 and that I once (at Lady Cloncurry's) transposed an accpt for Madame Trebelli, which far better pianists in the room were afraid to attempt.

When he entered Trinity, the Dublin University Choral Society (founded in 1837) gave him further scope for enjoying and promoting good music. An incident in 1887 involved the Society (and presumably Mahaffy as a prominent member and former officer) in a clash with a royal personage whose grandson he was later to count among his friends. That year being the jubilee of the Choral Society, as well as of Queen Victoria, the officers and

committee decided to perform Sullivan's *Golden Legend*, fresh
from its first production at the Leeds festival. The orchestration
required a special set of bells for one of its most dramatic
moments. Only one set existed, that cast for the Leeds festival.
These were ordered, and duly arrived in Dublin. Soon afterwards telegrams poured in – there are twenty-six, including
replies, in the Society's minute-book – requesting, urging,
demanding, beseeching, that the bells should be returned immediately, as they were needed in a special command performance
for the Kaiser, Wilhelm I, in Berlin. To the delight of Dublin
concert-goers and of patriotic Irishmen in general the Society
refused to yield. The concert, complete with bells, was a
spectacular success (even though owing to a ridiculous mis-
understanding *God save the Queen* was omitted). The Kaiser had
to be content with Chinese gongs.[2]

Though never a musician of more than local reputation,
Mahaffy had some lasting influence on Dublin music. He
specially admired Bach and did much to promote the revival
of interest in his work among Dublin choirmasters. As Precentor
of the College Chapel for many years, he spent much time and
energy in keeping up a high standard in the choral services. He
composed a few choral pieces, including an *Amen* set for eight
voices (which was sung at his funeral service), a robust setting
of the College grace-before-meat, a *Magnificat* and *Nunc dimittis*,
and a vocal quartet.[3] In 1891 the Dublin University made him
an honorary doctor in music. The robes of the degree – white
flowered silk faced with rose satin – were his favourite academic
dress among the many that he was entitled to wear. He liked to
recall how once, when he was wearing this elegant and impressive
robe in an academic procession at Louvain, mothers among the
bystanders held up their infants for him to bless, thinking that
he must be some very exalted prelate – and he blessed them.

One can catch a glimpse of Mahaffy's energy and enthusiasm
in musical matters in an incident described by a junior colleague,
though Mahaffy was then an old man:

> One Sunday morning Mahaffy and I were walking out of
> the Chapel . . . after service. Robin Gwynn had read the
> lesson (Genesis 1). He walked past us. Mahaffy stopped him.
> 'You read very well, but you made one mistake', he said. . . .

'Not – "And God said: Let there be light and there *was*
light", but "God said: Let there be light and there was
LIGHT!" ' He threw up his arms as he said this.[4]

Clearly Mahaffy was thinking of the great climax to the 'Let
there be light' chorus in Haydn's *Creation*.

Mahaffy often referred to musical matters in his conversation
and writings. Unpublished notes on his travels contain tran-
scripts of sounds that caught his ear – a cry of a muezzin at
Luxor, the crowing of cocks in Athos monasteries. These prove
his good musical memory, but the tradition that he could write
out the whole of Bach's St John Passion from memory sounds
like an exaggeration. He included a notable chapter on Greek
music in his Lowell Lectures of 1908–9. In all likelihood he
prompted his pupil H. S. Macran (afterwards a fellow of the
College and Professor of Moral Philosophy 1901–34) to produce
his masterly study on the harmonics of Aristoxenus. Probably,
too, the experience described in the following fragment of
autobiography from his Lowell Lectures may have led another of
his disciples to publish a notable book:

> I well remember persuading with great difficulty, a band
> of gipsies in Hungary, to play for me not the music of the
> Hungarians, for which they are so celebrated, but some of
> their own Oriental stuff which they play among themselves
> in private. I found it wholly unintelligible on account of the
> scale, which seemed to have thirteen or fourteen notes
> within the octave.[5]

Twenty years after that passage had been published Mahaffy's
godson, Walter Starkie (then a fellow of Trinity and Professor
of Spanish), went to Hungary and made a special study of gypsy
music, as described in his *Raggle-taggle* (1933). Starkie as a boy
had been discouraged by his father from spending much time
on music, but Mahaffy supported his godson and gave him his
Steiner violin which had been one of Mahaffy's 'great consola-
tions in life'.

Starkie has recalled how Mahaffy used to discourse on music
and morality:

> The older I become the more I am convinced that the
> moral characters of our musicians are directly influenced by

the music they cultivate. Hence the great lesson to be
derived from the singing of the Bach Cantatas, for Johann
Sebastian Bach was a most worthy representative of the
middle-classes – a traditional God-fearing German, educated
on the ancient German chorales, whose life was a model of
the domestic virtues. Alas, we moderns have unduly lost
sight of the moral side of music. Take, for example . . . the
passionate love songs of the newer Italian opera . . . they
are directly injurious to the character. In fact the more
beautifully and perfectly the music corresponds to the words
of those operas the more mischievous they are likely to be.[6]

Later, in reply to a listener's reference to 'the rapturous thrill'
she had experienced at performances of *Parsifal* and *Tristan
and Isolde*, Mahaffy (who had once made a pilgrimage to
Bayreuth with his daughter Elsie: her rather acidulous description of the journey has survived) continued:

Wagner . . . was an unutterable cad and should have
been hounded out of all decent society. When he was writing
the *Liebestod* he was living in sin with the wife of his
best friend, Wesendonck. Such music is most offensive to our
taste and must produce pernicious effects on the characters
of those who sing it. When, therefore, we hear it commonly
remarked that musicians are jealous, quarrelsome and rakish,
or that a young man with a good tenor voice is sure to go to
ruin, there may be musical reasons for such observations,
which did not escape the ancient Greeks, though they are
completely ignored nowadays.

This ethical theory of music was certainly Greek: Plato, among
others, has much to say about it. But the reference to the young
man with a good tenor voice goes back to his mother.

Starkie recounts another discourse of Mahaffy's after a meeting
– and an argument about the dangers of Wagner – with Hans
Richter when he came to Dublin to conduct the Hallé orchestra:

Today . . . I have proved to my satisfaction that the
celebrated quarrel of my youth between Wagnerites and the
Brahmsians is still as active as ever. . . . In College I never
agreed with Macran's craze for Wagner whom he idolized
as he did Hegel. I am still a Brahmsian, though . . . I would

except the Overture and Prelude to the third act of *Die Meistersinger* from my general condemnation of Wagner's art. Brahms and his friend, the violinist Joachim, personified all that was noble in music. Remember . . . it was Joachim who, by his classical style of violin-playing, raised the status of the soloist, and by his example as a quartet-player made the world familiar with the last quartets of Beethoven. Since his death . . . there had been no artist worthy to take his place, except the Belgian violinist Ysaye whom I look upon as the last of the Mohicans. Ysaye . . . is the only one who plays like a gentleman, he has the religion of his instrument, and he doesn't play with that abominable tremolo – a degenerate and effeminate habit which destroys the playing of most virtuosi today.[7]

Here, in this refusal to accept art for art's sake, one finds an example of Mahaffy's aesthetic and artistic 'impurity', which antagonized some of his contemporaries. Though music was clearly a source of great joy and delight to him, he also valued and cherished it as a powerful influence for good or evil in the body politic. In this, as in so many other principles of his, Mahaffy was a good Aristotelian, for Aristotle in his *Ethics* insists that the supreme values in human life are not those of any specific art or science but those of that architectonic art-and-science which controls society as a whole, namely, politics in its highest sense. In contrast, freedom-loving artists and writers have always been quick to see, behind this principle lurks a threat of censorship and interference. Yet, philosophically at least, Mahaffy's beliefs that art should serve the general welfare of society, and that forms of art which endanger this welfare should be discouraged, are not dishonourable. Further, if one is inclined to dislike praise of a musician for playing 'like a gentleman', one must remember that for Mahaffy the term essentially meant a man of high integrity and honourable principle.

Mahaffy was proud of his versatility. 'Take me all round, I am the best man in Trinity College', he remarked in his early prime.[8] He was thinking principally, perhaps, of his academic competence to lecture and examine in Hebrew, French, German, Italian, theology and music, as well as in his own special subjects, classics, ancient history and philosophy. His publications, too, extended over an unusually wide area. But he was also, no doubt, thinking of his excellence in cricket and field sports. As he saw it in his *Summary*, he had two reasons for being grateful to cricket: it had been 'of great social as well as of physical value' to him. He was first invited to the Viceregal Lodge when the Lord Lieutenant, Lord Carlisle, saw that he was a useful bowler. At that time, in the eighteen-sixties, while racing remained the sport of kings, cricket, which was just emerging from top-hats and under-arm bowling, was the sport of viceroys in Ireland. Later it became a rather perilous recreation for a while. Mahaffy wrote to a friend in 1882, 'It is curious nowadays to go to the Viceregal Lodge to dine or even to play cricket hedged about with soldiers and police.'[9]

Mahaffy was undoubtedly a cricketer of considerable ability, as the standard history of cricket in Ireland testified. Best as a bowler, his most notable achievement was that of taking thirteen wickets against an I Zingari team for the Gentlemen of Ireland in 1866. In another match against the same team in 1874 when rain caused the viceroy, the Duke of Abercorn, to retire from his captaincy in the field, Mahaffy took command and promptly put himself on to bowl, remarking, 'I am going to get the next five wickets: I love rain.' Then he rubbed the ball in the wet grass and got his wickets.[10]

Sometimes cricket led to less serious sports. After one match at the Viceregal Lodge some of the spectators organized a comic race between the Viceroy (the Duke of Abercorn, then aged sixty-four) and Mahaffy, whose advantage in age – he was thirty-six – was handicapped by his wearing cricket pads and carrying a cricket bat (or, according to another version, wearing a waterproof and carrying an open umbrella). Part of the fun was that Mahaffy was a very inelegant runner. As one spectator, Lord Frederick Hamilton, described him, 'he waddled and paddled slowly over the ground like a duck, with his feet turned outwards'. The contest ended farcically when two of the onlookers tripped Mahaffy up with a rope just as he was reaching the winning-post.[11]

He played several times for All Ireland against All England. His best recorded score as a bat in a first class match was 52 for Dublin University Past and Present against a United South of England XI captained by W. G. Grace and including some of

FROM AN ANCIENT GREEK POT—IN TRINITY COLLEGE
COLLECTION.

Mahaffy as a cricketer
(reproduced from a contemporary postcard)

the leading professionals of England, in 1876. Two years later as a vice-president of the Field Sports Section of the British Association on the occasion of the Association's visit to Dublin in 1878, after Grace had made his presidential speech Mahaffy proposed the vote of thanks and remarked that Grace's observations on bowling were 'worthy of attention'. One would like to know how Grace took this meed of praise. Both of them were experts in psychological gamesmanship. For example Mahaffy, when a ball of his was hit to the boundary, would solemnly walk down the pitch, shake hands with the batsman and congratulate him; and a phrase, which he liked to use when a batsman had a narrow escape, became a catch-word: 'That man was *morally* bowled.'

Until well into his fifties Mahaffy liked to go to the nets in the College Park and show the undergraduates how to bat. Perhaps a remark by an outspoken young American visitor, the celebrated J. B. King, helped to end these forays. One day he watched Mahaffy batting at the nets, not knowing his reputation in the College. After a while King went up to him and said, 'Well, Sir, if I was bowling to you, I would require only one fieldsman to take your wicket.' 'And where would you place your one fieldsman?' Mahaffy asked. 'Twenty yards behind the wicket, Sir, just to pick up the bails.'

Much as Mahaffy enjoyed cricket, he was happier still when he was shooting or fishing in good company. As a marksman he had won a place on the Irish team, and even when he was sixty years of age he outshot some of the crack military shots of Germany. A target, marked by his winning bullets and presented to him by Wilhelm II as a memento of his skill, still survives as a family heirloom. (This was the occasion when Mahaffy, having observed the conduct of the Prussian officers towards soldiers in the ranks, genially warned them, it is said, that their men would probably shoot them in the back in the next war.)

In the field his accuracy, especially at snipe, was far above the average. A frequent observer, Sir Shane Leslie, has recorded:

> I was present when the Professor made his wonderful shot at a snipe which he killed between 80 and 90 yards with a single pellet. I saw the gamekeeper, James Vogan, walk the yards out, and I picked the bird up, but it was not a jack snipe, which would not have been visible at that distance. . . . The snipe were very wild, and a great wisp of them rose ahead. The whole party stopped to congratulate the old Professor.
>
> He maintained a ritual of sport out snipe-shooting. He took the centre a little ahead with the head-keeper and dogs in attendance. We boys, family agents and friends, covered the flanks. If he brought a bird down, the line

halted till it was recovered. He fired desperately distant
shots – especially at woodcock. He could not believe he could
miss and demanded search. 'D'ye mean I did not even
hit that bird?', and the keeper would console him – 'Ye
did indeed – He went away lamenting his wounds.'

I remember him sallying forth on our jaunting car to face
the Monaghan bogs. With his old-fashioned gun and soft
clerical hat and gaiters he looked not unlike Mr. Pickwick
trundling ahead but certainly showing himself a Mr. Winkle in
sporting assiduity.

He held different theories as to the cooking as well as to
the shooting of the snipe. He held that the marksman should
fire in the split second he sighted the white glint of its
breast turning in the sun at whatever distance. I once saw
him kill a bird nearly ninety yards away with a single
pellet. He was over three-score years at the time.

Out on the lough or over the bogs his conversation
flagged no more than his keenness. He was impossible to
weary. Once we launched him on the slopes of Lough
Derg's Saints Island in pursuit of grouse. He struggled
gamely through the heavy moss and vegetable débris of
centuries until suddenly he disappeared leaving only the
barrels of his gun above ground. He was enormously interested
in his surroundings and was full of converse when we
rescued him. . . .

Theories delighted him. When I caught a specimen of that
rare fish a char, he insisted that it proved, like certain
wildered herbs, the monastic memories of the lake. He also
held that pike were introduced into Irish waters by the
Normans – to fill the fishponds of their Abbeys. There was
no old Irish word for the pike as there was for the trout,
who was like the native stock slowly dispossessed by the
more powerful alien. . . .

There were of course days when Mahaffy was missing
birds and his eye had to be politely wiped by the nearest
gun. When two or more had fired, the Professor could be
heard crying to the keepers – 'my bird, I think, my bird!'
and it was etiquette that he should not be contradicted.

In later life he liked to go to Donegal, his father's native county, for the trout fishing and grouse shooting in the autumn. According to Leslie, he was happier and more energetic there than anywhere else in Ireland. The quieter sport gave him more opportunities for conversations – or monologues. One of his favourite fishing stories was about a monstrous pike that he claimed to have seen floating on Lough Derg. Some of his hearers were inclined to discount it as Mahaffyian exaggeration, though he cited witnesses. But some years later when Lough Derg was netted for food supplies during the first world war fishermen caught what they thought was a drowned sheep in their net. It turned out to be a huge pen pike weighing sixty-two pounds (including a nine pound fish in its gullet), and Mahaffy was vindicated. Leslie in recalling Mahaffy's version of the monster's first appearance adds: 'The wonder and power of the story lay in the spaced sentences and subdued stress with which the Provost recited it amid the foam-streaked shallows of Lough Derg.' At other times when the fish were not taking he would recite passages from Gibbon – once in Leslie's hearing the whole account of the fall of Constantinople. Or else he would discourse on the historic associations of the district, recalling that the Blackwater in Co. Monaghan was the boundary separating O'Neill from MacMahon and from the English of the Pale, or plan an outrageous history of the local families, or (as he wrote to Leslie) interchange 'views of life in the boat, as in a Greek tragedy with Muldoon [a loquacious boatman] for a Chorus'.

chapter four

The art of conversation

with a challenge from Oscar Wilde

'Aristotle at an afternoon tea'

Helpful as Mahaffy's talents for cricket, field sports and music were as social assets, they had a limited scope compared with what he well knew to be the supreme social art, conversation. By common consent he was a master in it. 'A really great talker in a certain way',[1] was what Oscar Wilde called him. Gogarty went further – 'the finest talker in Europe'[2] – a superlative that would have been hard to authenticate. But at all events the voice of Dublin, a city famous for its conversation, was almost unanimous in admitting, though not in liking, his talking powers.

As a child he had been lucky in having excellent opportunities for observing good models:

> . . . my parents were exceptionally good talkers, and, what is far better, promoters of conversation. . . . I remember the orator Whiteside fresh from his triumph in the defence of O'Connell, and the centre of interest wherever he appeared by reason of his brilliant talk.

He was not slow in trying to rival them. His mother was 'perpetually warning him' that he was 'always disposed to talk too much'. There is early evidence that he tried to check this loquacity. A notebook, dating from when he was fifteen, contains two quotations on conversation. The first is from La Bruyère:

> It is a great misfortune not to have mind enough to talk well, nor judgement enough to be silent. The art of conversation consists much less in your own abundance than in

enabling others to find talk for themselves. Men do not wish to admire you: they want to please.

The second is La Rochefoucauld's:

> The reason why few persons are agreeable in conversation is because each thinks more of what to say than of what others are saying, and seldom listens but when he desires to speak.

Whether he also had ambitions at that early age to become a 'centre of interest' like Whiteside is not certain. But a prophetic passage in an early lecture that he gave in 1869 to the girls of Alexandra College, Dublin, shows that he may have had something of that kind in mind. Discoursing on the legend about William Tell, he asked his audience to notice how some of its elements seemed to have been transferred to it from earlier sources. This, he concluded, is 'but one more instance of the well-known tendency in the human mind of fitting a good story to the most suitable existing character that can be found':

> The very same good stories which were attached to the celebrated old Vice-Provost of Trinity College known as Jacky Barrett, in our parents' time, were, in my college days, transferred, at least in part, to Dr. Wall, the patriarch of the period; and even now these stories are floating about, waiting for another name, sufficiently venerable or eccentric, to which they will doubtless attach themselves and start into new existence. You may remember, in the same way, that a few years ago every good joke, however originated, used, in Dublin, to attach itself to the late Archbishop [Whately]. I venture to predict, that whenever there arises another man of equally high position, and of equally jocular disposition, these same stories will take refuge under his wing, and flourish beneath the shadow of his name.[3]

It was a curious foreshadowing – whether conscious or not – of what would eventually happen to John Pentland Mahaffy.

Eighteen years later he published his *Principles of the art of conversation* (1887), appropriately dedicated *To my silent friends*. Intent on intellectual discipline, he arranged his essay on strictly Aristotelian lines – Wilde headed his cutting review of it

F<small>M</small>

'Aristotle and afternoon tea' – defining the functions, analysing the conditions, and discussing the materials, of good conversation according to a formal classification. He listed the necessary qualities:

a   Physical: 1   A sweet tone of voice
              2   Absence of local accent
              3   Absence of tricks and catchwords

b   Mental: 1   Knowledge
              2   Quickness

c   Moral: 1   Modesty
              2   Simplicity
              3   Unselfishness
              4   Sympathy
              5   Tact

As qualities 'too wide to be called conditions of conversation' he added moral worth and truthfulness, and then, as 'too special ever to be obtained without great and peculiar gifts', wit and humour.

Strangely enough Mahaffy himself was not particularly well endowed in the required physical requirements. His voice was guttural and unpleasing, and as for 'absence of local accent', his English companions spoke of his 'brogue'. (Flinders Petrie recorded that in 1892 when he met Mahaffy in Rome, after seeing many places, Mahaffy suddenly grasped his arm and said, 'My dear choild, we're seeing a ghreat dheal too much!')[4] Surviving records of his conversational style certainly show freedom from catchwords and *clichés*, but in later life he seems to have returned often to the same topics and to have used carefully calculated gestures and pauses with theatrical effect, as when he would open his usually half-closed eyes to impress a special point – and their intense blueness – on a listener. He is conscious, however, in his *Conversation* that there could be exceptions to his rules, for 'we have all met great talkers whose Scotch burr or Irish brogue seemed an essential feature of their charm'; and 'a slight impediment or stammer' can add zest to conversation if 'what the speaker is hesitating to utter is worth waiting for'. His own lisping pronunciation of the letter *r* as *w*, whether natural or affected – in imitation of certain aristocrats, the malicious said – was renowned.

His greatest strength was in what he called the mental qualities. In knowledge, 'which may be either General (books, men)' – he was given the nickname 'the General' from this – or 'Special (great topics; the topic of the day)', he probably had few superiors in his time. An omnivorous polyglot reader with a tenacious memory he could excel in an extraordinary variety of topics. He had, too, more than most of his rivals 'the advantage of having seen and conversed with the greatest men of the day'. As he expressed it:

> The man who has just come from the society of kings and queens, or great generals, or politicians, or literary men whose names are exceptionally prominent at the time, can generally furnish some personal details by which people imagine they can explain to themselves great and unexpected results.

There was one empty shelf in Mahaffy's store of conversational topics – modern science. According to a critical observer, Lord Danesfort, he 'had not so much as a glimmering of scientific knowledge'.[5] Characteristically he was not prepared to acknowledge this as a deficiency or idiosyncrasy. When scientific discussion began in his presence, he would take the attitude of the artist, remembering with approval an incident with a colleague who when 'a scientific man' was 'boring us with his talk . . . turned to me and said with emphasis: "There is one golden rule of conversation – know nothing accurately"'. Sometimes like the proverbial barrister whose case is weak, he abused the leaders on the other side. In an essay on the decay of genius he pronounced that

> The mere making of great and useful discoveries, such as Newton's, though admirable in many ways, do not constitute genius in the strictest sense. All that Newton or most other scientific pioneers have discovered would have been put together or brought out by a number of lesser minds in the process of time. . . .

Elsewhere he wrote about 'the upstart man of science'. It looks as if he foresaw that the scientists were threatening to overthrow the classical domination of the older universities (where Greek and Latin were still compulsory for matriculation). So he denounced scientists and fought them, as he denounced and fought Home Rule and the Gaelic League, with equal lack of success. When he included a chapter on 'Greek science' in his *What have the Greeks done for civilization?* he made it brutally clear at the outset that he was using 'science' in 'the old and proper sense to include all strict reasoning, especially mathematics, and not merely the inferences from observation and experiment which now commonly assume and even monopolize the name of science'.

When Mahaffy goes on in his *Principles of the art of conversation* to discuss what he believes is the second essential quality for conversational ability, namely, intellectual quickness, he gives a warning that may have been partly directed against himself. Claiming that the Irish and French on the average are far superior to the English and Germans in this, he calls it 'a very dangerous advantage', which, 'if not deepened by solid acquirements, or chastened by moral restraints, may make a man rather the scourge than the delight of his company'. The quick-witted talker tends to be impatient, he says, and may 'interfere with and cow more modest minds, which might have contributed well to the feast of talk had they been allowed to work without hurry or pressure'. In contrast Mahaffy admired those, who like his parents, were 'promoters of conversation' in others.

Mahaffy describes an occasion when his ability to create lively talk in unpromising circumstances succeeded well:

> I have spent an evening shut up with a very unpromising
> commercial traveller in a remote country inn, and yet by
> trying honestly to find out what he knew and liked,
> succeeded in drawing from him a most interesting account
> of his experiences, first in tea-tasting, then in tea-selling
> to the Irish peasants in the remote glens of Donegal. What
> he told me was quite worthy to make an article in a good
> magazine. Yet a more unpromising subject for a long
> dialogue could hardly be found. He and I had apparently
> not a single interest in common. But when the right vein
> was touched one had to supply nothing but assent, or an

occasional question. People said that others found him morose and unapproachable. It was certainly their fault.[6]

But sometimes his attempts to make the company talk were less successful. Gogarty, describing him towards the end of his life, compared the effect of such efforts to that of a hawk on a brace of blackbirds.[7] Starkie, also writing about his later years, says much the same:

> As Dr Mahaffy believed that the *sine qua non* of good conversation was to establish equality among the members of a convivial party, he always tried to do so when he took his place at dinner. His smile, his slight touch of well-bred jocularity, his condescending dignity were all calculated to put the rest of the company at their ease. Nevertheless his commanding presence, his flat hair combed straight down both sides of his noble head, his open collar, and white clerical tie, at the outset overawed the guests. . . .[8]

Then, Starkie continues, when no one else offered, with encouragement from his host he would discourse uninterruptedly on St Paul, perhaps, or the classical tradition – such a discourse as 'a carping critic might have condemned as a deliberate breach of his own rule against selfish talkers'.

Augustus John (describing Mahaffy as 'this wonderful man', 'the great Illuminate') has recorded a similar impression. During a visit to Gogarty's house at Renvyle, Mahaffy 'displayed his accomplishment of an evening in a series of long, instructive and highly entertaining monologues which even Gogarty, try as he might was unable to interrupt'.[9] Another friend[10] has told of a dinner at Queen's College, Oxford, when James Russell Lowell, the American Minister at the Court of St James, was the guest of honour. Mahaffy talked incessantly, while Lowell contented himself mainly with monosyllables. Afterwards Lowell tactfully expressed his admiration for Mahaffy's powers. Mahaffy's comment was, 'Poor Lowell, never to have heard a cultivated Irishman talk before.'

Yet in fairness one must quote a more favourable witness. A colleague wrote in an obituary notice:

> We have no one now to stimulate X into uttering racy impertinencies; or to entice Y into disquisitions on Hindu

folklore. He dominated the conversation with a genial
masterfulness, like a musician who knows how to
evoke the finest harmonies of his instrument. And he would
be a patient and sympathetic listener.[11]

(But another colleague[12] commented that while Mahaffy always
insisted that conversation should be 'general' when he was at the
Common Room luncheon table, it meant in practice that he
talked while others listened.)

If one turns from Mahaffy's analysis of the 'mental conditions'
of a good conversationalist – knowledge and intellectual quickness – to the 'moral conditions' – modesty, simplicity, unselfish-
ness, sympathy and tact – at first sight Mahaffy might seem to
have been ill-qualified in them. In fact some of his chroniclers
have charged him with just the opposite qualities – arrogance,[13]
conceit, egotism, harshness and ruthless candour. For instance
when someone told him Provost Traill was ill, he replied,
'Nothing trivial, I hope.' An undergraduate at a *viva voce*
examination, after failure to answer two rather more relevant
questions, was asked 'Why was Dr Barlow made a fellow?,' he
replied, 'I don't know'. 'Correct. You get a mark for that. Nobody does.' When a waitress in a restaurant used the word
'manageress' – Mahaffy hated such hybrids – she was asked,
'How would you like it if I called you a sinneress?' A member of
the T.C.D. common room, then Professor of French, was even
more roughly handled. As he was having luncheon with his
colleagues Mahaffy marched in, exclaiming, 'Where's Rudmose-
Brown? Is he here? I've a letter I want translated into official
French.' In the silence that followed he added, 'There's no point
in keeping a dog and barking yourself, is there?', a phrase which
his exemplar Whately had used in similar circumstances before
him.

Brutal as these and other remarks may appear now, they
were in fact typical of many senior dons in T.C.D. – and indeed
of many lawyers and medical men – and even clergy – in Dublin
in nineteenth-century Ireland. Towards undergraduates and
junior colleagues alike the policy of the senior men was – in the
words of a well known successor to Mahaffy in the senior fellowship, John Fraser – 'Don't coddle them'. It was based on the
assumption that in a masculine world one could take hard knocks

and fairly brutal 'chaffing' without much pain. The entry of
women into the university world gradually induced gentler
manners. Even so, until well into the 1940s to see women in tears
and men in a state of nervous collapse after a *viva voce* with one
of the older fellows was not uncommon. Yet, though allowances
must be made for the custom of the time, some irony may still
be found in Mahaffy's dictum in his *Conversation*:

> A man who can say a good thing or make a person appear
> ridiculous may be so proud of his power that he exercises
> it at the cost of good taste and even of real humanity. The
> great wit is often cruel, and even glories in wounding to the
> quick the sensibilities of others. If he can carry some of the
> company with him he has a wicked enjoyment in making
> one of the rest a butt or target for his shafts, and so
> destroying all wholesome conversation. He may leave in the
> minds of his society an admiration of his talent, but often a
> serious dislike of his character. With such feelings abroad he
> will injure conversation far more than he promotes it.
> People may consent to go into his company to hear him
> talk, but will avoid talking in his presence.

As already noticed, some of Mahaffy's sallies were shock
tactics intended to provoke rather than to please. Addressing a
group of persons devoted to total abstinence, he remarked that
the only person he knew of in the New Testament who had prayed
for a drink of water had been in Hades. To a serious-minded
audience at a university extension lecture, who presumably were
expecting encouragement and advice on how to acquire superior
intellectual abilities, he offered the thought-provoking parable
of what had happened at the capture of Jericho by the Children
of Israel: they had entered the city blowing their own trumpets
and had found only the house of Rahab the harlot undestroyed.
Yet, here, too, one must make allowances for the way in which
such *boutades* were uttered: the scholar who records them emphasizes that though offence was sometimes taken at Mahaffy's
inopportune jocularity, his geniality and good humour were hard
to withstand and that, all in all, he was 'a singularly lovable and
sympathetic person'.[14]

In his *Conversation* Mahaffy did not try to define wit and
humour precisely, but he gave ten pages to these 'brilliant but

dangerous gifts'. As he saw it, wit consisted in 'quick flashes, in prompt repartee, in quaint comparison', while humour is sustained – 'a comic way of looking at serious things, a flavouring of narrative, a perception of a ludicrous vein in human life and character'. He insists on a quality of intellectual playfulness, like 'the playfulness of a young and happy animal', on spontaneity, on good-humoured satire – as in 'the social sketches in *Punch*, which for years have been the truest mirror of the vulgarities of English society' – and on the avoidance of pomposity, obsequiousness, conceit, hypocrisy, and provinciality. He recognizes that unless conversation is adapted to the mood of the company and unless it gives them pleasure it fails as an art – a hedonistic principle for which he could quote Aristotelian authority. Realistically he admits that modern audiences have less capacity for enjoying highly intellectual conversation than ancient audiences:

> There may have been times and nations where conversation was regarded as so serious and important an engine of education, that sound argument, brilliant illustration, and ample information took the highest place as qualities of talk. Perhaps they do in some cases now, as for example, everybody who knows him will concede to Mr. Gladstone the palm as a very charming man in society by reason of these qualities. But among hard-working and somewhat fatigued people, who have been pursuing information of various kinds in all their working hours, conversation must be of the nature of relaxation; it must be amusing first, constructive afterwards . . .

(As a younger man he had put this less gently in his *Social life*: 'Intellectually the bright and pleasure-loving Greeks would have hated the heavy pomp and stupid sameness of our large dinner parties.' Later, and even more pessimistically, he had pronounced in his *Decay of preaching*, 'Most people are very dull.')

He had his own two remedies for social dullness. Either he would find a subject on which even a dull talker has unusual information to give, as already exemplified. Or else, he would swing into action himself. Occasionally, however, there would be a crushing remark and then silence, as when a guest brashly exclaimed 'Oh, Dr Mahaffy. I hear you are *so* amusing. Do say something funny to me.' 'Well, I am delighted to have you beside me. Is that funny enough?'[15] Sometimes, however, a more playful piece of impertinence from someone in the company would stimulate him agreeably. He was boasting once about having shot forty-nine snipe in forty-nine successive shots. Someone asked why he hadn't made it up to the round figure of fifty in conversation. 'Do you think I would risk my immortal soul for the sake of a single snipe?' As Leslie has observed, here Mahaffy was using the same rhetorical device as Swift had done when describing a rat's tail as two yards long 'wanting an inch'.[16]

An Oxford scholar with a curiously apt name has recorded a certain liberality in Mahaffy's conversation which pained some of his acquaintants. G. B. Grundy met Mahaffy in Athens at the international congress of archaeologists in 1905, both staying with other dons and their wives at the Hôtel d'Angleterre:

> He was a very amusing companion, but at times rather embarrassing because he told in the drawing-room tales which were indeed amusing but not suitable for a mixed company. He brought one day to the drawing-room an evening paper and read out in a loud voice the following passage: 'The stupidity of our present government has been lately shown by an order to the effect that light women shall not be allowed in the streets of Athens during the International Congress. This cannot fail to give the foreign delegates the impression that Athens is not a European capital, but the type of a small provincial town.'[17]

Obviously these were shock tactics intended to provoke lethargic company. A few other examples have been recorded. One of his most effective gambits was to remark that he had once seen the mistress of the Prince Consort. When pressed to justify such an extraordinary claim about Albert the Good, he would explain – with how much detail, one can only speculate – that when Queen Victoria told her Prime Minister that she intended to marry Albert of Saxe-Coburg, Melbourne had taken specific measures with the practical help of a public-spirited German countess – whom Mahaffy claimed to have seen at Kissingen – to make sure that the proposed consort was capable of begetting heirs.[18] On other occasions if there were some

Irish nationalists within earshot he would cause lively argument by referring, no matter how obliquely, to the seventeenth-century traveller who reported that the womenfolk of an Ulster chieftain brought him politely into their house and 'having thrown off their mantles, sat down stark naked round the hearth inviting him to do likewise'.[19] Another excerpt has a similar flavour. Talking about old age, he said:

> 'The most marvellous old man I ever met was after the siege of Paris. It was at a civic banquet given to celebrate our deliverance from having to eat cats and dogs and rats and mice. He was one hundred and eight and as gay as a lark. But I am sorry to say there were some very wicked French actresses present, and he went away with the worst of them, and was found dead in his bed next morning.'
>
> 'Well (said one of the company) the moral is, I suppose, beware of wicked French actresses.'
>
> 'Ah, yes . . . when you are a hundred and eight.'[20]

At any rate whether the company enjoyed this kind of discourse or not, Mahaffy produced it quite deliberately. He had studied the pronouncements of his master Aristotle on the importance of correctly judging how, where, when, and to whom, various kinds of conversation should be employed, as his *Conversation* amply illustrates. And he was sensitive to changes in social conventions. 'I remember,' he says, 'when the word *girl* was thought rather improper in religious Dublin society, you should say "*young person*".' And he emphatically denied that conversational audacity, no matter how stimulating, should be condoned when it involved 'ignorance, rudeness, or graver vices'. On the other hand he refused to be 'the safe man' – as he called it in his *Decay of preaching* – or to regard his clerical ordination as prohibiting all liberality of discourse. If the time and the place and the company seemed to require a touch of impropriety to balance an excess of propriety – for virtue lies in the mean, if one follows Aristotle – he would give it. There was one invariable limit. He avoided *risqué* talk in the presence of young people. Juvenal's dictum, *maxima debetur puero reverentia*, was cardinal for him. And he went further. He believed that he, and others like him, should use their influence to curb the tendencies of younger men in matters of the kind. The strictest

Grundyite could hardly complain at this passage in his *Conversation*:

> There is no more valuable and useful check on the degenerating of talk into ribaldry, profanity, or indecency, than the presence of a mind of solid worth, which will not tolerate such licence. There are companies, especially of young men, where such things are taken for wit, and which thus show a degradation of the conception of talk that would very soon render conversation intolerable to any intelligent man, not only from its coarseness but from its dullness. . . . Every company of men ought to import two or three grave and reverend people into their circle for the purpose of checking such ruinous excesses, if there be any probability that the conversation may stray into the slough of mire.[21]

If Mahaffy was serious, this was going rather far; and just how such a plan would have worked in practice Mahaffy does not suggest. But at any rate it is not the recommendation of a man unconcerned with the difference between liberality and licence, unconventionality and impropriety, shock and outrage, piquancy and salaciousness.

As a humorist Mahaffy shared in the Victorian liking for jokes that required supporting action (often with inconvenience for the victim). Once, for instance, while cruising with a party of philhellenes in the Aegean, passing Thasos (others say Canea in Crete), though it was late in the night he insisted on going with his convivial companions and rousing the titular bishop of that region,[22] then sound asleep in his cabin, with 'Get up, get up, my lord. It may be the only time in your life that you'll see your diocese.' Again (though this may be another of those traditional stories that are passed on from one man of 'high position' and 'jocular disposition' to a successor) when an undergraduate entered 'sun-worshipper' as his religious denomination in his matriculation form, on the first morning after he had slept in his college rooms, he was awakened at dawn by a loud knocking on his door. Opening it, he saw a college porter: 'Provost's compliments, sir: it's time to say your prayers to the rising sun.' After some days of this he changed his religion. Mahaffy used the same kind of logic at a dance held for the milder and more fashionable patients in a Dublin lunatic asylum. A young woman danced a good deal with him and then became convinced that he was God. This was harmless enough – and perhaps not entirely unpleasing to the young don – until a violent thunderstorm came on. She came up to him, her face beginning to become distorted. 'What do you mean by bringing on this storm during our dance? We won't be able to sit out in the open air now . . .' 'My dear young lady,' Mahaffy lisped in reply, 'I'd wather not talk shop at a dance, if you don't mind.' The logic satisfied the lunatic, and an awkward scene was avoided.[23]

In his old age he delighted in entertaining children. He would invent conundrums for them in the Victorian style: 'My first is what I do: my second is what does it: my whole is a bird.' (Answer: a wagtail.) Once in frolicsome mood he decided to dress up in a tiger-skin rug for a children's party. Arriving in good time, he donned his disguise, crawled into the room where he believed the party was, and found himself confronted with a startled conference of clergy. Occasionally, it seems, his playfulness was not enjoyed: some children living in Howth used to travel in the same tram as Mahaffy; they wore open-toed sandals; Mahaffy used to poke at their toes with his walking stick; they were embarrassed, not amused, especially when it became a daily ritual. (It would have made a memorable scene in the tram if one of them had been precocious enough to quote from Mahaffy's *Conversation* – 'humour is its own antidote; and if a man has the true vein in him he will also have the tact to feel when he is tedious.')

But these were mere pranks. Mahaffy's special kind of conversational humour was usually not the humour of ingenious fancy like Lewis Carroll's or of paradoxical analogy like Sidney Smith's, or the ironical mockery of Bernard Shaw, or the broader comedy of Gogarty. It was more like the classical humour of Menander's comedies and of Theophrastus' *Characters*, a humour consisting in vivid, slightly satirical pictures of people and events, the humour, in fact, of an erudite and perceptive humanist as Mahaffy praised it in his *Conversation*:

> The humourist is the only good and effective storyteller; for if he is to monopolise a conversation, and require others to listen to him, it must be by presenting human life under a fresh and piquant aspect – in fact as a little comedy.

In this kind of conversation much depends, of course, on the personality and delivery of the speaker. But one can perhaps savour something of Mahaffy's style from his way of describing in his *Conversation* one of his more frustrating experiences as a talker:

> In a country house where I was staying, the host had invited the colonel commanding a neighbouring depôt and his wife to dinner, and the conversation was flagging seriously. Some mention of New Zealand in that day's papers suggested it as a topic, upon which a couple of us brought out all we knew about New Zealand, discussed the natives, then savages generally, and so restored the fortunes of the evening. The colonel and his wife sat silent. When they were gone, we said to the host that we thought it very hard work to entertain people who would not say anything to anybody. He replied that they *had* said something as they got into their carriage. What was it? The colonel observed that it was very impertinent of people to talk about countries they had never seen, especially in the presence of a man like himself, who had not only lived for years in New Zealand, but had written a book about it! This was the thanks we got.

Many of Mahaffy's acquaintances praised his gift for coining epigrams. Yet when one gleans among the surviving records for good specimens the harvest is slight. In fact most of his sayings are more like aphorisms or proverbs than finely polished epigrams in the manner of Wilde or Chesterfield. In reading them in cold print one must assume that their effect on the hearers who quote them so appreciatively must have been greatly enhanced by the voice and manner of the man himself. Some of the best authenticated are:

> In Ireland the inevitable never happens and the unexpected constantly occurs.
> An Irish Bull is always pregnant.
> If anyone is justly described as an old fool, you may rest assured that he was also a young fool.
> An Irish atheist is one who wishes to God he could believe in God.

The most popular speaker is the one who sits down before
he gets up.

Nemo repente fuit turpissimus: it takes forty years to
become a Senior Fellow of T.C.D.

We have no time in Ireland for a man who doesn't waste
both his money and his time.

It is sometimes suggested that Oscar Wilde may have derived
some of his conversational brilliance from his Trinity tutor and
friend.[24] No very clear influence has been adduced. Leslie and
others have suggested that phrases like 'poets are born, not paid',
'all art is perfectly useless', and 'it is the spectator and not life
that art mirrors' were originally Mahaffy's. And in attitude there
are some passages in his *Social life in Greece* which might almost
have been written by the early Wilde (though, just possibly,
these might have resulted from the 'improvements' for which
Wilde is thanked in the preface) for example:

> Thus it came to pass that Homer, in one sense 'the idle
> singer of an empty day', – because he sought no other object
> than the clear and deep delineation of human character
> and human passion – was degraded . . . into a moral teacher
> and accredited with definite theories of life and of duty.
> It was the same *sort* of blunder as we should make were we
> to dilate on the moral purposes of Shelley and Keats,
> and insist upon classing them with the school of Mr Tupper
> and Dr Watts.[25]

'Degraded . . . into a moral teacher' was an extraordinary phrase
for a young clerical don to use, though it becomes less challenging
to mid-Victorian standards when one inserts the omitted
qualifications 'if I may say so'. Yet even with that insertion its
attitude comes very close to the amorality of art for art's sake,
a Wildean doctrine which Mahaffy later rejected emphatically.

Whatever Wilde himself felt about Mahaffy's influence on his
early life, ten years after his fateful journey to Greece in 1877
he published what amounted to a declaration of independence
in devastating reviews of Mahaffy's *Greek life and thought* and
Principles of the art of conversation. These are all the more
unexpected – at least on the evidence now available – because
in the previous year Wilde had obviously still considered Mahaffy

his friend and benefactor. He had written to him in February 1886 asking for help in getting a post as an inspector of Schools in Ireland. Beginning: 'Dear Mahaffy' he first complimented him on a letter that had appeared over his name in the *Pall Mall Gazette* on 23 February: 'Your letter . . . is delightful. Though I should fight with you over some of the matter of it, the manner of it is most brilliant.'[26] (This would-be compliment was unfortunate, for the letter, as Mahaffy hastened to inform the *Gazette*'s readers in an amusingly written disclaimer, was a forgery.) Wilde went on to ask Mahaffy to write to Lord Spencer, formerly Viceroy of Ireland, recommending him as a suitable person to hold an Inspectorship of Schools, adding '. . . a word from you as to my capabilities would go far towards getting me what I want. I know Spencer has a great admiration for your powers and judgement,' and continuing 'Archie [Mahaffy's son Arthur] had tea with us at Christmas and looked delightful. He seems very clever. Very sincerely yours, Oscar Wilde.'[27]

Nothing is known of the consequences except that Wilde did not get the inspectorship. Possibly – but it is no more than a possibility – Mahaffy, being aware of Wilde's proclivities, refused to recommend him. Possibly Wilde felt that Mahaffy had let him down. At all events next year Wilde acted in a way that was likely to lead to the ending of their friendship. In November 1887, he wrote an anonymous scathing review of Mahaffy's *Greek life and thought* for the *Pall Mall Gazette*, stigmatizing the book – in terms that he knew would be specially wounding to Mahaffy – for being 'somewhat pedantic', 'rather awkward', 'inaccurate', 'if not parochial, at least provincial', though it had, he conceded 'a certain cheap popular value' and 'a plausible air of fairness'. He interspersed his knife-thrusts with occasional words of rather perfunctory commendation: Mahaffy was 'the distinguished professor of a distinguished university', and some of his sections were 'very pleasing reading indeed', 'extremely interesting' and even 'excellent'. But his general opinion was that the book with its political bias and literary blindness and its 'attempts to treat the Hellenic world as "Tipperary writ large"', to use Alexander the Great as a means of whitewashing Mr Smith, and to finish the battle of Chaeronea on the plains of Mitchelstown' would be 'a great disappointment to everybody except the Paper-Unionists and members of the

Primrose League'. In fact '. . . not merely does Mr Mahaffy miss the spirit of the true historian; but he often seems entirely devoid of the temperament of the true man of letters. He is clever, and, at times, even brilliant, but he lacks reasonableness, moderation, style and charm.'

Mahaffy had heard much of this kind of criticism before, especially about his inaccuracy and his refusal to treat history without pointing to modern parallels. But to be told that besides being a poor historian, he was also deficient in literary ability, reasonableness and charm, and to have his own favourite terms of contempt – pedantic, parochial, provincial, silly – turned against him must have been bitter enough.

At first, however, Mahaffy seems to have been more entertained than annoyed, apparently not having guessed that Wilde was the author. He wrote to his friend and publisher George Macmillan that he was 'highly amused' at the review adding that it was 'no doubt written by one of Madame's friends in politics'. He was probably less amused when he opened the *Gazette* for the day after Wilde's attack and read its editorial quotations from another anonymous correspondent:

> Irishmen of all creeds and parties will chuckle heartily over the deserved castigation which you have administered to Professor Mahaffy.

'The versatile professor', he (or she) alleged, had been an unscrupulous turncoat in politics: first he had supported Davitt's agitations for changes in land tenure; then 'under the delightful Spencers' he had been 'true to his character of Vice-regal tame-cat' in accepting the policy of coercion; he had turned his coat again under Carnarvon and Randolph Churchill; and now under 'the dear Londonderries' 'and that delightful fellow Balfour' he is again 'all for manacles and Manitoba'.

This was sheer venom, and perhaps Wilde himself regretted having evoked such a crude tirade. But, if he did, his regret did not last for long. In the same journal five weeks later, on December the sixteenth, just in time for Mahaffy's Christmas reading, he published over his own name a review of *The Principles of the art of conversation*. Now he adopted a different attitude, not that of one scholar castigating another, but more like that of someone trying to be kind to a less gifted friend. Consciously or unconsciously the tone is distinctly patronizing – 'a clever little book . . . a social guide without which no debutante or dandy should even dream of going out to dine. It fascinates in spite of its form and pleases in spite of its pedantry, and is the neatest approach, that we know of, in modern literature to meeting Aristotle at an afternoon tea.'

Wilde also gave a lively summary of the contents of the book. But he picked out for special attention some opinions which Mahaffy might have preferred to be left in their wider context, for example the view that 'even a consummate liar' was a better ingredient in a company than 'the scrupulously truthful man', and that 'the retailing of small personal points about great people always gives pleasure' – about 'Prince Bismarck, for example, or King Victor Emmanuel, or Mr Gladstone'. And he censured the style of the work both at the beginning and the ending of his review:

> . . . he has not merely followed the scientific method of Aristotle, which is perhaps excusable, but he has adopted the literary style of Aristotle, for which no excuse is possible . . .
>
> The only thing to be regretted in the volume is the arid and jejune character of the style. If Mr Mahaffy would only write as he talks, his book would be much pleasanter reading.

Ostensibly it was a much less scathing review than the earlier one. But its tone of condescension may have stung his old tutor more painfully than the outright attack on his classical book. On academic topics Mahaffy could dismiss Wilde's opinion as unprofessional. But in conversation the pupil already had a wider reputation than his master.

Taken together the two reviews look like Wilde's final rejection of Mahaffy's authority and influence – Mahaffy's conservatism in politics and morality, Mahaffy's Victorianism, Mahaffy's emphasis on wholesomeness and earnestness. This last word prompts a reference to Wilde's famous satire on this theme. But *The Importance of being earnest* could hardly have been another shaft at Mahaffy in particular, since earnestness was a common ideal of Arnoldian and post-Arnoldian England. On the other hand one of Wilde's less celebrated works, the essay entitled *The decay of lying*, published in January 1889, reads at times very like a parody of Mahaffy's style, especially in his *Decay of modern preaching* and *Principles of the art of conversation*. (In fact Wilde might well have called his essay 'The decay of the art of conversation' – but that would have made the parody, if intended, too obvious.) Though written in dialogue form, which Mahaffy did not use, Wilde's essay with its pseudo-Aristotelian approach and its references to ancient historians (who 'gave us delightful fiction in the form of fact', a remark that may echo Mahaffy's strictures on Thucydides), and in many turns of phrase, sounds extraordinarily like Mahaffy's work at times. Further, Wilde's blandly outrageous advocacy of mendacity as a fine art is little more than an extension of Mahaffy's assertions that excessive regard for truth could be socially pernicious. Here is what Mahaffy wrote in his *Conversation*:

> . . . there is such a thing in society – Aristotle saw it long ago – as being over-scrupulous in truthfulness. Even a consummate liar, though generally vulgar, and therefore offensive, is a better ingredient in a company than the scrupulously truthful man, who weighs every statement, questions every fact, and corrects every inaccuracy. In the presence of such a social scourge I have heard a witty talker pronounce it the golden rule of conversation to *know nothing accurately*. Far more important is it, in my mind, to *demand* no accuracy. There is no greater or more common blunder in society than to express disbelief or scepticism in a story told *for the amusement of the company*. The object of the speaker is not to instruct but to divert, and to ask him: Is that really true? or to exclaim Really that is too much to expect us to believe! shows that the objector is a blockhead unfit for any amusing conversation.

Here – and it might almost be a continuation of Mahaffy's remarks – is Wilde developing the same theme in his *Decay of lying*:

> Many a young man starts in life with a natural gift for exaggeration which, if nurtured in congenial and sympathetic surroundings, or by the imitation of the best models, might grow into something really great and wonderful. But, as a rule, he comes to nothing. He either falls into careless habits of accuracy, or takes to frequenting the

society of the aged and the well-informed. Both things are equally fatal to his imagination, as indeed they would be fatal to the imagination of anybody, and in a short time he develops a morbid and unhealthy faculty of truth-telling, begins to verify all statements made in his presence, has no hesitation in contradicting people who are much younger than himself, and often ends up writing novels which are so life-like that no one can possibly believe in their probability. This is no isolated instance that we are giving. It is simply one example out of many; and if something cannot be done to check, or at least to modify our monstrous worship of facts, Art will become sterile and beauty will pass away from the land.

What Wilde has done is to accept Mahaffy's basic principles, and to develop it to a serio-comic logical extreme, becoming deliberately more anarchical as the argument accelerates. (One may note in passing a pretty Mahaffyian qualification in his last sentence – 'if something cannot be done to check, *or at least to modify* our monstrous worship of facts'.)

Whether Wilde intended direct parody of Mahaffy or not, this proclamation of 'freedom from the dominion of hard facts' (which, as will be noticed later, a Scots reviewer had picked out as a Celtic trait in Mahaffy's *Social life*) was built on an inclination that Mahaffy never entirely overcame. As a boy he had copied out the following remark in his personal notebook. 'Swift said that universal as was the practice of lying and easy as it seemed, he did not remember to have heard three good lies in all his life.' As a don he had been chaffed by his colleagues for his fictional flights. An anecdote records how, when he remarked among a group of dons that he had only once been caned in his life and 'that was for telling the truth', Salmon observed: 'It certainly cured you, Mahaffy.' Late in life, too, he told a young man at Oxford, 'Never tell a story because it is true: tell it because it is a good story.'

But, as Wilde clearly saw, Mahaffy, being a clerical don in a highly respectable university, could not practise this doctrine fully and freely. Though Mahaffy had dared to assert in his *Conversation* that 'an overseriousness in morals may be detrimental to the ease and grace, above all the playfulness of talk' – a sentiment that Wilde could not fail to applaud – he had also, as we have seen, been careful to guard against libertinism with safeguards such as that of introducing 'two grave or reverend people' into youthful company to check 'ruinous excess' and the risk that 'the conversation may stray into the slough of mire'. (The concept and language might almost have prompted Wilde to compose a pleasing extravaganza based on the idea of an enterprising agency, ready at a moment's notice to provide such guides for parties verging on the slough.) In that respect Mahaffy, as Wilde clearly saw, was in a weak position. He was, attempting to keep a classical balance between the artist's need for freedom, with its inherent risk of licence and demoralization, and the moralist's demand for restraint, with its risk of dullness and mediocrity. Wilde's position, as argued to deliberate extremes in his *Decay of lying*, was a far stronger one theoretically. He rejected the notion inherent in Mahaffy's philosophy that ultimately art, any art, must be subject to any moral restraints. He was certainly not joking, despite the touch of flippancy, when he ended the passage just quoted,' . . . if something cannot be done to check, or at least to modify, our monstrous worship of facts, Art will become sterile and beauty will pass from the land.' And he was prepared to defend the same view against other moral restrictions. In fact he had accepted the dilemma that Yeats crystallized later in his lines:

> The intellect of man is bound to choose
> perfection of the life or of the work.

To Mahaffy what ultimately mattered most was the life: to Wilde, the work. Mahaffy had been honest enough at times to concede something like the artistic principle despite its contradiction of the moralists' code, and even to express sympathy for it. Perhaps the heredity of his painter ancestors, the Hones, influenced him in this. But the solid morality and piety of the clerical Mahaffys and his Pentland mother – no Speranza she – kept the mastery.

Whatever Mahaffy's final feelings about Wilde's hostile reviews were, he did not let any rancour prevent him from giving his name as a sponsor to a request for a grant from the Royal Literary Fund to Lady Wilde in 1888. Some years later he attended a performance of one of Wilde's plays at the Haymarket

Theatre in London. (It is uncertain whether it was *A woman of no importance* in 1893 or *An ideal husband* in 1895: perhaps the second is the more likely[28] as the Prince of Wales had attended the first performance and had expressed his approbation.) After it he wrote to congratulate Wilde, who replied:

> My dear Mahaffy, I am so pleased you like the play, and thank you for your charming letter, all the more flattering to me as it comes not merely from a man of high and distinguished culture, but from one to whom I owe so much personally, from my first and best teacher, from the scholar who showed me how to love Greek things.
>
> Let me sign myself, in affection and admiration, your old pupil and your old friend, Oscar Wilde.[29]

This was generous from a man at the height of his glory. Yet would one be wrong in detecting a tone of rather forced friendliness in it? Within two months – if the later dating of the letter is correct – the Marquess of Queensberry had delivered his fateful card at the Albemarle Club, and the storm broke. When Mahaffy heard of the accusations he is said to have asked 'Were they young boys?' Having received his reply, he said he hoped he would never hear Wilde's name again.[30] Later he refused to give his name in support of the petition to the Home Secretary in November 1895. (But his colleague Tyrrell did sign it, and in 1905 he wrote a compassionate review of Wilde's *De profundis*.[31]) If Wilde's name occurred in conversation Mahaffy would remark, 'We no longer speak of Mr Oscar Wilde', though he once mentioned him to a junior colleague[32] as 'the one blot of my tutorship'. In October 1897 an observation of Mahaffy's (in an address on education to the Mason College in Birmingham) must have seemed harsh to some readers. According to the report in *The Times* he said that 'among the many hundred people who had passed through T.C.D. during the fifty years that he had laboured there he had known some who in after life had become remarkable criminals. Every one of these was exceptional for his ability and for the high level of his intellectual education.'[33] Later on, however, he is said to have remarked to a writer in Dublin, 'Despite his extravagant garb and effeminate way . . . I rather liked Wilde' and to have praised his ability for writing Greek composition with a commendable grasp of 'the nuances of the Greek middle voice and conditional clauses'.[34]

Wilde towards the end of his life, according to one of his less reliable biographers, spoke of Mahaffy with gratitude:

> I got my love of the Greek ideal and my knowledge of the language at Trinity from Mahaffy and Tyrrell; they were Trinity to me; Mahaffy was especially valuable to me at that time. Though not so good a scholar as Tyrrell, he had been in Greece [not, in fact, until after Wilde had left T.C.D.], had lived there and saturated himself with Greek thought and Greek feeling. Besides he took deliberately the artistic standpoint towards everything. . . . He was a delightful talker too, a really great talker in a certain way – an artist in vivid words and eloquent pauses.[35]

chapter five

'My favourite emperor'

Few pleasures cause more envy and malice among observers than that of associating with exalted personages and talking about them to others. Mahaffy never tried to conceal either his liking for it or his contempt for those who misinterpreted, as he thought, his motives. His critics certainly did not spare him, alive or dead. A life of Oscar Wilde, written apparently on the principle of *de mortuis nil nisi malum* as far as Mahaffy was concerned, censures both his race and himself.

> The Anglo-Irish are a curiously snobbish people, and Mahaffy was a prime specimen of his kind. He was an out-and-out social snob: that is he would rather have sat down to a bad meal with a stupid aristocrat than to a good meal with an intelligent tradesman. . . . He loved a lord, adored a duke, and would have worshipped a prince. . . .[1]

During Mahaffy's lifetime George Moore, to be quoted in a later chapter, and others were even more venomous – 'vice-regal tame-cat', 'Castle lackey', 'tuft-hunter', they called him. Others who knew him better defended him against these crudities. Yet, even some of his friends conceded that he was something of a snob, but a dazzlingly successful snob. Here again one is on the frontier of what Mahaffy in his *Summary* called a 'difficult and delicate enquiry', which, unluckily for his biographers, he did not pursue.

As described earlier, Mahaffy when a child in Germany had

enjoyed the company of princes and their entourages. After he and his family had moved to Monaghan, social life had become sadly drab for him, then even gloomier in Dublin for a while, until cricket helped him to make aristocratic friends. (In his *Summary* he specially mentions St John Butler, a kinsman of Lord Dunboyne.) It was on one of his cricketing expeditions that the formidable warden of St Columba's College failed to overawe him with 'the awful dignity of his reception'.

Here at a very early stage in Mahaffy's life one finds a trait that marks his whole life – a determination not to be intimidated by overbearing people, whatever their rank or position. It was partly, no doubt, the result of an inbred independence and self-assurance. But it was also based on a clear view of his own rightful place in society as a whole. As he saw it, there were three main classes in the social order, the gentry, the business people, and what he described as 'the lower classes . . . the rabble, the poor, the socialists'[2] or 'the peasants'. Within the class of gentry there should be a sense of basic equality, irrespective of formal rank. He had no doubt that he himself was a gentleman:

> As regards my parentage I am neither like Admiral de Ruyter, whose epitaph at Amsterdam describes him as 'non claris natalibus sed ex ipso natus', nor am I of any distinguished ancestry, but belong to that class of lesser landed gentry which has furnished the Empire with many brilliant servants.

When Mahaffy became a fellow of Trinity in 1864, he entered what was in his own opinion 'so great a corporation, so wealthy and renowned in former days' that the fellows 'gave themselves airs of superiority, to which the Irish public willingly submitted'. To enter this *corps d'élite* was, he says, 'an introduction to the gentry all over Ireland' especially, of course, in mid-Victorian Dublin:

> The Dublin of that day, into which I came, and in which I lived, was so different from the present city and its society, that it is very difficult to make any modern reader realise it. Though the nobility no longer lived in Dublin, many of their houses were still occupied as dower houses. There was a large resident gentry, quite apart from the great

lawyers and doctors, judges of the Four Courts, some bishops and deans, not to speak of the Castle and the official Lodges of the Government, which were unknown to me till Lord Carlisle found me out as a useful bowler, and also as an educated youth.

As a result Mahaffy, helped by his other social graces, became a frequent guest at the Viceregal Lodge and Dublin Castle. There he made lasting friendships with the Abercorns, Marlboroughs and Londonderrys.[3]

A second focus of society in Dublin at that time was the Royal Hospital at Kilmainham, the residence of the commander of the forces in Ireland. Here in October 1886 Mahaffy met the genial and hospitable Prince and Princess Edward of Saxe-Weimar, who were afterwards to introduce him to members of the British royal family. In 1889 Mahaffy dedicated his *Sketches from a tour through Holland and Germany* (in which he praises the smaller German principalities) to the Prince 'in acknowledgement of many kindnesses', and in 1890 Mahaffy helped to collect subscriptions for a presentation to him on his departure from Ireland. In the following summer Prince Edward received an honorary doctorate in laws from Dublin University, presumably through Mahaffy's efforts. In 1901 a letter from the Prince says that he spoke to King Edward on Mahaffy's behalf asking the King to have luncheon or dinner in the college during his state visit.[4]

The succeeding commander, Lord Wolseley, also entertained Mahaffy at Kilmainham. It was at his invitation that Mahaffy in 1891 met the man who would eventually reject him for the provostship, Arthur Balfour. Wolseley and Mahaffy had a common interest in military science and military men, especially in Napoleon, whose strategy Wolseley was then studying for a forthcoming book. Mahaffy read the proofs of another book by Wolseley, presumably his life of Marlborough, in 1893.

His friendship with Prince Edward of Saxe-Weimar led to a meeting in 1893 between Mahaffy and a future Queen of England, Princess Mary, then the recently bereaved fiancée of the Duke of Clarence, eldest son of Edward VII, and soon to become engaged to the future George V. Mahaffy wrote about her, in the context of a characteristically energetic visit to England, to his daughter Elsie:

This is what happened to me in London. First I went to see Mr. Dasent, Lord Kimberley's secretary and secured I believe, a post at Lahore for Mr. Dallinger. Then I went and delivered an address for fully 40 minutes to the Oriental Congress – a very interesting affair. Then I had a note from Prince Edward of Saxe Weimar telling me on no account to miss coming to dinner with him. When I went I found myself one of a party of nine, only eight Princes and myself, viz. five Saxe Weimars and three Tecks. I was told off to take in the Princess May of Teck, and sat between her and her mother Princess Mary of Cambridge a great stout old lady, full of great vigour. But the girl was far nicer than I expected, tall and straight, about the size and look of Lady Southampton, without any *soupçon* of too much strength, as the other has. Her good brown eyes are rather close set and she is only the next thing to pretty, but exceedingly well made, a lovely skin and so healthy to look at. Quite sympathetic too and ready to talk agreeably, so that I felt ten times sorrier she was not sure to be Queen. I did not inquire of Prince Edward but other people say there is a chance of it yet. The dear old man was delighted that his scheme of making me meet these people succeeded. He considers it the most desirable thing in the world. Prince Hermann too was very nice and his gluttonous wife, so that the evening was a curious experience. That was *one* day in London in all. Then came Mr. Newbury [Newberry?] at the Oriental meeting to give me another great pile of Papyri, which Mr. Petrie had kept back. The latter is very ill and I fear the exploring is over.

Mr. Dallinger just writes that he has been sent for by the Secretary for India, that means that he is all right.[5]

If Mahaffy had customarily written or talked about his ducal and royal friends in that sober and unostentatious style, no one except the envious and malicious would have been likely to accuse him of snobbery. But he was not the kind of man to be always modest about his royal encounters. In later life his frequent references to 'my friend the King of Greece', and 'my favourite emperor' became proverbial. During the war of 1914–18 when these royal and imperial friends became military enemies, he was heard to remark, 'I'll cut that king the next time I meet him' and 'the Kaiser is not the man I knew'. Perhaps Mahaffy was responsible, too, for spreading a rumour that he had invited ex-King Manuel of Portugal, after his abdication in 1916, to come to Trinity as Professor of Portuguese, though more likely someone invented it for him. (At any rate he had met Manuel earlier when he was Duke of Braganza. In a letter to Mahaffy in May 1903 Manuel refers to their recent meeting in the transatlantic liner *Bremen*, inquires vaguely about a promotion which Mahaffy had said he wanted to get – presumably the provostship – and concludes amicably, 'Perhaps you will be transferred to the diplomacy and be sent to Vienna.')[6]

Other exuberancies were well remembered, 'Woodcock pie shot by lords', he once exclaimed to a group of students at supper with him. At dinner with the Leslies at Glaslough he once abruptly asked, 'Do you know what is wrong about Birmingham?' When no one replied, he gave the answer himself. 'No houses – no big houses', which became a source of mystification for the Leslie children who were led to believe that the citizens of Birmingham must live in tents or caravans. He made a similar remark to an undergraduate who said that his home was in Belfast – 'Where is that near? I've never had occasion to go there. There aren't any gentlemen's houses in that neighbourhood.'

His books, too – even his books on classical subjects – occasionally gave rather dragged-in glimpses of the author's regal and semi-regal acquaintances. 'My friend Prince Victor of Hohenlohe tells me . . .'[7] comes in a footnote to a book on Greek history. Even less aptly in a lecture originally delivered in republican Boston he observed:

> Quite recently when our King brought me to see the Mausoleum of Queen Victoria and her Consort at Frogmore, I was able to point out to him that the builders of this circular chamber, though they probably knew it not themselves, were copying the ancient and almost universal custom of a house for the dead.[8]

King Edward's reply is not recorded.

One of his most revealing letters was written to an American friend in 1886:

I am down here on a spree shooting with the De Vescis – nothing but Lords in the house except myself, Drogheda, Ormonde, Kingston, Castletown, . . . [another name, perhaps Ely] etc. and their wives – so I am really in a snob's paradise, if that were my object. We shoot from 500 to 700 things each day. But this is trifling.[9]

Similarly in 1894 he wrote to George Macmillan about 'luncheons with Duchesses etc.', adding with rather callous jocularity that they were too engrossing for him to call on his older friend.[10] By 1910 he was able to tell the same correspondent that he was 'larking with the Emperor in Berlin'.[11]

In later life Mahaffy liked to show friends the gifts that royalty had given him. At his second house in Howth, Earlscliff – which some unkind acquaintances suggested should be called at least Dukescliff – he used to show visitors the walking stick presented to him by King Edward and the tea-trolley from Queen Alexandra, both given to him in September 1904 perhaps as tokens of regret at his failure to win the provostship; and in the garden there were carnations from the same royal household. He was particularly proud of the target given to him by the Kaiser as a token of his skill as well as of imperial favour.

The most celebrated – or notorious – of these royal gifts was the fox-terrier presented to him by the King of Greece (or, according to another version, the King's niece). Oliver St John Gogarty, then an admiring acolyte of Mahaffy, was moved by its death in 1903 to write a *Threnody on the Death of Diogenes the Doctor's Dog*. It included the following verses:

DOCTOR MAHAFFY

When I rambled around
   In the ground that was Greece
I was given the hound
   By the King's little niece;
And rather were fined ere I found him to
   gaze on his saddest surcease.

CHORUS (SCHOLARS OF THE HOUSE)

He was given the hound
 By the seed of a King
For the wisdom profound
 Of his wide wandering.
But was it the donor, or owner, or dog
 that was led by a string?

* * *

DOCTOR

The eagle is Zeus's
 A *Bird* there may be
(the owl too obtuse is,
 The turtle too free),
To suitably serve as a symbol, a sign and
 a signal of me.

CHORUS

Leave Venus her turtles;
 Mock-turtle for thee,
Who not among myrtles,
 But rather wouldst be
Among the *élite* at a banquet, in the
 shade of a family tree.

DOCTOR

What Bird shall I get me
 That monarchs may know,
And ladies beset me
 Wherever I go –
All converts to my 'conversation', which
 only on these I bestow?

CHORUS

Get hence to the land
 Whereof Bion did sing,
When he wept on the strand
 And there wept on the wing
A bird that is called the Kingfisher
 and catch it to capture the King.[12]

To judge from this and from other comments in the students' paper, the undergraduates mostly regarded Mahaffy's liking for regal society as the amusing foible of a famous man. It printed plenty of friendly banter about him. In 1909, for example, it reported that:

> The King of Greece is in difficulties. We fear that Dr. M. has been paying too much attention to the affairs of the Georgian Society,

and in its customary 'Valentine Number' it sent him the following valentine in 1905:

> 'How sweetly he talks and tells news of this lord, and of that lady'

Even some of his more devoted young admirers were inclined to be critical, as, for example, Walter Starkie:

> All his life Dr. Mahaffy was renowned for his snobbery, but it would be very difficult to fit him into any of the categories of snobs enumerated by Thackeray, for he was too much of an Irishman and possessed too much wit and volatility of temperament. He wore his snobbery with such grace that it became an adornment to his personality and, besides, he would continually make fun of his own foibles. His snobbery sprang from his Anglo-Irish characteristics and it can be explained by a remark made by W. B. Yeats when he was asked whether Oscar Wilde was a snob: 'No, I would not say that: England is a strange country to the Irish. To Wilde the aristocrats of England were like the nobles of Bagdad.'[13]

Shane Leslie saw it rather differently:

> Mahaffy's view of Lords and Lordlings was based on Greek ideals, not on the social snobbery of which he was accused. He may have loved a Lord for practical reasons but not 'the tenth transmitter of a foolish face'. Good talk, good shooting and good cellars were not to be despised. Brilliancy came before blood. A Lord was expected to be worthy of his title. It would be a mistake to describe Mahaffy as 'a social snob who would rather have sat down to a bad meal with a

stupid aristocrat than to a good meal with an intelligent tradesman'. He had no use for the stupid or shabby-minded, but a bad meal he could tolerate in no company.

(This conflicts with a phrase in a letter by Mahaffy quoted elsewhere by Leslie: 'Better a dinner of herbs where love is than a stalled ox under any circumstances whatever'.)

. . . He could enjoy the company that George Borrow affected. He delighted in conversing with Irish gamekeepers, poachers or porters. He was amused and delighted when he found he could learn the experiences of travelling commercials or even of racing touts in railway carriages. The only type which never aroused his sympathy was the narrow Clerical, whatever his Church. It was a mistake for Catholics to argue controversy with him and a certain type of Protestant rasped his nerves. . . .

Another friend of Mahaffy, Swift MacNeill, has emphasized a fact often overlooked: 'He has been accused of being a seeker after the great and highly placed. In point of fact they sought him much more eagerly than he sought them.'[14]

There is clear evidence for this assertion in the tone of some surviving invitations, kept by Mahaffy perhaps for this very reason. To quote an example: in 1887 'Lord Sligo hopes that Mr. Mahaffy will not think him and Lady Sligo intrusive in seeking his acquaintance and asking him to stay at Losely Park . . .'.[15] Similarly Lord Fitzwilliam, faced with the task of entertaining Gladstone, invited Mahaffy to come to Coolattin and help to amuse the formidable visitor. Mahaffy, knowing Gladstone's interest in Greek studies, brought with him a copy of Browning's recent translation of the *Agamemnon* of Aeschylus (a work about which Tyrrell is said to have remarked that he had found the Greek most helpful in explaining its obscurities). A letter describes what followed:

As we were in the hall before a ceremonious 10 o'clock breakfast I told him I had brought it. Mr. Gladstone was highly interested and said at once: 'Read me that grand Ode about the Lion's whelp.' I did so and came to the last line of the first stanza which Browning translated literally: 'in belly's strict necessity'.

'Oh, that is horrid,' said Mr. Gladstone, 'not at all poetical. Do you know I translated that Ode years ago and this is how I did it.' He then recited it. . . .

Dear Lord Fitzwilliam came to us and said, 'I know your conversation must be most interesting but I am obliged to interrupt you for my lady is waiting.' 'Certainly,' said Mr. Gladstone, and then turning to me added, 'This is indeed "in belly's strict necessity".' I think it was the only joke, certainly the best I ever heard him make. The omission of such from Morley's *Life of Gladstone* (he could have got many personal details from others beside myself) is what makes that otherwise admirable book somewhat dull.[16]

Other glimpses of Mahaffy among his aristocratic friends show an ease and independence of manner far removed from the usual conception of a snob. Most celebrated, and a favourite of Mahaffy himself, was his encounter with the Kaiser. As often, several versions occur. The following is Leslie's account:

A certain visit to Windsor Castle always gave Mahaffy great satisfaction. King Edward had summoned him to deal as a buffer with the Kaiser whom he could talk down in his own language. On this occasion he met Queen Ena of Spain for the first time and entertained her with the famous division of proper uses between European languages – 'French to address a friend, Italian to make love to a mistress, Spanish to speak to God, and German to give orders to a dog!'

The Queen laughed heartily whereat the Kaiser rushed across the room to learn the joke. As he was more or less the subject of the pleasantry, Mahaffy saved the situation by saying: 'Your Majesty, I have only had the honour of the Queen's acquaintance for twenty minutes and we already share a secret.'[17]

This was by no means the only occasion when Mahaffy stood his ground against heavy social artillery. His friend Sayce described a brief passage of arms between him and the Duchess of Marlborough at the Viceregal Lodge in the summer of 1878:

When we joined the ladies in the drawing-room the Duchess asked Mahaffy if he would take a hand at whist.

'With pleasure,' he answered, 'provided you don't play for
more than penny points.' 'Oh, how mean of you, Mr.
Mahaffy,' said her Ladyship. 'Not so mean, your Grace, as
not to pay your debts.' The newspapers had recently been
accusing the Duchess of incurring debts which brought about
the sale of the collection of gems at Blenheim, though they
had really been incurred by her eldest son (Lord Blandford).
But Mahaffy was a favourite of the Duchess, and was
privileged to say what he liked.[18]

In fact there was a strong matter of principle behind Mahaffy's
behaviour here. All his life he retained an abhorrence of large-
scale gambling. When a young friend met him after a day at
Baldoyle Mahaffy said, 'I hear you have been to the races: I
hope you have lost all your money.' When she called it unkind, he
replied, 'It is the kindest thing I could possibly wish you. It is a
lesson you cannot learn too soon.'[19]

Sometimes Mahaffy's free and easy manners almost reached
the limits of his hosts' tolerance. When visiting Lord De Freyne
he took out a penknife and scraped off some of the paint on
the panelling of the staircase to show how much better it would
look unpainted. On another occasion, as described by Leslie, he

arrived at Pettigo to fish for trout in Lough Derg where he
was a great favourite with the boatmen whom he seemed to
understand as intimately as though they were the Ptolemaic
watermen on the Nile. His predecessor as a guest had been
Royalty, for whom a particular assortment of luxuries
had been imported from town. What was left over was used
to entertain the Professor who was expected to show polite
astonishment on finding such crumbs from the Royal table
falling upon the wilds of Tirconail. His only remark was:
'You know I really enjoy picknicking!' His hostess never
recovered from these words which she often repeated
whenever she had strained every effort to entertain a
guest 'Do you think he will enjoy our poor picknicking'?

On one long-remembered occasion Mahaffy's readiness to take
the initiative provoked an imperial snub. It happened in full view
of the viceregal court and its guests when Queen Victoria visited
Dublin in 1900. Mahaffy was presented to her in the line of guests

HM

at a *levée* in the Castle. Instead of passing on after her formal greeting, he delayed and remarked, 'Madam, I met your grandson lately', (meaning Kaiser Wilhelm II). She turned away, loudly asking one of her entourage, 'Who is that man?' Mahaffy made the best of it afterwards by remarking (according to various versions), 'What a disagreeable old lady!' or 'Poor old lady, she's at death's door: the Prince says she has been ailing lately', or 'She doesn't like the Kaiser, you know'.[20] Whatever he said, neither his enemies nor those of his friends who could enjoy a dramatic moment for its own sake let the incident be forgotten.

Another rebuff is described by Leslie. Mahaffy discovered that in remote times his predecessor as High Sheriff of Monaghan had been treated as a high provincial dignitary and consequently had been accorded an escort of javelin men on ceremonial occasions. But,

> The Monaghan Grand Jury did not sufficiently appreciate that a friend of Kings and Emperors had come amongst them. He was bitterly disappointed when the Lord Lieutenant of the County, Lord Rossmore, failed to meet him at the station with carriage and horses. It would not have been difficult to have provided him with javelin-men from the local gamekeepers, whom he had known in the field, armed with hauberks from the private armouries in County Monaghan castles. The great picturesque chance was missed.

A third incident was a private affair, but few incidents of the kind remain private for long in Dublin. Mahaffy once undertook to call on the Mother Superior of a convent to ask her to allow a neighbouring Protestant institution to let a new drain go through the convent's lands. Mahaffy, confident, perhaps, that everyone in Dublin knew him, presented his request without saying who he was. The Reverend Mother readily agreed, but something in her manner prompted him to identify himself. She then expressed her sense of being honoured at his visit, but, before Mahaffy had any time to acknowledge her compliment, added that up to that moment she had believed that he was the man who was in charge of the drainage scheme. For once Mahaffy seems to have found no adequate reply.[21]

To set in the scale against these incidents several examples of spontaneous generosity with no *arrières pensées* about rank or position, could be quoted. One, hitherto unrecorded, may suffice. A schoolboy who lived near Howth was reading a Greek author one day near the summit of that hill so dear to Mahaffy. An elderly clergyman approached, saw the Greek text, asked him about it, and later lent him books to help his classical studies. Then the clergyman – Mahaffy, of course – offered to arrange for his free education in classics at Trinity. At this point the boy's parents, suspecting proselytizing intentions, intervened to prevent further developments. But fifty years later as an old man he remembered Mahaffy's uncalculating kindness with warm gratitude.[22]

The question still remains undecided: was Mahaffy a snob? Definitions of that term vary so widely that a verdict satisfactory to everyone could hardly be reached. But two quite different social attitudes need to be distinguished. The first, and clearly the contemptible kind, is the desire not to be seen associating with undistinguished people. Mahaffy, on the clear evidence of many keen-eyed observers, must be acquitted of that. The other kind is to love and desire the company of 'the elegant or the eminent' and 'to yearn to be identified in the minds of others with the more powerful or decorative products of the human race'. (These are the phrases of a recent writer on good manners,[23] who judges the second attribute to be 'quite a noble form of aspiration'.)

Mahaffy would probably have agreed. Perhaps the fairest thing will be to let him speak for himself, from his *Principles of the art of conversation*:

> In conversing with superiors, we must broadly distinguish the socially from the intellectually superior. For the art of producing agreeable society in the former case differs widely from doing so in the latter. . . . The man or woman that succeeds among social superiors is not the timid or modest person, afraid to contradict, and ever ready to assent to what is said, but rather the free and independent intellect that suggests subjects, makes bold criticisms, and in fact introduces a bright and free tone into a company which is perhaps somewhat dull from its grandeur or even its extreme respectability. It is a case of the socially superior

acknowledging another kind of superiority, which redresses the balance. We need hardly add that the greatest stress must here be placed on tact, for to presume on either kind of superiority will cause offence, and so spoil every attempt at breaking the bonds set around us by the grades of the social hierarchy. . . . I may here dwell a moment upon conscious superiority and its companion, that conscious inferiority which is the great social barrier to conversation, and which in most cases actually prohibits all intercourse. In other European countries the separation of *noblesse* and *bourgeoisie* is carried so far as wellnigh to annihilate all free and intellectual society of the better kind. The intellectually-educated classes are so thoroughly excluded from social education in the urbanity and grace of noble society, that they sink into mere intellectual boors, while the aristocrats so seldom hear any intellectual discussion or take any interest in learning, that their society becomes either vapidly trivial or professionally narrow. . . .

The case is not so bad among us, where there are always great commoners, where eminent success in making money, or even in letters, brings men and women into the highest society, and where there are some of the greatest positions in the country from which our Peers are even excluded. There is no doubt that an intellectual man, or a man of strong and recognised character, whatever his origin, can easily take a place in high society among us. But how many lesser people are there of excellent social gifts who assume most falsely that they are not suited, and will not be welcome, to the higher classes, and so avoid both the pleasure and the profit to be derived from a more refined, though not more cultivated, stratum than their own! I am here talking of really modest and worthy people, not of those vain and vulgar persons who make it a boast – often a very dishonest one – that they have spurned associating with their superiors, from a profound contempt of what they call *toadyism*.

This term, which expresses the vicious relations of socially inferior and superior, is used in very vague senses, ranging from a just censure of meanness in others to a mistaken assertion of independence in ourselves. Nothing is more

inherent in all European society derived from the feudal
and ecclesiastical traditions of the Middle Ages – probably
in every cultivated society – than to honour rank and social
dignity as such, apart from the real worth of the person so
distinguished. This is the basis of that loyalty to sovrans
which even when irrational does not incur the imputation of
toadyism. People of independent rank and personal dignity
even still accept and prize semi-menial offices about a Court,
without losing either respect among ordinary people or
even self-respect.

There is then such a thing as respect for rank as such, and
a feeling of pride in the contact with it, which is regarded
as honourable. When does the virtue of loyalty pass into a
vice? Clearly when the higher and more important duties of
life are postponed to this love of outward dignity. The
man who neglects his equals for the purpose of courting his
superiors, still more who confesses or asserts his inferiority
when associating with them, and who submits to rebuffs and
indignities for the sake of being thought their associate,
above all, who condones in them vices which he would not
brook in an equal, is justly liable to the charge, which,
however, only asserts the exaggeration of a tendency affecting
almost all his censors.

The usual thing, however, is to hear people censured
for the *fact* of association with those above them, as if this
were in itself a crime. There is, too, not infrequently an
element of jealousy in our criticism, and of secret regret
that another has attained certain advantages, or supposed
advantages, to which we ourselves feel an equal claim. Yet
one thing is certain, that if the supposed toady exhibited
in the society which he courts the qualities ascribed to him
by his critics, he would very soon lose his position and miss
the very object of his ambition.[24]

chapter six

A sort of Irishman

'Wit is of no party' (*Berkeley*)

A ballad, expressing those mixed feelings of affection and dislike that Dublin citizens have often felt for Trinity and its champions, included this verse:

> *The Irish language, Mahaffy said*
> *Is a couple of books written clerkly,*
> *A dirty word in a song or two.*
> *Matter-a-damn, said Berkeley.*[1]

The reason for this moment of bardic fame for Mahaffy – though one must note the shrewd valuation implied in the contrast with Berkeley's loftier detachment – was that towards the end of the nineteenth century he had become involved in one of those acrimonious national controversies in which politics and philology ferment together to make a highly stimulating mixture. By that time the Irish nationalists were drawing strength and inspiration from a revival of the Irish language and a renaissance of the Gaelic literary tradition. Mahaffy, for reasons to be considered later, vehemently opposed these linguistic and literary movements. He summarized his opinions when he gave evidence to the Commission on Intermediate Education in Ireland in 1899: all the Irish-language text-books used in Irish schools were either silly or indecent, and it was 'almost impossible to get hold of a text in Irish which is not religious, or does not suffer from one or other of the objections referred to'. He also remarked that in his opinion 'Celtic' had no educational value and was a mischievous waste of time for schoolchildren. Asked by the chairman, Chief Baron Palles, whether he would admit that the Irish language was 'a very interesting study from a philological point of view', he answered laconically 'Yes'. Later he volunteered another concession, but one not likely to conciliate his opponents, 'it is sometimes useful to a man fishing for salmon or shooting grouse in the West. I have often found a few words very serviceable.'[2]

He had been writing in much the same tone in articles to the English press for some time. As early as 1882 in an essay on education in Hungary he had interpolated the remark, 'We are to be much congratulated that in Ireland the national system [of primary education] ignored Celtic, and this tended strongly to the destruction of that equally out-of-the-way and troublesome language.'[3] Now in 1899, for fear that anyone might have missed his testimony at the Commission, he made it the basis of another onslaught in a British journal: revival of Irish would be 'a retrograde step, a return to the dark ages, to the Tower of Babel'.[4] Some conversational remarks of his were also quickly circulated and widely remembered: 'I will always discourage the teaching of Gaelic wherever I can',[5] and 'If they must learn Irish, teach them that beautiful pre-Gaelic speech of which only three words remain. Anyone with a little aptitude can learn them in a week.'[6]

Naturally the supporters of the movement for the revival of Irish were indignant. George Russell (AE) denounced him as 'A blockhead of a professor drawn from the intellectual obscurity of Trinity and appointed as a commissioner to train the national mind according to British ideals.'[7] His most vigorous antagonist was a son of a Church of Ireland clergyman and a graduate of T.C.D., Douglas Hyde, then president of the Gaelic League and eventually to be the first President of the Republic of Ireland. He gave evidence before the Commission after Mahaffy. At an early stage he introduced a note of ridicule – he was fully Mahaffy's equal in that – by remarking apropos of the anglicization of Gaelic names, 'I hear the M'Gaffeys, a branch of the M'Devitt in Donegal, are calling themselves Mahaffy.' He quoted many eminent European scholars on the value of Irish, and denied Mahaffy's assertions that the movement for its revival was 'the outcry of a few enthusiasts' and that it was 'pandering to the clamour of false patriotism'. Then he attacked at the weak point in Mahaffy's armour: Mahaffy knew almost no Irish himself; so his evidence was 'beneath criticism'.

Hyde's evidence was published fully in the newspapers of February the fifteenth, his sally about the M'Gaffeys now calling themselves Mahaffy being credited with a burst of laughter (not recorded in the official reports). Next day the Dublin *Daily Express* printed an interview with Mahaffy, to give him an opportunity of making a prompt reply. The interviewer found him 'not indeed crushed by the satire and learning' of Hyde, 'but somewhat hurt by the astonishing ingratitude of the Gaelic League'. Mahaffy went on to make fun of his opponents:

> Extreme pugnacity is the essential feature of all true Irish scholars, and they usually try to murder one another in the second stage of a grammatical debate. I remember a distinguished Gaelic expert who called a colleague of the most approved Nationalist principles a 'Castle spy' over a difference about *cum* with the subjunctive. In the present case I have restored harmony in the Gaelic family by drawing their combined attack upon myself. I do not think that Dr. Hyde has been properly grateful.

Against the alleged Gaelic origin of the name Mahaffy he argued that it was more likely to be an example of how the English settlers sometimes took Irish names (citing the MacMahons and MacSwineys in Ulster). He reiterated his conviction that 'modern Irish has no literature worthy of the name' and that 'the folly of wasting the time of children who will have to work for their living on a language that is for all practical purposes dead is ridiculously obvious'. When the interviewer hinted 'with some diffidence' that according to Hyde there was an enormous mass of Irish literature in manuscript, Mahaffy replied that if they were genuine literature 'why doesn't somebody translate them? –

> . . . Gaelic scholars must not let the Intermediate Board buy a pig in a poke. They are morally bound to translate their treasured masterpieces for the ignorant people who know nothing but English and Greek and Latin. If they cannot do it, it is, perhaps, because the delicacies of the Irish language are as untranslatable as its indelicacies. If Dr. Hyde will do for his unknown authors what Macpherson did for Ossian we will gladly forgive him the falsifications of genius.

Then he attacked the credentials of the continental scholars cited by Hyde: except for one, they were no more competent to pronounce on modern Irish than 'the slighted Mr. Gwynn'.*

He (Mahaffy) had no objection to 'the theoretical study of Irish' as a branch of the Indo-European group of languages. But he did object to the waste of time and neglect of more important subjects which the teaching of the modern language would involve:

> In any case, no good end would be gained by touting for learners with extravagant rewards and absurdly easy examination papers, as is the present practice. A much more practical assistance to the cause would be to make it incumbent on Irish Nationalist members of Parliament to implead for Home Rule and other Irish causes in the Irish tongue alone. 'That', concluded Dr. Mahaffy, 'would not only be logical but would save the House of Commons from a good deal of incompetent oratory'.

Hyde replied in the next issue. He had expected, he wrote, that Mahaffy 'would come up smiling' and had not been disappointed. He gave evidence that in fact the scholars depreciated by Mahaffy were well qualified to offer a verdict on modern Irish, so

> Dr. Mahaffy . . . should not presume too far upon that Stygian flood of black ignorance about everything Irish which, Lethe-like, rolls through the portals of my beloved Alma Mater.

On the following day a gentler correspondent, Alice Milligan, took Mahaffy up on his remarks about the lack of translations from the Irish, citing Standish O'Grady's work, and adding

> I do hope Gaelic workers are not going to lose their temper with Dr. Mahaffy, for I verily believe that if they went the right way about it they would find in him the making of a Gaelic enthusiast.

Mahaffy did not reply to either the lion or the lamb.

Hyde returned to the attack in December 1899. In an article

---

* E. J. Gwynn, an eminent Celtic scholar, later Provost of T.C.D. (1927-37), who had supported Mahaffy's view in part.

entitled 'A university scandal'[8] he described Mahaffy as 'a man whom everyone knows to be utterly, absolutely, and grotesquely ignorant of the very subject upon which he gave his evidence, and who, to do him justice, does not now pretend for one moment to have ever been anything else'. He ended more peaceably:

> How I wish that Dr. Mahaffy, for whose brilliant versatility, learning and genuine goodness where the interests of his students are concerned I have nothing but a sincere admiration, would not put himself forward clad in the intellectual garments of a Dublin Castle official of the eighteenth century. . . . Knowing Dr. Mahaffy's genuine interest in all intellectual movements, I shall not despair of his sympathy if he ever succeeds in mastering from the inside the bearing of this and other native Irish questions.

Mahaffy had in fact relied on the opinions of a gifted but cross-grained English-born Professor of Comparative Philology in Trinity, Robert Atkinson. A brilliant linguist – Mahaffy was once heard to remark that he knew the language of every country in Europe except the one he happened to be in – he contributed usefully to the philological study of Irish. But with Irish literature he had no sympathy at all.[9] Much of it he ranked as folklore and in his opinion all folklore was 'at bottom abominable'. He told the chairman of the Commission that in ancient Irish literature, 'I would say that it would be difficult to find a book in which there is not some passage so silly or indecent as to give you a shock from which you would not recover for the rest of your life.' These and other outbursts gave Mahaffy plenty of ammunition to use with his more expert marksmanship. But academic bullets to be effective must be moulded from personal knowledge.

This he must have realized. Why, then, the ill-advised attack? Once again the element of over-confidence seems clear. He was at the height of his own prestige as a classical scholar, and in the eighteen-nineties any member of the classical ascendancy might still believe that he was entitled to give an authoritative judgement on all matters of education and culture. At the same time, he sensed that what seemed then to be an innocuous educational and cultural movement could be the life-blood of a political

A photograph of Mahaffy in the 1890s

revolution likely to overthrow the religious, political, and cultural
ascendancy on which his fortunes and, he believed, those of his
class and college essentially depended. So he hit at it with all his
force.

What had stimulated his first main attack in his article in
1896[10] had been the support given by some Irish Protestants
(besides Hyde) to the newly founded Gaelic League. This he
considered an act of betrayal:

> It is only recently that I was sent a pronouncement
> regarding the Irish (Celtic) language, signed, I grieve to
> say, by a Protestant bishop and canon, among other names
> which represent either hostility to England or mere
> gratuitous folly, recommending that an agitation should be
> commenced to prevent the appointment of any officials in
> the south and west who could not speak Irish, and
> suggesting other means of galvanising into life a most
> difficult and useless tongue – not only useless, but a
> mischievous obstacle to civilisation.

He had no doubt what the result of that policy would be:

> There is no country in which sham excuses, political
> and religious, for appointing incompetent men to
> responsible posts flourish more signally than in Ireland.
> Are we to add a new sham, the linguistic excuse?

He refused to concede that a knowledge of Irish would make
Irishmen more valuable to Ireland or to the world:

> If . . . Berkeley and Swift, Goldsmith and Sheridan,
> Grattan and Burke, had been compelled to speak and
> write in Irish for the sake of official promotion, or to
> soothe national sensibilities, not only would the English-
> speaking world, but Ireland herself, have suffered
> immeasurable damage.

In another article written in 1898, just a year before the
Commission sat, he had unmasked what he considered to be a
piece of specious hypocrisy on the part of those who claimed that
to increase the marks given to Irish in the state examinations
was simply an educational, and not a political, matter:

A famous Scotsman has held that, if he could control a people's songs, he cared not who made their laws. In the unfortunate twentieth century the adage is likely to take another form: Give me a nation's examination papers, and I defy the politicians to control its sentiments.[11]

In general, as Mahaffy saw it, the ultimate effect of a revival of Irish would be 'provincialism', a separation from 'the great republic of letters'[12] (in which since Latin had gone out of use, only three languages, English, French and German, were now, he believed, valid), 'a return to the dark ages, to the tower of Babel'. It would give greater scope to jobbery and obscurantism, without providing any educational or literary gains.

Clearly, on all except the last of these arguments Mahaffy was fully competent to express an opinion, whether one agreed with it or not. But obviously he was rash to depreciate Irish literature, one of the richest of the early vernacular literatures of Europe, especially when he had no first-hand knowledge of it.

In 1899 so far as practical results were in question, his side of the linguistic controversy won a temporary victory. As a result of the report of the Commissioners, Irish was not included among the compulsory subjects in the new syllabus for Irish Intermediate Education, which controlled most of the secondary schools in Ireland. Further, French and German were allocated more marks than Irish, and German was given preference to French – 'Mahaffy and the King speak German', Hyde remarked. Mahaffy himself was made a member of the new board of commissioners, an appointment which the supporters of Irish took as a direct insult to their efforts.

Meanwhile in 1899 and the following years Mahaffy's opponents pressed him hard. Douglas Hyde, being of similar social origins, knew how to inflict the sorest blows. He kept recalling that the name Mahaffy had originally been Gaelic, and he attacked him mercilessly in an Aristophanic satire *Pleusgadh na Bul-goide* (*The Bursting of the Bubble*), which a biographer had described as 'one of the few things Hyde has written which could be considered malicious', and as showing 'Hyde's capacity for amusing mischief'.[13] The plot turns on a terrible curse pronounced on the professors of Trinity, including a certain MacEathfaidh (Mahaffy) who speaks with a strong lisp. It compels them to speak that 'appalling jargon', Irish, on the very day when a visit is expected from the Lord Lieutenant, with grotesque results. The squib reads harmlessly enough now in an era of far more savage satire. But the intention to ridicule and humiliate is clear in its imputations of lackeyism, pedantry and boastfulness.

Most venomous of his attackers was George Moore. Having retreated with fastidious distaste from the vulgar jingoism which jarred on him in England, he had come to Ireland aglow with enthusiasm for his romantic conception of the Gaelic revival. Naturally enough he was soon exasperated by Mahaffy in the role of the robust realist. Moore turned on him with feline force and made him the first victim in his series of Dublin caricatures. In an article in a Dublin journal[14] in July 1901 he reached a level of vituperative spitefulness that made some of Mahaffy's worst enemies feel uncomfortable. Moore denounced Mahaffy as a comedian, an ignoramus, a liar, a careerist, and a snob. As a comic figure (he wrote)

> Dr. Mahaffy is a character as well known in London as the most celebrated creations of fiction, as Handy Andy, Mickey Free, or any other stage Irishman in dramas of Boucicault. London people go to the theatre in order to digest their dinners, and they invite Dr. Mahaffy, whose pleasant stories at the expense of his country begin the process which the theatre completes. . . . Nature did not intend him for a dusty book-worm. Nature meant him for the stage. On the stage he would have given an individuality even to the stage Irishman; in the parts of valets or Squireens, and in certain parts which are known as travesty, he would have secured a permanent fame. . . . The mere sound of his name provokes a smile. . . .

Mahaffy, Moore asserts, is an ignoramus not only about the Irish language but also about Greek art. He is an incorrigible liar. (Here Moore quoted Salmon's retort when Mahaffy complained about having been caned for telling the truth – 'It certainly cured you'). Mahaffy is a careerist with hopes – vain hopes – of becoming provost of T.C.D.: 'he understudies the Provost in public because he is a born comedian, capable of enjoying in mimetics the fruit that he may never enjoy under his teeth', and it was partly in order to have a better chance of the provostship that he had denigrated Irish. To prove him a snob and a 'tuft hunter' Moore cites his own version of the incidents with Queen Victoria in Dublin Castle, the German Emperor, Lady Londonderry and others. He adds one anecdote not recorded elsewhere (presumably because of its total incredibility):

> According to the legends Lord Randolph [Churchill] said
> when he was in Dublin, to someone who offered to help
> him to find his overcoat: 'Never mind, my little dog,
> Mahaffy, has it in his mouth, and he will bring it to me
> presently.'

Mahaffy made no public reply to this diatribe.[15] The more fair-minded of his critics felt that Moore had gone too far. Besides, Mahaffy, whether one liked him and his opinions or not, was now a celebrated Dubliner, while Moore was an interloper.

Mahaffy, Hyde, and Moore, all came to regret their acerbities. Mahaffy in the last of his publications on the language question admitted that a friend whose opinion he respected had assured him that some passages in Irish literature showed 'a fine feeling and a certain poetic beauty'.[16] Hyde in later life said he had some regrets for having written his *Bursting of the Bubble*,[17] and in his autobiography he conceded that at least the Mahaffys were 'great fighters'.[18] It is a quality that Irishmen have generally admired. Mahaffy's most implacable antagonists, even when they believed him to be most deplorably in the wrong, would respect him for it. In fact one perceptive writer on the period, Stephen Gwynn, has stated that 'despite all, the average Irish nationalist liked and admired Mahaffy'.[19]

Moore, looking back on the controversy after many years in his *Salve*, wrote this brief elegy of regret for the barrier which political bitterness had built between men who might have been congenial companions:

> Provost Mahaffy sometimes walks in the path under the
> railings shaded by beautiful trees, and if it had not been
> for a ferocious article published at the time, attacking
> him for his lack of sympathy with the Gaelic Movement, we
> might have spent many pleasant hours together under the
> hawthorns.[20]

Mahaffy's attitude to other aspects of the Irish cultural renaissance was less unsympathetic. In 1898 he sent a subscription to the Irish National Theatre, writing:

Dear Lady Gregory,
I am ready to risk up to £5 on your scheme and hope they may yet play their dramas in Irish. It will be as intelligible to the nation as Italian, which we so often hear on our stage. I wish you every success *except* to force Irish on unwilling students who want a practical education.
Yours always,
J. P. Mahaffy[21]

Later, too, in 1914 he supported the efforts of Lady Gregory's nephew Hugh Lane, to provide Dublin with a gallery of modern art. He suggested that it could be housed in the former College of Science, which he heard was going to be taken over by the Board of Works. 'Surely,' he wrote, 'one of the forty-nine boards that swallow up so much of Dublin could not stand in the way of such a great national object.'

Perhaps in supporting these particular projects he was influenced by the fact that their chief promoters came from the ranks of the protestant and catholic gentry. Besides, neither of them was exclusively nationalistic in policy. Lane intended to provide a cosmopolitan collection of paintings, and the National Theatre proposed to perform European masterpieces. The Lane project failed; the National Theatre prospered; but after Mahaffy had attended the inaugural dinner he does not appear to have given it any active support. He was never an ardent theatre-goer. He preferred the drama of conversation and life. Besides, the romantic mysticism of plays and poems like those of Yeats in his earlier period had not impressed him. According to Starkie, he once remarked:

Dowden gave me some of the little poems of Yeats to read: it is twilight stuff, vague and insubstantial: I couldn't read them. Poor fellow! He is an autodidaktos – he never worked under a Master.[22]

Yeats and Mahaffy met in 1911 when the poet was interested in the possibility of his succeeding Edward Dowden as Professor of English Literature in Trinity.[23] Yeats had an interview with

Mahaffy, and recorded in a letter Mahaffy's rather contemptuous attitude towards literature as an educational subject:

> It has been of great value to this University having Professor Dowden associated with it, because he has a reputation as a scholar; but he has been teaching here for thirty years and hasn't done a pennyworth of good to anybody. Literature is not a subject for tuition![24]

Yeats goes on to wonder whether this disparagement of Dowden was due to jealousy – 'I had always heard that the Fellows were jealous of Dowden. . . .' But it seems more likely that Mahaffy was expressing his lifelong devotion to history as a superior discipline to literature.

As it happened, Dowden did not resign from his post then. But after his death in 1913 the suggestion was made that a special professorship of poetry should be established, so Yeats made another overture. Mahaffy, recognizing, no doubt, that Yeats's eminence as a man of letters would bring lustre to Trinity supported his candidature energetically. But Provost Traill and a majority of the board defeated him.

Soon Yeats was given a good opportunity of showing his magnanimity. As will be described in more detail in a later chapter, in November 1914 Mahaffy banned a meeting of the College Gaelic Society, because it was to be addressed by 'a man called Pearse' – another one of Mahaffy's phrases that caused hostility against Trinity in the minds of nationalistic Irishmen, though in fact Patrick Pearse was not a widely celebrated figure at that time. The meeting was then held outside the college. Yeats spoke at it. He chose to say the healing, not the wounding, word:

> I am very sorry Professor Mahaffy is not here tonight. I am not more vehemently opposed to the Unionism of Professor Mahaffy than I am to the pro-Germanism of Mr. Pearse, but we are here to talk about literature and about history. In Ireland above all nations, where we have so many bitter divisions, it is necessary to keep always unbroken the truce of the Muses. I am sorry the Vice-Provost of Trinity should have broken that ancient truce. It would have been a great pleasure to have stood on the

same platform with Dr. Mahaffy, who has done so much
good service for English literature, and with Mr. Pearse
who has done such good service to Irish literature.[25]

The tragic sense of waste in Yeats's phrase 'in Ireland above
all nations, where we have so many bitter divisions', is a recurrent theme in the writings and sayings of almost every Irish
patriot who has valued the complex Irish tradition as a whole.
Mahaffy, too, felt this tragedy of a country so long divided
against itself. Four months after the Easter insurrection some
citizens of Dublin presented him with a commemorative silver
cup (now in the possession of his grandson). In his speech of
thanks Mahaffy recalled that exactly one hundred years previously his great-grandfather, John Pentland, had been presented with a silver snuff-box by unanimous vote of the Lord
Mayor, Sheriffs, and Commons of the city of Dublin for his
services 'in suppression of Defenderism and the preservation of
the public peace'. He went on to say (as reported in an obituary
notice in the *Irish Times*):

> The Defenders, against whom his great-grandfather,
> John Pentland, held his house for a whole night in Finglas,
> corresponded to the Sinn Feiners of the present day – both
> Irishmen, both citizens of the city, both people who had
> either real or imaginary grievances to redress. They knew
> now very well that the Defenders of 1796 had many great
> grievances. He was not able to ascertain whether the Sinn
> Feiners of the other day had any grievance, except that
> they were not allowed to form a republic and join the
> Germans against the power of England. But, still, it was
> of the nature of a civil war, and he was very sorry
> indeed, that the virtues of his family should have been
> shown in combating not an external enemy, but the
> dangers of home rebellion.

'Very sorry indeed' – the strong note of regret is noteworthy.
It came from a man who knew well from classical history how
destructive civil war could be, and it came from a man who
loved his country as deeply, in his way, as Yeats and Pearse.
(He might have added, if he had wished, that in May 1867 as a
very junior fellow he had been among the nineteen fellows and

professors of the College who headed a petition to the Lord
Lieutenant for commutation of the death sentence on the
Fenians.)[26] The fact is that in contrast with his attitude to the
Irish language his admiration and affection for Ireland as a
country was deep and strong.

For example, in his *Rambles* (1876) a description of the
Parthenon prompted this eulogy of the Rock of Cashel:

> The prospect from the Irish sanctuary has, indeed,
> endless contrasts to that from the pagan stronghold, but
> they are suggestive contrasts, and such as are not without
> a certain harmony. The plains around both are framed by
> mountains, of which the Irish are probably the more
> picturesque; and if the light upon the Greek hills is the
> fairest, the native colour of the Irish is infinitely more
> rich. So, again, the soil of Attica is light and dusty,
> whereas the Golden Vale of Tipperary is among the richest
> and greenest in the world. Still, both places were the noblest
> homes, each in their own country, of religions which
> civilised, humanised, and exalted the human race; and if
> the Irish Acropolis is left in dim obscurity by the historical
> splendour of the Parthenon, on the other hand, the gods of
> the Athenian stronghold have faded out before the moral
> greatness of the faith preached from the Rock of Cashel.[27]

Later in the same book he compared the treasury of Atreus
at Mycenae with the Irish chamber tomb at New Grange, preferring the Irish monument in ornamentation though not in
general design. He also contrasted the way in which the Irish
fondness for elaborate detail (as, for example, in 'the glorious
intricacy of the illuminations of the Book of Kells') with the
Greek preference for design and order which culminated in 'the
severe symmetry of the Doric temple'. In these comparisons he
treated the Greek and the Irish artistic achievements as equals
in excellence.

His attitude to his fellow Irishmen, as distinct from Irish
art, was more mixed. During his boyhood in County Monaghan
he had felt a warmer regard for what he called 'the delightful,
sympathetic R.C. peasants' than for the less agreeable protestant
tenants on his mother's estate. That was in the eighteen-fifties
when the prevailing attitude, especially in the northern border

counties like Monaghan, did not encourage any such liking for 'the other side'. A passage from Mahaffy's *Social life in Greece* makes this clear. In a discussion of Theognis' 'exhortations . . . against trusting in any of the lower classes who will ever be found false and ungrateful' he remarks:

It is precisely the feeling entertained towards Roman Catholics by the old-school Orangemen of Ireland. Hundreds of times have I myself been warned not to trust the 'false papists', whose religion was full of lies, and whose word could not be believed, who had been known to betray their best friends, and to violate the holiest ties.[28]

(He continues in a footnote)

This antipathy sometimes assumes a very grotesque form. 'How are you getting on, James?' said a friend of mine to one of these Orangemen. 'Badly enough, your honour; sure the country is gone to the divil.' 'Why do you say that? I see your farm in good order, with plenty of stock on it.' 'What matter about that, doesn't your honour know that if you shot a Papist now you'd be *tried* for it?' When my friend looked amused, the Orangeman added with much warmth:
'*Well with the blessing of God, I'll have one day's fowling among them before I die.*' Another was known to object vehemently to controversial sermons whereby the Papists might be converted. 'Till hell with them,' he exclaimed, 'I wouldn't convert them.' Such anecdotes might be multiplied *ad libitum*. The Roman Catholic party have just as strong sentiments, but do not express them so boldly.

Though Mahaffy obviously detested this protestant extremism, yet he was not prepared to reject completely the warnings against 'false papists'. So he went on to say:

Unfortunately, there are certain real facts sufficient to vamp up such a frightful theory. In the first place, the pure Celt, who is always a Catholic, has less regard for truth than the Protestant, with his touch of Saxon breeding. Secondly, the long oppression of the Roman Catholics, and their enforced separation from Protestant society, has created a clan feeling, which in times of what one side translate as faith towards country and religion, the other call traitorous betrayal of friends and relations. Thus any thoughtful man who has lived in Ireland comes to understand Greek political hate with peculiar bitterness.

Yet he was quick to defend his Roman Catholic fellow-countrymen from unjust accusations. For example in one of his earliest articles on Greek society, in 1876,[29] in attacking the hypocrisy of conventional mourning at modern funerals he expresses his approval of the traditional merriment at an Irish wake, and then bursts out:

> The Irish an unfeeling people! They have faults enough and they are patent. But anyone who sees their charity to the widow and the orphan, with whom they share their wretched living, who sees in every village the adopted child sitting at the scanty meal, and the beggar receiving alms from ragged benefactors; anyone who knows that every turn of their language, every idiom, even every imprecation speaks deep feeling, who knows how the poorest man can converse freely, because he has the quick tact to feel with his hearer . . .

Though Mahaffy's liking for the countryfolk of Ireland was clear from such remarks, his way of expressing it sometimes gave more offence than pleasure. The following passage written in the year of his attacks on the Irish language was probably phrased in deliberately patronizing terms:

> For many years back I have noted these linguistic facts [about the use of Irish in rural parts] with interest, and with a real love for the people who will always be to me the most charming peasantry in Europe. No one desires more than I that they should preserve their delightful peculiarities. Even the frieze *frac*, with knee breeches and blue stockings, which was the usual dress of old men twenty years ago, and which was, of course, not really Irish, but borrowed from England – even that costume I should desire to preserve: it is picturesque in its way, and is now at least a sign of the old times in Ireland.[30]

On the other hand he certainly did not idolize the English. This remark is typical:

> The English people possess (I suppose) only two attributes which are also to be found prominently among the Greeks – an overweening self-conceit and contempt for all outsiders, and this remarkable mixture of seriousness and sport.[31]

Similarly in his writings on Irish history he readily condemned what was wrong in the British administration in Ireland. The fact that Queen Elizabeth had founded the College to which he was so devoted – he described it as 'the only English foundation that ever succeeded in Ireland'[32] – did not inhibit him from criticizing the faults of her Irish policy.

Surprisingly enough Mahaffy was a severe critic of the Irish landed classes, 'the pompous absurdity of the encumbered Irish squire' as he called it.[33] In the early eighties, at a time when Irish landlords would regard any criticism of their order by a man of their own class as bordering on treachery, he castigated their faults in a trenchant article.[34] He admired the larger landlords who had sufficient resources to manage their estates successfully (and whose houses he enjoyed visiting), but he complained that the Irish gentry as a body were inefficient and lacking in public spirit. They had failed to stand up to the land league; they were idle and condoned idleness in their tenants; they had little respect for education. They did not send their sons to a university and 'the splendid libraries so common before the famine times are scattered and it is now an exception to find a good library in any country house'. But there was one section of the Irish gentry which he highly praised, the section to which he himself belonged, the clergy of the established church, 'an enlightened and educated class of country gentleman', and he declared that the loss of this class (brought about by Gladstone) was the irreparable social damage suffered by Ireland in the nineteenth century.

In his way of hitting out all round Mahaffy was as typically Irish as many another writer whose Irishness has been less questioned – his friend Bernard Shaw, for example. In fact the mixture of affection and scorn that he showed for his fellow-countrymen, combined with a confident feeling of superiority towards the English, was very characteristic of the nineteenth-century Anglo-Irish in general. John Butler Yeats, the poet's father, has described this attitude frankly:

> As regards Ireland our feelings were curious and though exceedingly selfish not altogether so. We intended as good Protestants and Loyalists to keep the papists under our feet. We impoverished them, though we loved them; and their religion by its doctrine of submission and obedience unintentionally helped us; yet we were convinced that an Irishman, whether a Protestant or Catholic, was superior to every Englishman, and that he was a better comrade and physically stronger and of greater courage.[35]

Mahaffy took great pride in being one of those 'splendid mongrels' as he called the Anglo-Irish. He eulogized them extravagantly in one of his later books, *An epoch in Irish history* – but with a characteristic twist in the last sentence which was bound to infuriate his more Irish Anglo-Irish readers:

> He [John Stearne, father of Bishop Stearne] shows how superior the Anglo-Irish intellect, when properly trained, was to the pure English so largely imported in those early days into Trinity College. [He was] the first example of that peculiar type which distinguishes Trinity College, Dublin, to the present day. Instead of devoting all his life to one study, he mastered several branches. . . . From that day to the close of the nineteenth century this manysidedness has been the peculiar fashion of the College, and has produced men whom specialists have acknowledged as masters in each of their studies. . . . The real cause seems to be the versatility of the Anglo-Irish intellect, that type represented all over the world in so many successful soldiers, traders, lawyers, statesmen, that it may fairly be regarded as the most valuable strain in the very composite Anglo-Saxon race.[36]

In view of Mahaffy's readiness to see the virtues as well as the failings of other aspects of Ireland and the Irish, his implacable hostility towards the Gaelic element requires some further explanation. Here, as has been illustrated earlier, he was prepared even to make an attack on territory which he had never personally surveyed and to set his second-hand opinions against the authority of acknowledged experts. Psychologists might explain this irrationality as the result of a complex which derived from conflict between Mahaffy's Gaelic ancestry in the male line and from the Anglo-Irish on his mother's side. Politicians might see it as a deliberately chosen line of propaganda against an ideology that obviously threatened the Anglo-Irish ascendancy. Classical historians might emphasize the influence of those nineteenth-century German writers on Roman history who in the interests of imperialism, ancient and modern, depreciated the culture and ethical qualities of the disruptive Celts.

This last influence had certainly affected him strongly as a young scholar. In the lectures he had given at the age of thirty to the young ladies of Alexandra College, Dublin, he had quoted Mommsen – whose words he claimed might pass for a description of the present Irish peasantry – on the inferior political stamina of the Celts, and on their laziness, ostentatiousness, curiosity, credulity, childlike piety, fervent national feeling, antipathy to strangers, tendency to exaggerate, and delight in 'tippling and brawling'. He cited Mommsen in detail about the Celts' utter incapacity to preserve a self-reliant courage equally remote from presumption and from pusillanimity – to perceive the right time for waiting and for striking – to attain, or even barely to tolerate any organization, any sort of fixed military or political discipline. 'It is,' he concludes, 'and remains, at all times and places, the same indolent and poetical, irresolute and fervid, inquisitive, credulous, amiable, clever, but – in a political point of view – thoroughly useless nation; and, therefore, its fate has been always and everywhere the same.'[37]

'Always . . . everywhere . . . at all times and places . . .' – when historians use such phrases about complex races and civilizations one may reasonably suspect that history has yielded to rhetoric. It was no doubt impressive doctrine for Dublin schoolgirls of ascendancy stock, especially when presented by a gallant young fellow of Trinity – just as its original pronouncement by Mommsen must have pleased the eaglets of Bismarck's Germany.

There was one obvious flaw in Mahaffy's denigration of Celts and Gaels. How could he explain the high level of art and architecture in pre-Norman Ireland and the traditional native Irish talent for music? He had freely expressed his admiration for these in his early writings. What could he say now in maturer years when he was trying to prove the general uselessness of the Celts and Gaels? Undismayed, he produced a bold theory: the Gaels, he claimed, deserved none of the credit for the artistic achievements of ancient Ireland. It was the Firbolgs, their predecessors, who had been the creative artists, and no one could prove that the Firbolgs were Celts. As audience for this ingenious explanation he chose a meeting of the National Literary Society of Ireland in London in 1914.[38] Whatever the assembled literary nationalists thought of its truth, at least the nationalists could hardly deny that in terms of sheer audacity Mahaffy had exemplified what Yeats would call 'the indomitable Irishry'.

Naturally there were Irish nationalists who asserted that by opposing Gaelicization Mahaffy forfeited his right to be considered truly Irish. He repudiated this. In his final article on his clash with the Gaelic League – 'Recent fuss about the Irish language', as he nonchalantly called it – he exclaimed:

> I . . . may protest that I am Irish of the Irish, that I have lived all my days since boyhood in Ireland, striving to help young Irishmen to get on in the world.

And, unlike so many other Irishmen who for social, political or cosmopolitan reasons have discarded their nationality abroad, Mahaffy spoke and wrote as an Irishman or Anglo-Irishman. Late in life he stigmatized the tactlessness of the would-be compliment that the English often paid to Irish people if they found them 'civil in manners and education' – 'I had no idea that you were Irish'.[39] At the same time he seems never to have suffered from those uncertainties of loyalty which have troubled some of his Anglo-Irish fellow-countrymen, often driving them to extremes of thought and action. He released himself from any anxieties about his true nationality by flatly denying that there was, or ever had been, any such thing as a genuine Irish nation (a view strongly contrasting with that of another graduate of Trinity, Thomas Davis, in his famous song, *A nation once again*):

> Ireland [unlike Scotland, he claimed] never had been a nation, in any sense, but a conglomeration of tribes and

sects, always at variance, and never gathered in historical times, I believe not even in mythical, under a single head.[40]

He admitted that there was of course an Irish race and an Anglo-Irish race: but that was quite a different thing from true nationality. As for Ireland's right to political freedom, the world was, always had been, and always would be, better off without small, independent, nationalistic states. In asserting this he was not just asserting a matter of political expediency for himself and his class. From his early days as a scholar he had preferred the large Hellenistic kingdoms to the smaller city-states of classical Greece. He was a cosmopolitan, 'a citizen of the world' to use the term that his admired Stoics had invented under the influence of Alexander's empire. Since there was no prospect during Mahaffy's lifetime of a truly cosmopolitan world-state or even a United States of Europe, he gave his loyalty to the most cosmopolitan empire of the time. Similarly in matters of art and intellect he preferred 'the great republic of letters' and English as the *lingua franca* of five continents to anything that the Gaelic tradition could offer. Politically and culturally this unionism was certainly not a negative creed, nor in principle a selfish one, no matter how his opponents might dislike it.

In what sense was he an Irishman, then? Failing an agreed definition of the term, the question can hardly be answered conclusively. Though he had had a name of Gaelic origin and though he showed some of the traits considered to be most typically Irish – a love of conflict (the 'Donnybrook fair' quality), a gift for invective, a scathing wit, a tendency to exaggerate – yet his political enemies implied that he was not truly Irish at all. They believed that a love of the Irish language and a determination to establish an independent Irish state were essentials of true Irish nationality, and that even a man of entirely Irish descent forfeited his claims to be considered genuinely Irish if he lacked those essentials. His contemporaries could not even agree whether he looked like an Irishman or not. Stephen MacKenna, the translator of Plotinus, defended Mahaffy's Irishness against the assaults of the Irish press with the remark, 'Just look at the Irish gob on him.'[41] But T. P. O'Connor asserted that he looked much more like a

Scandinavian or a German or an Englishman of Saxon descent.
Again, failing agreement on racial types, one can hardly make a
firm decision. He did, however, as his portraits show, have one
feature that is often accepted as characteristically Irish, a long
upper lip.

If one prefers to judge by deeds and not by opinions or
features, two facts must not be forgotten. First, Mahaffy chose
to stay in Ireland, his homeland, though at times he felt that
it was an *ultima Thule* for a scholar. Other gifted Irish classical
scholars of his time preferred to seek wider scope in England –
Jebb, Ridgeway and Bury, for example. Oscar Wilde had gone,
too, and Carson, and Shaw. When the first Lord Birkenhead
asked Gogarty why Mahaffy with so much wit and intellectual
ability had chosen to remain on in Dublin, Gogarty flippantly
replied, 'He was Provost. He was knighted. What Fellow in
Oxford can be knighted without being benighted first?'[42] More
seriously and more truly, Mahaffy stayed on in Ireland because
he never wanted to live anywhere else.

Secondly, he tried to make young Irishmen by birth into full
Irishmen, according to his ideals, wherever he could exert his
influence. Letters to Shane Leslie and his mother[43] illustrate his
feelings in this respect (though the motive may partly have been,
as Leslie has suggested, a desire to persuade members of the
Irish aristocracy to send their sons to Trinity as they had in
earlier centuries). He wrote to Shane Leslie in 1904:

. . . Now I am indeed without prejudice in this matter. Of
my two sons I sent one to Oxford and the other to
Cambridge. But then I had no prospects for them in
Ireland, and intended them to earn their livelihood
elsewhere which they have since done.

But to you, who will have an estate in Ireland and who
will, I trust, not be an absentee, drawing rents from this
country, and taking no further interest in it – to you it is
vital that you should learn what is the best of the intellect
and of the rising talent in Ireland and to you I
recommend very strongly to come here. As far as education
goes, I can assure you, with my intimate knowledge of my
sons' work and with much intimacy as to Oxford and
Cambridge, that you will learn more and better here.

And if your father thinks you will meet 'finer men and
better society' at Oxford, I should like to have his definition
of both before I could agree with him. In so far as Society
goes, I can tell you that no Common Room at Oxford can
compare for one moment in life and brilliancy with ours
and as to fine men I think I could show far more from
our smaller numbers in the last twenty years than could
be drawn from Oxford. But that is a smaller matter. The
more serious thing is that if you live your next four years
at Oxford, you will never learn to understand Ireland and
you will never be really at home here for years and years
to come. Two of the best such country gentlemen I have
ever known here . . . would have infallibly represented this
University, and been most leading Irishmen, but that they
laboured under the incurable disadvantage of being Oxford
men. This separated them from us and from other Irish
interests so completely that the one died and the other
lives a disappointed man, and we are as much disappointed
as either of them, for we have had to promote inferior
men.

If these things don't persuade you, I pray you not to
decide till you and I can talk over the whole matter. For
I look upon it as no small matter that a boy of your
position and brought up in your way does think about
Ireland and does feel that his duties towards this very
misguided country should influence the methods of his life.

In the same year he wrote to Shane Leslie's mother, ending:

Here we are now tossed about between poor place-hunting
people, when the future of Ireland is at stake, and the
whole condition of the country wants able and single-hearted
gentlemen to save it from ruin.

Don't you be persuaded to try and make him an
English gentleman residing by accident in Ireland, but a
real Irishman in the highest and best sense and don't
deprive me of the great pleasure and the great privilege of
teaching him what I know and saving him from humbug
and imposture.

'A real Irishman in the highest and best sense' – whatever

Mahaffy's fellow-countrymen may have thought of his interpretation of such an ideal, it was not the ideal of an alien or of a spiritual exile in Ireland, nor that of a man embittered by harsh – even if deserved – criticism. In the latter years of his life, as described in another chapter, he saw that much of what he had so vehemently opposed in Irish politics was gradually winning. So he tried to preserve what had been good in the old *régime* within the context of the new. He resolutely resisted the effort to exempt Trinity from the jurisdiction of the new Irish parliament, and in 1914 when he saw the danger that Ulster, or at any rate some of the northern counties, might demand and obtain exemption from Home Rule, he did all he could to hold the country together. Among other efforts, he wrote a powerful letter to *The Times* attacking the suggestion of a separate jurisdiction for Northern Ireland, which he considered was simply a reversion to the inveterate English policy of 'divide and rule'. The letter clearly combined a southern protestant's pride in Ireland with a fear of finding himself left as a member of a small minority in a small country.

Fortunately for his peace of mind Mahaffy never had to accept or reject loyalty to an Ireland entirely separated from Britain and a part of Ulster. How he would have reacted if that decision had been forced on him in his youth, one cannot tell. At any rate, as things were he never, after his brief notion in his twenties of entering the Indian civil service, seems to have contemplated a career outside Ireland. Though he was proud of being a citizen of the world, a cosmopolitan in the old stoic sense, at heart he was no restless wanderer. He travelled so as to return home, enriched by knowledge and experience. The home that he returned to was always in Ireland; and Ireland, the country of his ancestors with their Gaelic and Saxon names, was always his homeland.

chapter seven

An unclerical cleric

Not in any offensive sense

Opinions varied widely on Mahaffy's religious convictions. His young friends, Gogarty and Starkie, found it hard to believe that he was a Christian at all, and portrayed him as essentially a pagan Greek at heart.[1] Another friend who had a great regard for him personally did not ask him to officiate at her wedding 'because he hardly seemed to be fully a clergyman'. Some of his colleagues accused him of heresy. A Jesuit biographer of John Sullivan, S.J. – Mahaffy's only student to have his cause promoted in Rome for beatification – described him as 'all too like a thinly disguised abbé of the unbelieving Enlightenment.'[2] On the other hand others to be quoted later who knew him intimately have denied that he lost or repudiated his faith and have suggested that his unorthodoxy masked a genuinely religious disposition.

His appearance and his remarks were certainly unconventional for a clergyman of the Church of Ireland. As an obituarist described him,

... there probably was never a more unclerical cleric than Dr Mahaffy. His clothes were entirely unecclesiastical except for a white tie. If he had lived in England he would have looked like what is called a Squarson – the man who divided his time between sport and the duties to his church and to his congregation.[3]

In fact the reason why Mahaffy wore the old-fashioned white tie of the early nineteenth-century clergyman to the end of his life was probably because he wished to keep aloof from a new kind of clericalism which he disliked. Whether one called the salient feature of the new clerical dress for anglicans 'the Roman collar' or 'the dog-collar', neither it nor its implications would appeal to a man of his protestant background and independent intellect.

Some of his best-remembered remarks have been taken as proofs of a mocking attitude towards religion and the church. When asked by a stranger, perplexed perhaps by his unconventional dress, whether he was indeed a clergyman, he is said to have replied, 'Yes, but not in any offensive sense of the term' (or, according to another tradition, 'Slightly, madam, slightly'). But a junior colleague[4] who knew him well has affirmed that this was intended less as a disparagement of the clergy than as a repudiation of the common prejudice which imputed narrow-mindedness and bigotry to every clergyman. On another occasion Mahaffy was challenged on that question so vital to evangelical protestants – 'Are you saved, Dr Mahaffy?' His reply varies in the tradition: the authentic version seems to be – 'Yes, but it was such a vewwy nawwow squeak that I never boast about it.' Whatever the wording was, it was essentially no more than a refusal to discuss his personal religion with a stranger. Another anecdote, if authentic, implies a rather puerile flippancy likely to be offensive to many: when Mahaffy saw an undergraduate coming without an academic gown to a college ceremony at which gowns were required, he called him over with, we are told, 'an imperious beckoning finger' – 'Come here, boy! Who's your tutor? . . . Don't you know that you are imperilling your immortal soul by being without a gown?' And then after a slight pause: 'And what is worse the fine is five shillings.'[5] Similarly when he asked an entrant to the College what his religion was and was told 'Christian, sir', he is said to have replied, 'Oh no, we don't have that here at all – you must answer Catholic or Protestant.'[6] In fact, so far as the folklore of Mahaffy goes, the prevailing image is that of what his more evangelical contemporaries would have called a scoffer and a worldling.

Mahaffy himself thought of giving his own account of his religious beliefs. At the end of his autobiographical *Summary* he says that he had 'long hesitated' whether he should say anything in it about his 'convictions on religion, politics and social problems'. He decided to postpone the matter and never went further with it. But, as noticed in an earlier chapter, several passages in the *Summary* refer to the climate in which his earliest beliefs were planted and nurtured, that of evangelical protestantism – the daily Bible-reading, the long Sunday services beginning at noon and lasting until a quarter past two, the fervent sermons, ample prayers and deeply emotional hymns. Several Irish contemporaries of Mahaffy's father had written hymns that still rank as classics of low-church anglican hymnology – notably H. F. Lyte with his 'Abide with me', 'Pleasant are thy courts above', 'Praise, my soul, the King of heaven', and Thomas Kelly with 'Zion's King shall reign victorious', 'Hark, ten thousand voices sounding', 'Look, ye saints, the sight is glorious', and 'Saviour, send a blessing to us'. They blended a firm post-Augustan diction with a warm spirit of devotion, and combined a confident reliance on Christ as guide, redeemer and friend, with an agonizing sense of personal unworthiness. In a single service the impressionable soul might experience the terrors of hell, the joys of heaven, a heart-breaking sympathy for Christ on the cross, a conviction of Christ's constant personal affection day by day, a warm feeling of all being 'saints' together, a cold dread of Satan prowling about to snatch away the heedless ones, and a glowing desire to be holy, good and useful.

To any normal child the appeal of all this eloquence, poetry, music, emotionalism, and 'togetherness', was bound to be deep and unforgettable. Obviously there were dangers of over-enthusiasm, to be followed perhaps by a violent reaction. Mahaffy's mother and father were people of too much common-sense and social experience to encourage any excessive fervour; and, besides, as members of the established church of Ireland they had to be on their guard against unruly individualism. His mother's influence – 'a great soul' was how he described her in his *Summary* – remained a steadying force in his religion to the end of his life.

Intellectually, however, many aspects of early Victorian piety could not satisfy his growing critical powers. His reading of Whately's *Elements of Logic* at the age of fourteen 'very soon led to asking questions about the extremely illogical evangelicalism wherein all serious society in Dublin had its being'. Soon, too, his ever-increasing admiration for ancient Greece and Egypt led him to question monopolistic claims that Christianity was the unique source of goodness and truth in western civilization. In his first major work of scholarship, *Prolegomena to ancient history* (1871), he asserted:

> There is indeed hardly a great and fruitful idea in the Jewish or Christian systems which has not its analogy in the Egyptian faith. The development of the one God into a Trinity; the incarnation of the Mediating Deity in a virgin, and without a father; his conflict and his momentary defeat by the powers of darkness; his resurrection and reign over an eternal kingdom with his justified saints; his distinction from, and yet identity with, the uncreated, incomprehensible Father, whose form is unknown, and who dwelleth not in temples made with hands – all these theological conceptions pervade the oldest religion of Egypt. So too the contrast, and even the apparent inconsistencies between our moral and theological beliefs – the vacillating attribution of sin and guilt partly to moral weakness, partly to the interference of evil spirits, and likewise of righteousness to moral worth, and again to the help of good genii or angels; the immortality of the soul and its final judgment, the purgatorial fire, the tortures of the damned – all these things have met us in the Egyptian ritual and moral treatises. So, too, the purely human side of morals, and the catalogue of virtues and vices, are by natural consequence as like as are the theoretical systems. But I recoil from opening this great subject now; it is enough to have lifted the veil and shown the scene of many a future contest.[7]

Three years later he wrote in his *Social life in Greece*:

> But I confess that when I compare the religion of Christ with that of Zeus and Apollo, and Aphrodite, and consider the enormous, the unspeakable contrasts, I wonder not at the greatness, but at the smallness of the advance in public morality that has been attained. It is accordingly here, where the differences ought to be greatest, that we are led to wonder most at the superiority of Greek genius which, in spite of an immoral and worthless theology, worked out

in its higher manifestations a morality equal to the best
type of modern Christianity.[8]

He constantly emphasized the debt of Christianity to the
pagan Greeks. Much of St Paul's teaching, he claimed, was
derived from stoicism; St John owed much to Platonism; the
plan of the New Jerusalem in the Revelation was modelled on
that of a Hellenistic city; Christ himself, coming from a hellenized
area of Palestine, probably spoke Greek at times.

This kind of exegesis was distinctly unpalatable to the more
evangelical theologians of his time, with their strongly judaic
inclinations. For them ancient Greece was pagan Greece, and the
less said about its morals and theology the better. Eventually he
was accused of heresy. He wrote about it to a friend in November
1881:

> The charge of heresy was duly brought, and sent down to me
> by the Board. I sent up a reply which made them hop,
> and I have not heard one more word about it. I have asked
> to have the correspondence printed but they wouldn't have
> it at all. So my lovely correspondence is merely filed on
> their minutes, and will no more be seen.[9]

Mahaffy's prediction was only too true. His 'lovely correspondence' is not now to be found in the College archives, and the
board's minutes contain no record of what he may have hoped
would become a theological *cause célèbre*. Nor, it seems, has the
substance of the heresy been recorded elsewhere. Perhaps the
accusation resulted from a sermon he preached in the College
Chapel on what St Paul meant by his reference to 'an unknown
god' in his address to the Athenians. At all events, according to
Gogarty, Mahaffy was suspended from preaching in the College
Chapel as a result of his interpretations (whereupon Tyrrell is
said to have complained of insomnia at the Chapel services).[10]
A footnote in his *Decay of modern preaching* may perhaps give
the substance of what he said on that occasion:

> St Paul's sermon at Athens, for example, is nothing but a
> statement of the Stoical morality, with the doctrine of
> Jesus Christ and the Resurrection superadded. And it is
> quite plain that if these were his precise words he was

KM

arguing on the Stoical side against the Epicurean, just as
he took the Pharisee's side against the Sadducee on a
memorable occasion. Any one who knows what the Stoic
theodicy and morals were, cannot possibly deny this.[11]

Perhaps Mahaffy expressed these views rather more forcibly
in his sermon than in the cooler medium of the written word. At
any rate Leslie has recorded that when Mahaffy talked about
St Paul in conversation he used a racier tone:

> Think of the impertinence of this impudent little Hebrew
> talking to the sages of the ancient world in that manner.
> I can never forgive St Paul. There was an excellent
> university at Antioch, but he never seems to have availed
> himself of it.[12]

As a preacher Mahaffy was by common consent ineffectual.
In an obituary notice *The Times*, with its accustomed tact,
described his sermons as 'scholarly and restrained, more practical
than eloquent'. The *Daily Telegraph* was less gentle:

> He was about as unimpressive a preacher as ever faced a
> congregation: he knew nothing of the art of gesture, his
> voice was metallic and monotonous; nor did his sermons –
> he preached but seldom – display any signs of that
> originality and proneness to innovation which can be
> found abundantly in his historical and philosophical
> writings.

Mahaffy himself once wistfully remarked to his cousin Margaret
Stokes, a woman of forthright speech, 'I wonder why men of far
inferior ability can preach so much better than I.' 'Because,
John, you have no gospel,' she replied.[13]

In the year after the abortive inquisition for heresy he
published what was clearly an *apologia* as well as a critique, his
Decay of modern preaching. This rather harsh attack was
ostensibly aimed at the whole of Christendom but in fact was
limited in scope to the small, post-disestablishment Church of
Ireland. The reader is often conscious that Mahaffy is trying to
work some of his own feelings out of his system. The general
state of preaching is bad, he asserts: 'It is in fact only the simplest
or the most old-fashioned congregations who are now-a-days

satisfied with preaching.' The common view that all a preacher needs for success is piety, is wrong-headed: 'Many a well-meaning Christian, for the very want of being wise as a serpent, has not been harmless as a dove, but mischievous to the great cause he rashly or feebly advocates.' Preaching, he claims, has become stereotyped, anachronistic, formulaic, unworthy of well-educated congregations.

He goes on to emphasize the inconsistency between the doctrine of what was known as 'the call' – which he defines as 'a special motion of the Spirit' – as a requisite for holy orders, and the secular view of clerical life as a profession:

> The general public . . . and the majority of serious parents, regard the ministry as a profession to be ranked with law or medicine, and they assume that any man who feels a turn for it, in the ordinary sense of the word, is entitled to enter it. This is indeed a true and practical view, because if the higher requirement were maintained, so few would dare to present themselves as to render our pulpits empty, and the maintenance of our churches impossible. Even the most pious bishop would hesitate to enforce such a condition, were he given an insight into the hearts of the candidates; nor would he venture to reject those who were honestly disposed to do their duty as professional men, without possessing a higher calling.

(Elsewhere he commends the military officers, some of them veterans of Waterloo, whom he had known as a boy after they had become clergymen of the Church of Ireland: they were unlearned in theology but 'in other respects they made excellent parsons, for they never lost their military air and the habit of command they had acquired in their youth'.)[14] He continues, perhaps partly in self-defence:

> This criticism does not apply to preaching only; it is equally true in the case of all the higher offices in our churches, which require sense and vigour in dealing with human affairs. Thus we need not hesitate to affirm that an honest and sensible, though worldly man, if endowed with a quick insight into character, would make a better bishop, in the strictest sense of *better*, than a simple and

unintellectual man of the deepest piety, whose very
devotion to things unseen leaves him liable to deception
by hypocrites, and to mistakes in action through the
influence of selfish and designing men.

Yet Mahaffy took care to make it clear that he did not despise
piety as such. He pays a tribute to its dignity and beauty:

It is indeed most ungrateful to urge anything against
that one feature in mankind, so rare, so holy, so majestic,
that in this, and in this alone, we may be said to approach
the perfection of a future state.

Such piety, he readily admits, may enable a man, even without education, natural gifts or special training, to preach
effectively. But 'it is a gift of the Spirit, rare, like genius'. It
cannot be learned. But the art of rhetoric, of which preaching is
a branch, and the wide store of information that is needed for
an intellectually arresting sermon, could and should be learned:

I remember seeing the most popular evangelical preacher
of his day in Ireland borrowing an encyclopaedia from a
friend, who asked him what need he, a busy and devoted
minister, could have for such a book. He answered that it
was necessary to keep storing his mind with all manner of
information, otherwise he could not make his sermons
interesting to his hearers. This was a practical man, a man
of sound common sense as well as of deep piety.

The decay of modern preaching, despite its deliberate formalism
in the style of an Aristotelian treatise, is a very personal document. It is partly a justification of his own inability to preach
an effective sermon, partly an attack on hypocrisy, partly a
defence of art against naïve naturalism, and partly a criticism
of narrow doctrinalism in 'the Church which I desire loyally to
serve'. Its general tone is that of – to use his own words – 'a
practical man, a man of sound common sense'. Naturally some
readers found the book 'worldly' and disliked its insistence on
the need for art and preparation in preaching; they preferred
the comfortable doctrine that the Holy Spirit would always
guide an earnest extempore preacher.

Twenty-one years later, in 1903, Mahaffy returned to ecclesi-

astical controversy in an article for the first number of *The
Hibbert Journal*, founded 'to offer to religious thought a genuinely
open field'. His title was 'The drifting of doctrine', and his
theme, 'those tendencies which operate gradually and without
open declaration, often without the knowledge of the orthodox,
upon their creed, and modify vital doctrines without pretending
any influence at all'. As an example he chose a topic very congenial to a man who was now a friend of kings and princes, the
popular conception of kingship. In New Testament times the
dominant conception of a ruler was that of an absolute monarch
who assumed that the lives of his subjects were his personal
property. Consequently any act of benevolence on his part
evoked gratitude, while, on the other hand, his severities could
not be considered reprehensible: he was entitled to do what he
liked with his own. But now, in the early twentieth century, the
prevailing concept was that of a constitutional monarch volun-
tarily bound by laws and by the defined rights of his subjects.
Hence one finds a 'silent drifting of opinion', rather than any
new and conscious heresy.

Instead of the old view that an action was right because
God does it, the new view is that God does it because it is right.
Similarly the importance of miracles as a proof of divine power
must diminish 'as being suited to a ruder age and less devoted
people, and not perfectly consistent with the establishment of
wise laws by an omniscient power'. Also, he claims, belief in the
literal infallibility of the Bible and in eternal punishment has
declined. But we need not now fear that moral dissolution will
follow if the terror of hell is removed, for

> . . . if our forefathers, who inflicted capital punishment for
> a whole catalogue of offences, had been told that their
> descendants would mitigate this severity, and even set
> down as barbarous the penalties formerly inflicted, they
> would have exclaimed that crime and vice would become
> rampant and society dissolve by such unheard-of laxity.
> Nevertheless the change has taken place, and society has
> not dissolved. In the same way, the disappearance of this
> dogma of external and extreme punishment from the
> practical creed of most Christians does not seem to have
> brought with it any corresponding laxity in moral life.

He ends with a series of questions. Can a non-miraculous Christianity be called Christianity at all? Can we maintain Christianity as the highest and noblest rule of life, even for those who do not believe in future rewards and punishments? Is it not, even so, greater and better than worldliness, or selfishness or idleness? Is it a worthy thing to advocate Christianity as a security for the future life, rather than, as a rule, perfect and noble, for our conduct in this life? Finally, has not the Church yet to find a better conception of the future life than that of the mere continuance of the rewards and punishments in this life?

Meanwhile scattered remarks published by Mahaffy elsewhere had expressed other religious convictions and prejudices. The influence of his strongly protestant upbringing affected him to the end of his life. At the Commission on University Education in 1901 he referred to his going to hear Cardinal Newman preach in Dublin, adding, 'We delighted to hear him preach, and preach Catholic doctrine, and we were not the least bit afraid that he would convert us, because we had been taught our own creed properly.'[15] He disliked medievalism in architecture and doctrine: 'The Gothic fane was no doubt the ideal gloom wherein to worship a relentless God and his tortured Christ: The Renaissance palace was a place of light and gladness.'[16] He condemned asceticism and ritualism, as when he ended his *Greek pictures* with a diatribe against the monks of Mount Athos:

> . . . the traveller can not only wonder at the Providence which has made all things beautiful in their kind, but also the strange devices of men to serve Him, not by enjoying with thankful and reasonable devotion, the good things of life which He has given them with large hand, but by reversing His laws, and making the practice of religion a thing of fasting, of abstinence, of ritual, and of mental stagnation.

In another place he denounces priests who 'mumble through services they do not understand, to people who come to hear them as mere enchantments'.[17] Roman Catholicism, with its elements of medievalism and ritualism, he generally condemned, often using the current protestant term of disparagement, 'superstitious', for its forms of piety and discipline. But he also condemned what he believed to be excessive zeal on the other side. In his *Epoch in Irish History* he pilloried the more puritanical Protestants of the seventeenth century as:

> harsh iconoclasts whose first anxiety was to insult and
> destroy the venerable relics or high places held in
> superstitious reverence by all the old inhabitants. Such
> a form of controversy is needlessly and stupidly irritating;
> we may see it even in our own day in the Protestant
> hatred or suspicion shown towards the sign of the Cross,
> the great emblem of all Christianity.[18]

In contrast he praised the seventeenth-century Jesuits whose 'consummate ability, energy, zeal and devotion command the admiration of any fair-minded historian'.[19]

He regarded the political influence of the Roman Catholic bishops and priests of his own time as obnoxious, and he fought it in two forceful articles, 'The Romanisation of Ireland' (1901) and 'Will Home Rule be Rome Rule?' (1912). In 1886 he suspected that the Roman Catholic Archbishop of Dublin was hostile to T.C.D. 'Archbishop Walsh,' he wrote to a friend, 'is bent on destroying us if he can, as he cannot by any means prevent the best RCs from coming to us as long as we last.'[20] (But he came to respect and admire Walsh later.) He considered that the Roman Catholic Church had failed to teach the Irish to tell the truth – he was always sensitive on that point – but he commended them for making the Irish chaste.

Some of his more narrowly protestant contemporaries disliked his readiness to meet and be friendly with Roman Catholic clergy. As a young don in 1868 he had been given an audience with Pope Pius IX, and subsequently had not disguised his respect for the Vatican and its splendours. Many years later he remarked to a friend (after a reference to recent conversions to Roman Catholicism in Magdalen College, Oxford):

> I think if I could turn an R.C. priest for a year and spend
> it at Rome in the confidence of the Pope and Cardinals, it
> might be worth while.[21]

According to Leslie, whose kinsman Mr Leslie of Ballybay accompanied Mahaffy at the papal audience, a curious story, which Mahaffy liked to relate in detail, emerged from that event. The Pope, having been informed that the two Irishmen

came from County Monaghan, made some inquiries from them
about a family named Foster there. This naturally aroused their
curiosity. Eventually they discovered the reason. As a young
layman, the Pope had met Agnes Foster, daughter of the
Church of Ireland Bishop of Clogher, when she was visiting Rome
on a holiday. He and she fell in love, and an unofficial
engagement followed. Later, after the Fosters had returned to
Ireland, higher authorities in Rome intervened, letters were
intercepted, the engagement lapsed, Giovanni Mastai-Feretti
was ordained, and eventually became Pope.[22]

Though opposed to religious intolerance and fanaticism,
Mahaffy like many others in his time certainly did not accept
the doctrine of loving one's enemies – or even the old testament
principle that 'vengeance belongeth unto the Lord' – as a
sovereign rule. Writing about Napoleon in 1913, he remarked:

> Of course he was one of the greatest and most fascinating
> men that ever lived but also one of the greatest liars and
> scoundrels. Any torture inflicted on him at St. Helena served
> him right, though I do not therefore admire or like the
> torturers. But Napoleon inflicted far more than he got.[23]

During the first world war, he wrote to another friend on the
destruction of a German submarine (in 1916):

> *The Baralong* treated the German U boat as a pirate
> ship, which it was, and all merchants have always killed
> pirates wherever they could. All I hope is that the U boat
> was that which torpedoed the *Lusitania* and I think it was.
> If so, it was Divine Justice to have that villain captain
> swimming about and holding up his hands for mercy
> before being shot. Serve him right. This is what brutality
> in war brings us to. It breeds itself like other vermin at a
> terrible rate.[24]

One can see just how fast this brutality could breed by
reading the lecture that he gave to a clerical conference in
T.C.D. in July 1918. By that time he had ceased to be half-
apologetic about a policy of retaliation. He believed now that
he could prove it a quite justifiable policy for Christian people.
The principles of the Sermon on the Mount, he argued, though
suitable for 'the Roman peace' of Christ's time, were not tenable

in 1918, and he spoke scornfully of those 'foolish pacificists' who thought that they still applied. His own attitude towards the Germans was, 'If you use poisonous gases in warfare, we shall adopt them. . . . If you kill unarmed prisoners, we must do it also,' and:

> So long as the Germans openly repudiate all the
> limitations of justice and humanity, and strive to make
> brutality and cruelty the attributes of victory, so long are
> we bound to regard them as poisonous reptiles, which the
> most Christian man does not feel it any violation of his
> duty to exterminate.[25]

Some of his acquaintances seem to have found Mahaffy's loyalties in 1914–18 rather inconsistent with his well-known acquaintance with the German Emperor. But he had his answer – 'The Kaiser is not the man I knew.' Others probably saw inconsistency, too, with what Mahaffy had written in an article entitled 'International jealousy' in 1896.

> What has become of the so-called Christianising of the
> world? What has become of the dreams that, as religion
> was more widely taught and enlightenment spread abroad,
> wars would become impossible, and be regarded as a piece
> of barbarism, superseded by higher methods of arranging
> disputes? Have we abandoned the 'peace on earth, good will
> to men', which was heralded at the birth of Christ, and are
> we now to have no bridle on our mutual hatreds but the fear
> of losing our money?

But on that occasion he was writing to defend the British empire from attacks in the press and from alleged jealousy on the part of other great powers.

This fusion of Christian ethics with imperialistic politics is also illustrated in a letter Mahaffy wrote to Leslie (who had just told him of his forthcoming marriage) in 1912:

> I doubt if any letter from anyone else in the world could
> have given me more pleasure than yours announcing that
> for once you had taken my advice and were passing from
> the ascetic (and often selfish) type of Christianity to the
> more human and altruistic. I always told you that the

highest life for a Christian man is to marry a good wife
and bring up a family in the fear of God and in loyalty to
the Empire.

If challenged Mahaffy would, no doubt, have replied that Christ
had prescribed duties to Caesar as well as to God.

Remarks of this kind won Mahaffy a reputation for being a
pragmatical believer in the efficacy of good works who had little
or no faith. In later life he repudiated this doctrine emphatically.
Writing in 1917 to one of his closest friends at that time, Lady
Woods, he told her that he was planning a sermon for West-
minster Abbey in the following year:

> My discourse there last year on the inherent aristocracy of
> the Church of England has brought me so much criticism
> and correspondence that it is apparently worth while
> thinking out a topic for that great audience. . . .[26]

He now proposed to argue against the current view 'that a man's
faith does not signify a straw, provided his life is good'. He
intended to show that this was untrue both in religion and in
other spheres of life:

> In politics, *e.g.*, it is a man's political *creed*, and not his
> life or acts, that is thought all important. In art, it is not
> because Fra Angelico and Blake produced better works than
> other men – they did not – but because of their religious
> and artistic creeds that they speak to us as no mere
> craftsman ever can. So that after [? insert 'all'], faith is the
> force that has moved the world.

When one tries to find a consistent pattern of development
in such scattered evidence as this, nothing very distinctive
emerges, apart from the usual contrast between a young man's
challenging criticisms and an old man's return to orthodoxy.
What is peculiar is the difference of opinion on whether Mahaffy
was a sceptic or not. Examples of the hostile view have already
been quoted. Justice demands that some favourable opinions
should also be considered.

Mahaffy's rector in Howth from 1905–12 (Dr Arthur Barton,
later Archbishop of Dublin) has recorded[27] that Mahaffy,

though he refused to preach – his weakness there, Barton thought, was due to lack of emotional appeal – often helped in the Sunday services, though he characteristically omitted the part of the fourth commandment, beginning 'for in six days the Lord made heaven and earth . . .', because, as he explained, 'we do not believe that God made the world in six days'. Most significantly, Mahaffy readily undertook the most solemn task of a Christian priest, the service of holy communion, a ceremony which no gentleman – to judge simply by the social ideal which Mahaffy so constantly upheld – would undertake without genuine belief in its truth and efficacy. As Barton testifies, he conducted this service 'with great reverence', though his sense of reverence did not prevent him from introducing a personal touch into the ceremony: in the formula used in administering the sacrament according to the anglican rite he emphasized the words in such a way as to exclude any narrow doctrine of 'the chosen few' so dear to the kind of person who had asked him 'Are you saved, Dr Mahaffy?'

Another witness – also to become a bishop in later life – is the late Dr Arnold Harvey, who as a young divinity student met Mahaffy in his old age and was told, 'at my time of life I have abandoned speculation and have come to rest upon the old, simple truths of the Faith'.[28] On the other hand, Harvey's successor as Bishop of Cashel, Dr Cecil de Pauley, remembered that if Mahaffy's rationalism had been muted by old age his egotism had not. When he heard Mahaffy in the College Chapel reading the phrase from the Revelation 'I am *alpha* and *omega*', he felt that the emphasis on the first word seemed to suggest a new interpretation of the personal pronoun.[29]

Among laymen, Leslie has denied that Mahaffy was essentially a sceptic or a scoffer. Mahaffy's attacks, he holds, were seldom, if ever, on Christianity or the Church (as distinct from pietistic excesses and narrow-minded churchmen); noticeably, too, Mahaffy rarely turned his critical powers against the Bible (except the early chapters of Genesis) or the creeds. Leslie records an incident illustrating his dislike of flippant criticism of the Bible:

I remember a brilliant lady – one of the 'Souls' or at least a hoverer round that intellectual harem which was

swayed by Lords Curzon and Balfour. She poured contempt
on the Book of Lamentations – so depressing and
unnecessary etc. Mahaffy stiffened like a ramrod, and called
attention to and explained its literary beauty.

Another friend reveals a rather unexpected element of
irrationalism. According to Swift MacNeill, Mahaffy believed in
ghosts and claimed to have seen them more than once. Mahaffy
seems to have kept remarkably quiet about this. Perhaps he
had used the word 'superstitious' too freely to risk having it
turned against him.[30] He showed an interest, however, in the
work of the Society for Psychical Research, and was invited to
become a vice-president in 1913.[31] Most significantly, as a proof
of his faith in the world of spirits, he inscribed on his wife's tomb-
stone 'awaiting the glorious resurrection and the life everlasting'.
He was not the kind of man to record hypocrisy on stone.

But what was his inner personal creed as distinct from the
communal creeds of the church to which he assented? Mahaffy
never stated it explicitly. He was no Pascal or Newman, to
reveal the secrets of his soul in diaries or letters. Yet here and
there in his published works passages occur which seem to
speak from the heart. In his *Decay of preaching* he described and
defended the kind of preacher who

> may feel all the value of goodness . . . may sincerely believe
> in the truth and value of his creed and yet . . . may not
> have attained that inner calm of the soul, that closer walk
> with God, which is the privilege of the few among men.

A second passage, written later when he was fifty-seven,
perhaps comes closest to defining his intellectual position:

> . . . there is the increasing tendency to thrust aside or
> forget the great unifying principle of all our life and
> knowledge – that all our thought, all our science, all our
> history, all our speculation of every kind, nay, even all the
> vast complex of worlds in which myriads of other beings
> may be prosecuting similar inquiries – these are the product
> or the outcome of the design of one Almighty God, who has
> created the world according to his infinite goodness. A
> recognition of this great fact on our part is the proper link
> or common ground of all the various and minute special

researches we may make into the laws of the universe,
or the history of any part of it. Nay, more, it is the proper
defence, the only defence we can make, if we are checked
by the warning that in the few years vouchsafed to us on
this earth we have no right to spend one moment of our
precious time upon things of no eternal import; that the
study of religion and our future condition under the
providence of God is our only proper employment. We can
reply in the most thorough earnest that the exclusive study
of what we have separated and called moral or religious
science is not the best way to promote that very science.
The most remarkable illustrations, the most powerful
vindications of God's providence, are found in probing the
secrets of nature, the varieties in the course of human
history. He we may see working in practice what we learn
from our theology in theory, and if in our feebleness and
blindness we are unable to accommodate all the phenomena
of science or of history to these laws, surely the worst way
out of the difficulty is to ignore it, to shut our eyes to the
facts, instead of using them to correct or enlarge our
theory.[32]

Finally, what Mahaffy wrote as a young man in commenting,
not disparagingly, on the religious orthodoxy of ancient Greece,
may perhaps serve as a description of his own:

It was not the faith of mystics, nor an absorption of the
mind in the contemplation of Divine perfections and Divine
mysteries, but rather the religion of a shrewd and practical
people, who . . . blessed God, not like Fénelon, because he
was ideally perfect, but like Bossuet, because they received
from him many substantial favours.[33]

chapter eight

A militant scholar

When in the last few months of his life Mahaffy looked back over his achievements as a scholar and writer, as recorded in his autobiographical summary, he had good reason for feeling satisfied, even triumphant. Viewed retrospectively his scholastic career might seem like a steady, undeviating ascent to the heights. He had produced over thirty books on classical, historical and philosophical subjects, some of them best sellers, others highly praised by specialists, besides a huge corpus of contributions to learned periodicals and popular magazines. He had done pioneer work in two neglected fields of classical study, which had later become major centres of interest. Men of such eminence in the world of scholarship as Schliemann, Wilamowitz, and Theodore Reinach had praised and admired him. Five famous universities and eight of the most distinguished academies of Europe had awarded him their highest honours.

It was an impressive record. But, as Mahaffy well knew, he had had to fight hard against faults of temperament, errors of judgement, and severe censure – censure that for a less robust character might have been overwhelming – before he was accepted as a meritorious scholar. Even at the end of his life there were still some critics who held that his faults outweighed his merits. In his younger days he fought them hard. Later he grew to regard them as being at best mildly eccentric. How could they be right? 'I was told,' he patiently explained in 1896 when his work as a classical scholar was almost completed, 'that I was introducing the heat of modern disputes into the calm

atmosphere of classical learning.'[1] But in fact he was told very
much more. He was accused of superficiality, irrelevancy, rash
judgement, exaggeration and inaccuracy. For example, Basil
Gildersleeve, founder-editor of *The American Journal of
Philology*, wittiest and most erudite of nineteenth-century
American scholars (piqued a little perhaps by his cavalier reception by Mahaffy in Dublin as described in chapter 2), reviewing
one of Mahaffy's books on Hellenistic Greece declared:

> Mr Mahaffy's *Greek Life and Thought from the Age of
> Alexander to the Roman Conquest* . . . is a bright and
> suggestive book. This is a matter of course. It is equally a
> matter of course that the book is not to be taken in dead
> earnest, that the investigator of the period must be at pains
> to verify, and that the young student must not give way to
> the fascination of the many parallels that the author's wide
> vision discerns between ancient and modern history. But
> after all, Mr Mahaffy's *Greek Life and Thought* is hardly
> intended to be anything else than a running commentary
> on the latter half of the nineteenth century, and, when,
> fatigued by the long contemplation of this bright mosaic,
> one closes the eyes for the reproduction of the total effect,
> but two lines come out distinctly – the miserable narrowness
> of English scholarship and the unreason of Home Rule.[2]

Another critic, D. B. Monro, later celebrated as a Homeric
scholar, writing on Mahaffy's first really successful book, *Social
life in Greece*, remarked: 'Mr Mahaffy has the advantage of being
one of a people, with whom the imagination, if it has not attained
to the Greek perfection of form, has at least the Greek freedom
from the domination of hard fact.'[3]

Both of these critics struck at one of Mahaffy's greatest
failings – inaccuracy. It was a surprising, indeed a humiliating,
weakness in a classical scholar. Carefulness and accuracy always
ranked high among the virtues inculcated by a good classical
education. But Mahaffy had not toiled in the harsh treadmill of a
Victorian school, where the slightest error in grammar or
quantity would have been mercilessly castigated. 'Probably
absurdly self-confident' was how, in later years, he described
himself as an undergraduate. He was only too willing to cherish
the warning which, he twice asserts,[4] was given to him as a

young man by two senior colleagues, Jellett and Salmon. 'If you have anything to say,' they told him, 'don't be afraid, print it and don't mind the idlers and scorners. And if you do make a mistake, what matter? In fact, no man is a real man until he has learned that he has made a mistake and is ready to acknowledge it.' Even in his eightieth year he still apparently considered it good advice.

Mahaffy had plenty to say and he was a remarkably rapid worker. For instance, when he had finished his *Social Life in Greece*, he wrote to his publisher, 'the whole manuscript is ready with the exception of one short chapter on the business habits of the Greeks, which I can write in about a week after a week of collecting material. The summer is my only leisure time, and I am sometimes away fishing and shooting.'[5] Productivity, not perfectionism, was his ideal. He was inclined to view with contempt, 'the cold, calm college don, loving cautious statement and accurate rendering as the highest of virtues'.[6] He despised 'herd of specialists . . . each master of his own subject, but absolutely ignorant and careless of all that is going on around him in kindred subjects'.[7] Often he suggested that his lapses were 'trivial' (a favourite word of his) and that it was unworthy of a gentleman to draw attention to them. When a reviewer in an English classical journal charged him with serious inaccuracies, he defended himself on the grounds that in works of genius errors in matters of detail were not merely forgivable but inevitable, quoting the Greek *Essay on the sublime* to the effect that 'lofty genius is far removed from flawlessness, for invariable accuracy incurs the risk of pettiness, and in the sublime, as in great fortunes, there must be something overlooked.'[8] (His 'pedantic' critics – to use another favourite term of his – no doubt remembered that this licence was granted to poets, not to professors of ancient history.) To be fair to Mahaffy, he conscientiously corrected his clear mistakes, and modified his more egotistic statements in later editions.[9] But he never adopted an apologetic tone. Sometimes, indeed, he implied he was exercising a Christian virtue in accepting correction. 'In no case,' he wrote in the preface to the second edition of his *Rambles and studies in Greece*, 'has the tone of a criticism, however supercilious, prevented me from profiting by the matter of it, very thankfully, too, whenever it saved me from any serious error.'

Inaccuracy was not the only fault alleged. He was also charged with superficiality and exaggeration, with indulging in reckless generalizations, and with sprinkling his works with prejudiced and irrelevant allusions to current personalities and events. To these accusations Mahaffy had a simple answer. 'The real difficulty . . . is this. "Can the dry bones live?" I found it impossible to make them do so without fusing strong modern or personal elements into the writing.'[10] He had never forgotten his mother's warning, which he once quoted with devastating effect after a tedious orator at a college meeting – 'Johnny, never be a bore.' His worst enemies could not accuse him of that fault. If he wanted positive assurance of his success in making history lively and colourful he could remember what Acton had said in a letter in 1899 asking him as 'the most brilliant writer we can obtain' to contribute a chapter on sea-power in the Napoleonic era to the *Cambridge Modern History*: 'Will you not give the Cambridge History a purple patch? Will you not give us *the* purple patch of all?'[11] Similarly against the often repeated charge of superficiality – 'a clever popular summariser of Greek history . . . never supreme in any branch of knowledge'[12] – he could quote the verdict of Henry Jackson, one of his few admirers in Cambridge: 'The truth about Mahaffy is that he knows enough in three distinct lines to have a European reputation in each of them, and people do not believe this possible, so they think him superficial.'[13]

There was one other foible, the product, no doubt, of the evangelical fervour of his early upbringing, which even his most loyal supporters could not deny. He constantly used ancient history as a vehicle for moralizing and preaching. Despite censure, he refused to abandon this 'naïve demand for moral earnestness', as one reviewer styled it.[14] His creed was firm: 'I hold that one of the greatest lessons of ancient history is to suggest guiding posts for the perplexities of modern life.'[15] 'Is it worth anybody's while to sit down and endeavour to unravel the tangled skeins of Hellenistic history if he cannot find a single lesson for life, a single corroboration of the adage that human nature is the same in all places and at all times?'[16] The fact that many historians, and among them his celebrated pupil, J. B. Bury, would strongly maintain that it *was* worth while – and better history, too – did not perturb him at all.

A scholar of less self-confidence and resilience might well have been daunted by the running fire of rebuke and censure that almost all his major works provoked from 'pure' scholars. In fact Mahaffy seems to have enjoyed the opportunities for controversy and conflict. As an eminent fellow-countryman said in an obituary notice, Mahaffy was 'rather of the Donnybrook type of Irishman that trailed his coat looking for a fight . . . he liked being in hot water.'[17] Others saw a 'streak of impishness'[18] in him. Gildersleeve, always alert to pinpoint his faults, called it 'a certain Robin Goodfellow malice'.[19] Like his friend Bernard Shaw, he enjoyed being the provocative iconoclast, revelling in the sheer joy of battle. So with a hibernian talent for invective and denunciation, he attacked popular idols like Sophocles and Thucydides and raised doubts about the truthfulness of the ancient Greeks and the originality of Professor Jebb. He had a similarly Irish sense of the ridiculous, as when in his *Rambles and studies in Greece* he noted with evident amusement that in a 'battle' during the Greek war of independence 'the quantity of ammunition expended was enormous and the result was one man wounded'.[20] In criticizing others he hit hard – sometimes rather wildly – and generally bore no rancour when 'the scholastic trade union which thinks that all Greek authors are to be lauded as perfect'[21] retaliated vigorously. Occasionally, but not often, he found their touchiness rather tiresome and stupid:

> The present scholarship both of Germany and of England has been positively vitiated by the fashion among professors of taking criticism as an act of hostility and pursuing the critic, so that no quiet man thinks it worth while to set his neighbour right or expose, however gently, a piece of literary imposture at the cost of being annoyed and maligned for the rest of his life.[22]

Though Irish provocativeness may have prompted many of Mahaffy's attacks on established figures and beliefs, there was a matter of principle involved too. Ironically, in view of the complaints about his disregard for truth, some of the most serious troubles in his rise to academic fame were caused by sheer truthfulness. Honest discussion, he believed, demanded recognition of the whole truth without suppression of unpalatable features: a picture was not a true picture unless it showed the shadows as well as the sunlight. So he refused, for example, to pass over the faults of the modern Greeks – 'the Greek public is too intelligent to resent friendly comment on its failings'[23] – or to be silent on the homosexual tendencies of the classical Greeks. In this, as in other aspects of his life, he refused to 'play safe'.

Qualities of Mahaffy's kind can be given a good name or a bad name according to the inclinations of the observer: honest candour or lack of due reticence; commendable moral earnestness or unscholarly tendentiousness; courage and initiative or foolhardiness and rashness; avoidance of boredom or over-eagerness to entertain; imaginativeness or disregard for the facts; versatility or inability to specialize; 'love of large principles' (to use his own phrase)[24] or carelessness in matters of detail; wide scope or superficiality; self-confidence or arrogance; masterly detachment or what one critic called 'the usual tone of super-cilious superiority which distinguishes the average insular voyager'.[25] If one asks why he resisted so many of the self-improvements, which even his friendliest critics often suggested, the answer may be that he realized how deeply the faults complained of were rooted in his inner nature. Remove them, and he might have lost the dynamism that made his work so forceful and effective. As he saw it, 'The existence of such defects is merely human, and should be condoned. It is only their number and quality which can make them the object of fair censure. To delay the publication of any large work until all possible flaws are removed, is to postpone it, if not indefinitely, at least till some remote period and to sacrifice any freshness or vigour it possesses for no certain equivalent.'[26] In other words, the choice for Mahaffy was not between flawlessness and faultiness, but between living flesh and dry bones, between 'gentlemanly' scholarship and pedantry.

Up to now the emphasis in this chapter has been on Mahaffy's more ambiguous qualities. But he would, of course, never have reached final recognition as a meritorious scholar had he not possessed the basic capacities that all work of academic merit requires. He had a tenacious memory – 'like a rat-trap' as one obituarist described it[27] – a keen critical faculty, a high degree of originality, solid common-sense, and an exceptional talent for discerning latent affinities and implicit causes. A fluent linguist, he kept himself fully familiar with the latest discoveries and developments in continental scholarship. Most valuably for his work as a social historian, he had a profound insight into human nature, and an unflagging interest in man as a political and social animal. Finally, despite the impression of gentlemanly leisure that he habitually gave, he had the quality essential for all substantial achievement, sheer industry. Early in life he had made it 'an iron rule' never to write less than five pages a day as 'an irreducible minimum'.[28] One of his favourite quotations was 'Seest thou a man diligent in his business? He shall stand before kings.' His own career proved that it could be literally as well as metaphorically true.

When one turns from these generalities to consider Mahaffy's publications specifically, the first surprising fact is that he had not originally intended to be a classical scholar at all. 'The thrill of delight' which Whately's *Elements of Logic* gave him as a boy of fourteen had set him, he thought, on the road to being a philosopher. After winning his fellowship in 1864 he prudently saw that he could combine this interest in philosophy with his useful knowledge of German in elucidating the obscurities of Immanuel Kant. Two years later he published a translation, from the German, of the section of Kuno Fischer's *History of Modern Philosophy* dealing with Kant's *Critique of Pure Reason*. In his footnotes and long introduction Mahaffy not only put Fischer right on some points but vigorously challenged Mill and G. H. Lewes, then well established leaders of British philosophic thought. (Mill generously praised it, all the same, as 'a valuable contribution to the literature of philosophy' in a letter to Mahaffy later.)[29] The book must have met a definite need: within a few years it was almost sold out, and Mahaffy, having come to the conclusion that it 'was a common mistake to think that because a man talks German or holds a chair in a German university he must know more of the subject than ourselves', decided to produce a detailed commentary on Kant's *Analytic* and *Dialectic* in three volumes. In 1872 he published volume one of this work, an introduction to Kant, largely devoted to attacking J. S. Mill and Bain, outstanding members of what Mahaffy called the 'sensual' school. Volume three followed in 1874, the preface containing the ominous sentence, 'I must plead my numerous and exacting duties, not indeed to cloak any defects in the matter of the book, but for any negligences that a more careful revision of my proof-sheets might have removed.' Volume two never appeared.[30]

In his *Summary* Mahaffy gives a practical reason for turning away from philosophical work. 'Had I been elected,' he wrote, 'to the chair of Moral Philosophy for which I had strong letters from Grote, Mill, Mansel etc. metaphysics would have been the main pursuit of my life.' But another junior fellow, T. K. Abbott, was elected to the vacant chair in 1867, which was scarcely surprising since Abbott had published an able attack on the Berkleian theory of vision and was ten years Mahaffy's senior.

Though Mahaffy may have felt that by rejection for the chair of philosophy he had been baulked of a successful career as a philosopher, he had in fact been moved into a field where his powers would be much better employed. As a writer of philosophy he was argumentative and at times acute, but he lacked subtlety and any notable faculty for abstract metaphysical thought. Essentially interested in people and events rather than in purely intellectual concepts, he found his true *métier* in history. Yet the logic and the skill in discerning fallacies which he had learned from Whately gave a clarity and firmness to his thought that lasted all his life.

Mahaffy now turned to his second dominant interest, ancient history, inspired by his early reading of Grote's *History of Greece*. The college was not slow in giving him encouragement. In 1869 a special lectureship in ancient history was created for him, and in 1871 it was raised to a professorship. Ancient history was added to the moderatorship course in classics – later it became an independent subject by itself – and Mahaffy was appointed examiner. Further, the board gave him permission to order whatever foreign books and periodicals he required. Mahaffy quickly collected a quantity of valuable material, though the siege of Paris delayed his French orders.

Perhaps his appointment as a lecturer had been partly prompted by his success before a fashionable Dublin audience. During the sixties Dubliners were flocking to the theatre of the Royal College of Science to hear eminent local and visiting figures – Ruskin was among the latter – discourse on literature and art. Mahaffy spoke there in 1867 on 'Three epochs in the social development of the ancient Greeks'. Clearly he set out to be challenging and provocative. He asserted that the Homeric Greeks were neither very courageous nor scrupulously honest (though they had good manners); that Euripides was superior to Sophocles, Herodotus to Thucydides; and that the epoch of the Macedonian monarchs showed much more refinement than the classical periods. He also mounted hobby-horses that he would ride hard in future books – the justice of woman's claim to emancipation and the squalidness of old age.

Dublin society, accustomed to eulogistic discourses on classical antiquity, may well have been shocked at these *boutades*. But Mahaffy had made a good impression. Soon the governors of the recently founded Alexandra College, Dublin, prompted partly perhaps by his forthright views on women's rights, invited him to lecture there on political geography and ethnology, and he consented. Founded in 1866 on the model of Queen's College, London, for 'the general education of ladies', Alexandra soon became the leading school for girls in Dublin. Its premises in Earlsfort Terrace were only a short walk from Trinity, and several Trinity dons accepted invitations to lecture there. Mahaffy highly approved of the new foundation, because, he wrote (probably not altogether to the liking of its founders), 'it never aimed at unattainable objects. . . . No more is intended than to make girls better sisters, wives and mothers than they were hitherto.' Mahaffy also approved of the fact that the girls would be enabled to understand something about 'the more serious subjects which are discussed among men in general society'.

He soon transformed his prescribed course in geography and ethnology into nothing less than a survey of all ancient history in the near east and ancient Greece. This he published in 1869 as *Twelve lectures on primitive civilizations and their physical conditions*. They made no pretensions to original scholarship, but they had flashes of prophetic intuition, emphasizing, for example, the historical significance of Minos and Mycenae before Schliemann and Evans had made this view commonplace. They still make good reading. Already one can see Mahaffy's guiding principles being put into practice. He offers 'stimulant rather than nutriment'. History should be useful, he avers, and not a 'mere compendium of barren facts and dates'. He aims – not with full success – at avoiding dogmatism. He digresses freely, as when he commends the English aristocracy for marrying outside their class so that 'our nobility is still a living, growing, thinking power, and all the lower classes are stimulated by the hope of attaining the highest positions in the country by their own efforts', and he censures his fellow-countryman abroad for being 'still the same turbulent, interesting, unmanageable being', as he is at home.

After his promotion to the Professorship of Ancient History in 1871, he published in that year his first historical study addressed to scholars, *Prolegomena to ancient history*. In the opening chapter he again attacked the prevailing view fostered by Thomas Arnold and Jowett among others, that Thucydides – or Thukydides, as he then preferred to spell it – was a better historian than Herodotus. (He showed some uncharacteristic qualms about this in his preface: 'Perhaps it was unwise to put forth in the outset an adverse judgement on Thukydides without going more fully into the evidence.') He discussed the historical value of myths and thoroughly enjoyed himself in ridiculing the solar theory of heroic legends. Most of the remaining pages were given to a description of ancient Egypt, with special attention to the deciphering of the hieroglyphs and of the Asian cuneiform scripts.

This discussion of ancient Egypt was a fortunate preparation for his papyrological work twenty years later. Probably his interest had been stirred a few years earlier, in 1866, by obituaries of a former fellow of the College, Edward Hincks (mentioned seven times in *Prolegomena*), who from a remote rectory in Co. Down had published papers of capital importance on the hieroglyphic and cuneiform scripts, and had come to be regarded as one of the leading pioneers in that field. (His bust was later given a place of honour in the Cairo Museum.) In Mahaffy's opinion Hincks and William Rowan Hamilton, the mathematician, were the only men of international reputation – the only two 'world-men',[31] as he put it – that Trinity produced after 1800. He was determined to equal them if he could.

In his preface Mahaffy implies that he tried to make his *Prolegomena* a disciplined work of pure scholarship. But he failed to eliminate all digressions. Scholars may have been surprised to find such entries in the index as, 'Irish Protestants, their bigotry', 'Irish Catholics, their bigotry'. One can guess, too, whom he had in mind when he wrote:

> If I am right, that mind is best imbued – perhaps that mind is alone really imbued – with liberal and just principles on religion and politics, which has been brought up in honest bigotry, and which *thinks itself free.*[32]

Nor could he restrain himself from remarking that the Egyptian farmers apparently 'required a Land Act more urgently than even the Irish tenantry', or hold back from impish mockery of a German professor who claimed to have entered into the inner feelings of Pericles' mistress, Aspasia. Another stricture on the Germans has ironical overtones in the light of Mahaffy's own practice: 'Even the most brilliant German historians seem tainted with the impropriety of displaying their political opinions through a thin veil of history.'

Mahaffy in his *Summary* described the book's reception as a *succès d'estime*. The *estime* had sharp edges. A reviewer in *The Academy* described it as a 'volume of clear and sparkling essays', erudite, suggestive, pleasant: but he called the title 'somewhat ambitious', spoke of inaccuracies and irrelevancies, and noticed its 'zest for theological controversies'.[33] Mahaffy accepted the blame with the praise – happily so, for the sake of his own future, since the reviewer was the Oxford scholar A. H. Sayce, who soon became his firm friend and eventually introduced him to the Petrie papyri.

Sayce in his memoirs over fifty years later (1923) asserted that *Prolegomena* was Mahaffy's best book. (He added rather an unexpected reason: 'If any corroboration of my opinion is needed, it is the fact that it was the only one of his books which had what he considered a poor sale.'[34]) It certainly is remarkably talented – zestful, versatile, wide-ranging, well-informed, challenging and independent-minded. In it Mahaffy frames his own criteria for the highest achievements in historical writing. He finds 'the distinctive quality of a *great* historian' (Mahaffy was fond of emphatic italics) in the 'formation of an historical theory based upon his facts, and the sober balancing of probable evidence and of uncontradicted though unsubstantial tradition'. 'In history, genius appears to me to mean this strong stamp with which the writer's mind marks all his materials – this frame into

which he fits all his figures.' And later: 'Broad views are doubtless
the finest features in our great historians.'

His next publication, *Social Life in Greece from Homer to
Menander* (1874), brought Mahaffy his first full taste of popular
favour. As he himself wrote in his *Summary*:

> This book, drawn directly from a fresh study of the Greek
> texts from a social point of view, had an immediate and
> great success, not indeed financially, for out of the 1st
> edition, which ran out in 6 months, I was shown by the
> publisher's accounts to have emerged a debtor to him! But
> the public read and praised the book: it was easy and
> popular, and soon became a habitual prize-book given at
> classical schools to diligent pupils. The book is still alive
> after nearly 50 years in its 7th edition, and, at all events,
> did its work in making Greek life familiar to many who had
> thought it was mere ancient history.

As a book to interest and instruct both the expert and the
general reader it was a masterly achievement, and its emphasis
on sociology rather than on military and political history was in
many ways original. It gave the general reader a lively impression of the ancient Greeks seen as 'men of like passions with ourselves'. It also gave an impression – and a true one – of impartial
judgement. Its frank strictures on the failings of a people so
long revered as paragons of beauty and virtue must have seemed
almost as iconoclastic as Lytton Strachey's later assaults on
eminent Victorians. Those marmoreal Greeks of Flaxman and
Keats were (one learned) prone to lying and dishonesty and, at
times, to a 'strange and to us revolting perversion, the Asiatic
custom of attachments among men'. Further, the age of democracy was a time of decadence; the tyrants were better rulers
than the democrats; classical civilization depended on slavery;
and the status of women was sadly degraded. As for himself, he
affirms in the preface what was to remain his lifelong claim: 'I
have endeavoured to take homely and common sense views, and
have thus arrived at many results opposed to what I consider
sentimentalism or pedantry.' In case obtuse critics should complain about omissions – as they did – he asserts: 'It is . . .
generally true that no work is so disappointing as that which
professes completeness.'

His wide-ranging comments on Greek life gave him ample opportunity for introducing modern parallels. He praised the 'Irish peasants' for their care of orphans. He deplored the failure of English law in Ireland, believing that 'the harshest despotism would be more successful, and perhaps in the end more humane'. He attacked Froude's views on Irish morals and the ridiculousness of menu French. A vivid footnote on the agonies of a criminal condemned to be hanged reads now almost like an introduction to *The Ballad of Reading Jail* by his pupil Oscar Wilde, who read the proofs. (Mahaffy derived his information on this from *Principles of Animal Mechanics* published in 1873, by his senior colleague Samuel Haughton, F.R.S., whose researches are said to have led to the introduction of the modern method of hanging by dislocation of the spinal vertebrae, instead of by strangulation.)

The reviewers received the book with mixed feelings. They praised the liveliness of its style, the freshness of its approach, and the independence of its judgements. But several deplored its aggressive and censorious tone, and the Scots scholar, D. B. Monro, as quoted earlier, while praising it for many good qualities, asserted that it relied too much on an Irish imagination.

It was an anonymous reviewer[35] who ventured to refer to the topic that others had chosen to pass over in silence. In his last sentence he accused Mahaffy of palliating a certain kind of Greek immorality in an 'indefensible' way. This clearly referred to Mahaffy's descriptions of the 'Asiatic custom'. Greek homosexuality had not previously been frankly discussed in any book on the classics designed for popular reading in the English-speaking countries, though many Victorian Englishmen, especially in the universities and public schools, were well aware of it. Jowett in the introduction to his celebrated translation of Plato's *Symposium* in 1871 had handled the topic very discreetly, not to say reticently. Mahaffy was careful to stigmatize this aspect of Greek social life as a 'strange and to us revolting perversion'. But with his ingrained honesty and candour he had tried to see how 'this peculiar delight and excitement felt by the Greeks in the society of handsome youths' fitted into the perspective of its epoch. Certainly this homosexuality – he used other terms, as that word was not yet current in English – led to 'strange and odious consequences', but modern romantic passion among men and women could lead to 'consequences socially more serious, though less revolting (of course) to *our* tastes'. He named several alleged homosexuals in ancient times, among them Parmenides, Sophocles, and Alexander the Great. Though 'these things are so repugnant and disgusting that all mention of them is usually omitted in treating of Greek culture', he felt it his duty 'to show how from its sentimental side, this feature of Greek life can be conceived as co-existing with purity and refinement'. He also thought it fair to point out that some of the customs of modern heterosexual society – ballroom dancing, for example – would have been immoral and shocking to the ancient Greeks, and he snatched an opportunity of making a slash at a *bête noire* of his by asserting that 'a modern gentleman who marries for the reason admitted by St Paul would be justly stigmatized as a low and brutal creature, who was dishonouring the so-called object of his affections'.

One can easily imagine what effect these remarks had on more conventional readers in 1874. In the second edition, next year, Mahaffy yielded to pressure and omitted most of what he had said about the unmentionable topic. As he wrote to George Macmillan in 1875: 'I have now done what I can to make the book accurate and have taken out some strongly flavoured things and put in some more interesting facts.' In place of the offending pages he had adroitly substituted an appreciation of 'female beauty' in ancient Greece and a discussion of other matters of wholesome feminine interest. As a result he hoped that the book would now be 'suited to all classes of readers' and could be 'made of general use for school and family reading'.

This was the most notable occasion on which Mahaffy yielded to criticism in an important matter of personal judgement. But he was neither apologetic nor mealy-mouthed about it. On the contrary, he combined firmness and flexibility. He made no recantation of any kind, but referred any reader who required information on these 'male romantic attachments' to his first edition (which seems to have become something of a collector's piece to judge from a request from Lord Houghton to him for a copy in 1885).[36] He even added some new classical references on the topic. For those who might ask why he had withdrawn his first frank pages he had a resolute reply:

There were certain phases in Greek morals, which had
hitherto not been fairly discussed and had been consequently
misunderstood and upon these I wrote freely what I thought
due to the Greeks and to their culture. I see no reason to
retract one word I have written . . . but there are things
which ought to be said once, and which it is nevertheless
inexpedient to repeat.

The delicate operation was entirely successful, and the book
lived on in high popular esteem for over fifty years, not merely as
'a habitual prize-book' for 'diligent pupils', but as a source of
illumination and stimulus to every classical scholar sensible
enough to read it. Mahaffy's critics and rivals never – so far as
the present writers can discover – publicly used his candour as a
weapon against him – whether from delicacy or magnanimity
or respect for the law of libel, one can only speculate. At all
events, the cumulative evidence of Mahaffy's life and work is
against the notion that he had any intention of encouraging a
revival of this feature in Hellenism. Whether his frank discussion
of it had any effect on his pupil, Oscar Wilde, who is thanked in
the preface for having made 'improvements and corrections all
through the book', there is no clear evidence to decide.[37] The
first reference to homosexuality in Wilde's letters occurs two
years after he had left Trinity.

Apart from this clash with conventionality, Mahaffy had good
reason for being elated in the early months of 1876. The first
edition of his *Social life* had sold out, and the second edition was
already going well. He had visited Greece for the first time in
the previous year, and had found it extremely exhilarating, as
his lively articles in the intellectual journals had already shown.
He was now completing a full account of that visit in his *Rambles
and studies in Greece*. He could feel reasonably confident that
this book would be quite as popular and successful as his *Social
life*. But while he had good reason to be elated, he might also,
as a classical scholar, have remembered the familiar maxim of
ancient Greek ethics that great success often leads to arrogance,
and arrogance to a recklessness that may have tragic consequences. What actually happened was no great tragedy – some,
indeed, found it rather comic – but it antagonized a powerful
faction of British classical scholars for the rest of his life.

In February 1876 Richard Claverhouse Jebb published the two volumes of his *Attic orators from Antiphon to Isaeos*, a work still highly valued and frequently consulted. He was then in his thirty-fifth year,[38] just two years younger than Mahaffy. He, too, was something of an admirable Crichton, as well as being an Irishman by ancestry and upbringing. (Mahaffy discovered with some amusement after their controversy that he and Jebb were third cousins.)[39] His first schooling had been at St Columba's College near Dublin, the school which Mahaffy had sardonically referred to in describing the social slights he had to endure as a boy. Jebb spent the year 1853–4 there, during which his headmaster had written to his parents that he had been surprised to perceive 'how wretched a few words of blame made the boy, and his misery lasted for days': in fact he had 'talked to him seriously on the mistake of having too much *amour propre*'. Jebb left in the following year, going on to Charterhouse and Cambridge, where Oscar Browning saw his early promise as 'a purely Celtic genius, like a flame of fire'. Before his book on Attic oratory provoked Mahaffy's attack he had previously published two short but valuable editions of Greek literary works. But *The Attic Orators* was his first *magnum opus*.

There is evidence of some sharpness of feeling between Mahaffy and Jebb before their public conflict. Jebb had written in January 1876 to his publisher Alexander Macmillan[40] about an advertisement which had been printed in the end papers of his *Attic Orators*. After asking to have the whole sheet removed, he wrote:

If, however, you insist on it, at least do me this favour. Remove Prof. Mahaffy's book from the list. I must absolutely decline to have my book made a vehicle for advertising a book which I believe is more calculated to destroy the study of Greek literature at the very root than any other I have ever read. Of its merits in other respects I am not called upon to say anything. But, as far as it deals with Greek literature, it is simply 'impudently absurd', as Mr. Matthew Arnold renders the French *saugrenu*. Excue my freedom of speech, but I feel strongly on this point.

Meanwhile Alexander Macmillan had presumably come to

know about a letter from Mahaffy to Grove (editor of *Macmillan's Magazine*) in 1875,[41] mentioning a small but obviously wounding incident. A letter to Mahaffy had been forwarded by mistake to Cambridge (presumably because it had been addressed to 'Trinity College' without the 'Dublin'). It eventually reached Mahaffy marked 'Not Known', which he took to be a deliberate insult on the part of what he called 'the Cambridge authorities'.

Clearly war might break out at any moment. The first shot was fired by a hidden marksman. On 25 March 1876, the *Spectator* carried an unsigned review of Jebb's new book. After a courteous prelude about 'so eminent a Greek scholar as Mr Jebb' the anonymous writer went on to describe the work as 'wearisome', 'unprofitable', 'these mouldy bones', 'singularly tasteless', 'misdirected industry', 'often pedantic', 'We suspect that the whole of his theory about ancient oratory being one of the fine arts is a blunder', 'The Professor has strung together a number of hazy statements and nearly all of them are false.' In the end the criticism became sheer invective.

Jebb immediately wrote to Alexander Macmillan:

> You see Mahaffy has wreaked his spite in the *Spectator*. I do not think it will do me lasting harm. His venom is a little too evident, and the abuse is too coarse. But I hope that your eyes are now opened to the real character of the man. There is not a single statement of his which I could not blow to the winds. But silence is wisest, and I shall say nothing. There is my present resolve, at least . . .

A week later, on 1 April, *The Academy* published a much longer review signed by Mahaffy. Though more temperately worded than the earlier one, it was quite as destructive. 'It would be a poor compliment,' he urbanely began, 'to this long-expected book from a mature scholar, were it to be disposed of with a simple eulogy.' The book, he pronounced, was disappointingly unoriginal: worse still, it was seriously plagiaristic. To prove this Mahaffy cited a list of 'coincidences' between Jebb's exposition and that of the German scholar Friedrich Blass, who had already published three books on the subject. (On this he is said to have remarked, 'Jebb will carry a Blassted reputation for the rest of his life.') He added accusations of inaccuracy, omission, exaggeration and faulty judgement. On the good side, the book, he said, showed enthusiasm, style and 'refined taste': Mr Jebb had 'few rivals, and certainly no superior' in one department of classics, namely, 'accurate and elegant translation'. After some further strictures, Mahaffy concluded with the hope that Jebb would not misunderstand the 'great freedom' with which his book had been treated: the criticisms were solely prompted by a 'sincere interest in a great subject', and by a desire to be of service in promoting knowledge of it.

This last protestation would have carried more weight if Mahaffy had not in an earlier paragraph revealed some personal pique. Talking of Jebb's 'long and interesting introduction' he remarked that the liveliest part of it was 'a polemic . . . against some person or persons unknown, who have ventured to put Euripides as a tragic poet above Sophocles, owing to a mistaken view of the plastic character of Greek art'. Every well informed reader would have known that Jebb was referring to Mahaffy's *Social life*. Mahaffy's playful irony – 'It is a pity Prof. Jebb did not name these critics, as most people will be disposed to doubt their existence or at least their sanity' – would deceive few.

Jebb, against Alexander Macmillan's advice – 'it is absolutely certain that your pamphlet or paper will be answered again and with greater animus, and time and temper and labour, all in your case of the highest value, will be wasted' – decided to produce a detailed reply. He published it as a sixty-page pamphlet before the end of 1876. He began by showing that Mahaffy had understated the extent of his (Mahaffy's) high opinion of Euripides, and hinted that Mahaffy's hostility was due to the omission of his name from among the authorities cited in the *Attic Orators*. (Here some readers may have wondered whether this omission was not due in turn to Mahaffy's neglect of Jebb in his *Social Life*.) Jebb went on to a detailed examination of the charges of inaccuracy. His refutation of the accusation of plagiarism was simple: he had written to Blass and had received a letter stating that he had not found a single instance of Jebb's having adopted a conjecture of his without explicit acknowledgement.

Towards the end of his reply Jebb struck at Mahaffy's pride and prestige as a scholar: his omission of Mahaffy's name from

The Attic Orators as an authority on a certain point of chrono-
logy was not occasioned by insensibility to Mahaffy's clever-
ness – 'everything he does is clever' – but by a conviction that a
scholar who could censure Thucydides for surly silence and
Pindar for bombast, and Sophocles for incompetence in portray-
ing heroines, was not worth studying. As he put it, 'I came to
the conclusion that Prof. Mahaffy's general appreciation was
not such as to permit of my deriving any solid advantage from
his teaching.' He ends by saying that his 'earnest wish and
endeavour' in writing his reply had been to keep personal
elements out of it: he believed that 'it was in the general interests
of literature' that he should speak.

Mahaffy – there is no evidence that *he* consulted anyone –
quickly published twenty-eight pages entitled *Reply to the
'Remarks' of Mr. Jebb*, promising in a letter to a friend to make
it 'as gentle and impersonal as possible'. He took what in the
eyes of precise scholars must have seemed rather a weak line of
defence, announcing in his first paragraph that: 'the business
of reviewing is not one of fastidious leisure, nor are its words
of praise or blame intended as monumental records worthy of
microscopic attention', which might have been more convincing
if he had not cited so many details in his original review. He
claimed that Jebb's microscopic attention had only discovered
two or three trifling weaknesses and one misstatement in his
review. He had not been able to examine all Jebb's 'complaints'
in detail since 'the time of one who has yet so much to learn' is
'too precious to be spent in defending his own opinions'. He
regretted that 'two scholars, of whatever respective merits,
should appear before the world in the character of controver-
sialists', because quarrels in philology are 'almost invariably a
waste of time and temper'. He then, rather inconsistently,
appended twenty-six pages of detailed refutation of Jebb's
'carefully planned attack'. Blass's letter he brushed aside as a
mere kindness. To reinforce his former charges he added another,
that Jebb had failed to understand German correctly at times.
He found it unfair of Jebb not to acknowledge the review's praise
of his diligence and elegance – 'but it almost seems that in Prof.
Jebb's camp no such independent respect is tolerated; he must
have absolute submission, or war to the knife'. Finally he
assured Jebb that there had been no deliberate ill-will in any of

his criticisms, and hoped that this public disclaimer might save him 'from the misfortune of being again compelled to refute so polished a scholar, and so painstaking a controversialist'.

Jebb replied again in 1877, mostly repeating the main arguments from his earlier paper. But he now insinuated that Mahaffy had been disingenuous, noting how one passage had 'dwelt with such remarkable accuracy in Mr. Mahaffy's memory, while other things on which the light of the past would have been interesting have faded'. He ended 'I have no taste for controversy. But I shall not regret the time bestowed on a detailed refutation of Prof. Mahaffy, if he should in future be more on his guard against making grave charges which he cannot justify, and converting the responsible office of criticism into the opportunity of a petulant attack.'

Mahaffy did not reply. Perhaps he recalled the aphorism from Menander quoted in his *Prolegomena*: 'This sharpness of spirit and excessive bitterness is an immediate proof of small-mindedness to every witness.' He was glad later that he had let the dispute lapse. He wrote to a friend in 1880: 'The longer I live, the more I see that controversy is no use. Keep preaching the right thing and let the other fellow alone.'

Reading the arguments and accusations on each side after an interval of ninety years, most scholars would probably judge that Jebb, the more careful and exact writer of the two, had won the battle. In controversies of that kind the rifle is more effective than the shotgun. Besides, Jebb was fighting mainly on his own favourite ground of style, syntax and literary criticism, though matters of history were also involved. Mahaffy had clearly over-reached himself in his initial onslaught. His rejoinder to Jebb's reply had wavered between expressions of gentlemanly scorn for sustained controversy and an inadequate attempt to answer Jebb in detail. On the other hand, he had kept his temper better than Jebb, and to the general reader, whose opinion Mahaffy valued as highly as that of the expert, that was victory in itself. In general Mahaffy seems to have taken the view that, to use a favourite cricketing phrase of his, Jebb had been 'morally bowled'.

What may perhaps jar most disagreeably on a present-day reader is the contrast between the high-minded protestations of public spirit and the obvious self-assertion on both sides. When

MM

Mahaffy described his motive as 'a sincere interest in a great subject', and when Jebb in turn affirmed that he was only speaking 'in the general interest of literature', readers might have been more impressed if so many personal denigrations had not been included. In fact both Mahaffy and Jebb were high-flying young Irishmen, both destined to be highly honoured as brilliant Hellenists in different fields of classical studies.

Jebb remained sore about this encounter for some time afterwards. He wrote to Alexander Macmillan in December 1878:

> The elaborate lying of Mr. Mahaffy, and the ravings of two drunken school-masters, cannot have done any appreciable harm, I should think. I exposed Mr. Mahaffy in a way from which his reputation will not recover.

But controversy broke out again in 1881,[42] the year when Mahaffy and Jebb were simultaneously elected members of the Athenaeum (with seven other candidates, Matthew Arnold being one of Mahaffy's sponsors). Jebb, smarting from criticism by Mahaffy of his contributions to the *Encyclopaedia Britannica*, wrote an article for the *Journal of Hellenic Studies* attacking some of Schliemann's (and by implication Mahaffy's) views on the site of ancient Troy. Mahaffy replied. Sayce came in to support him, D. B. Monro to support Jebb (which resulted in a brief Monro-Mahaffy duel over Monro's *Homeric grammar* in December 1882). An innocent American scholar, W. W. Goodwin, was dragged in as a witness much against his will. Once again Jebb was allowed to have the last word. But, so far as archaeology was concerned, here he had probably the weaker case, and the verdict of posterity has gone against his views.

Mahaffy, to judge from references in his correspondence, seems to have been less perturbed than Jebb by these controversies. But he remained at feud with Jebb and his supporters for long afterwards. Writing to George Macmillan in 1882 he gibes at 'exaggerated and fulsome praise of Jebb', and he remarks to him in February 1884:

> How can you say that Jebb is not reviewed after my paper in the Academy? He has been writing furious letters all round ever since and is thinking seriously of suicide. . . .
> Jebb's *Sophocles* is handsome and carefully done but

contains nothing new and people who want merely a good translation will properly object to paying 15 sh. a play for it. He has no talent for conjectures, and besides has made a good many small mistakes.

The majority of classical scholars would probably consider Mahaffy wrong in his judgement on Jebb here, too. But at any rate Mahaffy's self-confidence clearly remained unshaken: as he wrote to a friend in 1885 (with reference to his reply to Jebb): 'I can imagine the old Master of Trinity chuckling over Jebb's case. He always hated him.'[43] In 1906 when Henry Jackson, always a supporter of Mahaffy in Cambridge, succeeded Jebb as Regius Professor of Greek there, Mahaffy wrote to him: 'I wish to add my tribute of sympathy with your appointment. I wish it had taken place twenty years ago and it would have put Classics on a better footing in Cambridge. This however is strictly "entre nous".'[44]

The feud dragged on. Mahaffy wrote to Macmillan in 1886:

Jebb's name was again proposed for an honorary degree here by his friends, but had to be withdrawn. It is rather undignified of them to be so perpetually begging for this honour for him and without success. I suspect no one would feel more strongly about it than he himself.

Later, in 1888, Tyrrell did manage to get Jebb an honorary LL.D. But Cambridge did not join the universities that honoured Mahaffy in his later years. Nor was Mahaffy elected a Fellow of the British Academy (where Jebb's influence was powerful since its foundation) though Tyrrell and his junior colleagues, L. C. Purser and J. B. Bury, were. An influential section of British classical scholars maintained a vendetta against him even after his death. The historian of the Athenaeum in 1926, after a biased account of the 'unfortunate literary quarrel' (in which Jebb took Mahaffy's criticisms 'much too seriously'), dismissed Mahaffy as 'a clever popular summarizer of Greek history'.[45] If Mahaffy had lived to read it, the denigration would hardly have surprised him, for he had declared on a post-card to his Cambridge friend and admirer, Henry Jackson: 'The God of the Cantabs, like the God of the Hebrews, is a jealous God.'[46] Happily Oxford would eventually offer Mahaffy some comforting honours. But there was irony in the contrast between his reputation in the two universities, for, as Mahaffy and Jebb well knew, Trinity College, Dublin, had been cherished chiefly by Cambridge men in its earlier years.

Mahaffy's mock-heroic battle with Jebb in 1876 was by no means his only literary effort in that year. He was also engaged in writing two of his best-known popular books. The first, and more original, was *Rambles and Studies in Greece*, the product of his first visit to Greece in 1875. In his own words it:

> was not only an immediate success, but . . . has survived
> for 45 years and is now to be had in a sixth edition printed
> in America. [A seventh appeared later.] The reason why
> this book has survived a score of others written then and
> since on Greece is that it is essentially a *sentimental* journey,
> like a few others that have likewise survived their
> generation. The greatest of them are Kinglake's *Eothen* and
> Curzon's *Monasteries of the Levant*. The chapter on Arcadia
> in my book, besides its new information, is the most
> carefully written chapter in all my books.

The title, *Rambles and Studies*, describes it well. On the one hand there is a sense of relaxed enjoyment as of a gentleman on the Grand Tour, a *dilettante* in the better sense of that word so suspect among austere scholars. On the other hand while it has the zest of an amateur, one is clearly in the company of an erudite, alert, professional classical scholar who takes nothing on trust. His critical attitude is apparent from the outset. 'I am no enthusiast about the modern, any more than about the ancient Greeks, as I have elsewhere plainly shown', he announces in his preface, and goes on to prescribe the cure for Greece's political troubles *vis-à-vis* 'the turbulent and mischievous Servians'. He does not spare the faults of Greek politicians, or the incompetence and squalor of Greek domestic life. He finds the famous honey of Hymettus inferior stuff, and described Marathon as the place 'where a few thousand ill-disciplined men repulsed a larger number of still worse disciplined Orientals, without any recondite tactics – perhaps even without any very extraordinary heroism'. He defends his strictures with a side-blow at a famous philhellene:

surely any real lover of Greece must feel that plain
speaking about the faults of the nation is much wanted.
The worship lavished on them by Byron and his school had
done its good, and can now only do harm.

Then his sense of fair play, together with his reverence for
genius, compels him to add: 'But here, as elsewhere, the folly
of a great genius has more truth in it than the wisdom of his
feebler critics.'

As he says in his *Summary*, it was essentially a sentimental
journey. Among other personal traits, his love of landscape, and
especially – since his early days in Switzerland – his love of
mountains, add vividness to his narrative. At times he becomes
lyrical, as in his widely admired description of the site of Plato's
Academy:

> I have wandered whole days in these delightful woods,
> listening to the nightingales, which sing all the day in the
> deep shade and solitude, as it were in a prolonged twilight
> and hearing the plane tree whispering to the elm, as
> Aristophanes has it, and seeing the white-poplar show its
> silvery leaves in the breeze, and wondering whether the
> huge old olive stems, so like the old pollarded stumps in
> Windsor Forest, could be the actual sacred trees, the
> μορίαι under which the youth of Athens ran their races. The
> banks of the Kephissus, too, are lined with great reeds, and
> sedgy marsh plants, which stoop over into its sandy
> shallows and wave idly in the current of its stream. The
> ouzel and the kingfisher start from under one's feet, and
> bright fish move out lazily from their sunny bay into the
> deeper pool. Now and then through a vista, the Acropolis
> shows itself in a framework of green foliage, nor do I know
> any more enchanting view of that great ruin.

In parenthesis one may note that Mahaffy, with typical pre-
science, foresaw that these rural delights would not last for much
longer. This elegiac passage was written eight years later:

> When roads and rails have been brought into Greece,
> hundreds of people will go to see its beauty and its
> monuments, and will congratulate themselves that the
> country is at last accessible. But the real charm will be

gone. There will be no riding at dawn through orchards of
oranges and lemons, with the rich fruit lying on the ground,
and the nightingales, that will not end their long hours of
song, still out-singing from the deep-green gloom the
sounds of opening day. There will be no more watching the
glowing east across the silver-grey glitter of dewy
meadows; no more wandering among grassy slopes, where
the scarlet anemones, all drenched with the draughts of
night, are striving to raise their drooping heads and open
their splendid eyes to meet the sun. There will be no more
watching the serpent and the tortoise, the eagle and the
vulture, and all the living things, whose ways and habits
animate the sunny solitudes of the south.[47]

Reviews of *Rambles and Studies* were mostly enthusiastic,
though one American reviewer complained of its supercilious
tone and deplored such irrelevant and partisan remarks as that
on the advantages of a dictatorship for the Greeks and Irish
alike. A friend of Jebb, the influential Sidney Colvin, writing in
The Academy for 27 January 1877, conceded that the book was
lively, fresh and vivid; but, he claimed, it contained facts and
judgements that were 'sweeping', 'unguarded', 'not sound',
'inexact', 'inept'. Indeed, he found it 'hard to see what a book of
this kind would do'. This went too far. Undeniably the book had
some faults, but certainly not enough to damn it.

Mahaffy ignored Colvin's review until he was writing the
preface to the second edition where he replied to it obliquely.
But in a letter written to a friend five years later he expressed
his personal reactions:

Colvin is a cross between a prig and an ass. His main
cause of hatred of me, apart from his friend Jebb, is that
he tried to slaughter my *Rambles and Studies* in the *Academy*
in such a way that the Editor Appleton wrote to apologise
about it. But the second edition came out in spite of him
in six months. This was slap in the face from the public
No. 1. No. 2 when I next met him, and he took it for
granted I must cut him. I walked up to him blandly and
said 'my dear Colvin, how do you do? Of course you don't
imagine I am going to cut up rough, and make a fool of
myself like Jebb, because you treated me unjustly and

spitefully. I will pay you off some other way.' This was
altogether too much for him, and he looked so red and
awkward that I could not help laughing at him to his face.
Hence his rage. *Humanum est odisse quem laeseris*, says
Sallust. [Tacitus in fact, with a different wording.] It is also
human to hate the man whom you could not succeed in
injuring.[48]

The other book that Mahaffy produced in the year of his
controversy with Jebb, 1876, was scholastically slight, but it
became internationally popular, appearing in Spanish, French,
Hungarian and Russian translations. This was his *Old Greek
Life* (republished as *Greek Antiquities*), a shilling primer in a
very successful series issued by Macmillan under the general
editorship of Mahaffy's friend J. R. Green. Mahaffy wrote it in
three weeks, he says, at his country house in Howth, without
any books of reference.

Euripides, also published by Macmillan as a primer, in 1879,
was equally competent. Though intended for beginners, it was
by no means negligible for scholars, especially in a period when
Euripides was still generally regarded as inferior to Sophocles.
Mahaffy had mixed feelings about it: he wrote to a friend, 'if
you read my Euripides carefully, you will find all sorts of literary
points in it, which are new. But perhaps 'tis not worth the
trouble.'[49] Yet even in a comparatively slight undertaking of
this kind he was ready to spend time and trouble to provide
touches of distinction. He wrote to Robert Browning asking
him to translate a choric passage for it. In reply he got a cordial
letter and a not very memorable rendering, which he duly
printed (and economically used again in his *Survey of Greek
Civilization*, with a tribute to 'this great poet').[50] He produced
another primer of this kind two years later, *Old Greek Education*,
published by Kegan Paul in 1881. Meanwhile he was also dashing
off articles for *Macmillan's Magazine*, *The Athenaeum*, and *The
Academy*.

In 1880 he returned to his first intellectual love with a book
on Descartes, published by Blackwood. (His range of publishers
remained remarkably wide until the end of his life.) He paid less
attention to Descartes' philosophy than to the man himself and
his social background. At times, indeed, Mahaffy seems to have

allowed his own personal interests to predominate in his choice of topics, as when he discourses on the advantages of not going to school too early, on the nature of a gentleman, on the language that a courtier should use, on the importance of logic and clarity in style, and on the 'mysterious law' of genius. In connection with the last theme he wrote a paragraph that might be taken as autobiographical:

> These details are of interest as affording one more instance of that mysterious law in the production of genius which selects from a series of ordinary children, born of average parents, and makes us wonder what subtle combination, what momentary variation in physical conditions, can produce so marvellous a result.

In the same year he produced one of his major works, his four-volume *History of Classical Greek Literature*. (Its first publishers were Longmans, but after Mahaffy had quarrelled with them, Macmillan took it over for the subsequent editions.) It was generally accepted as a valuable survey, independent-minded, fresh, and often original. But it was criticized for being too partisan at times. Thucydides was attacked, as before, for being 'curt', 'stingy', and for producing 'barren chronicles of petty raids and ineffectual campaigns'; Sophocles was considered inferior to Aeschylus in poetry, and to both Aeschylus and Euripides (with his 'great and earnest work') in philosophy; Pindar was far from being faultless. Personal loyalties made him exaggerate at times: the Irish Virgilian scholar, Dr James Henry, is described as having known 'more than all the rest of the world put together' about Virgil. His strictures on other scholars and critics, especially the Germans, provoked retaliation. A German reviewer[51] counter-attacked by saying that the book was no improvement on its main English predecessor (by Jevons), and worse still that Mahaffy was not so familiar with either the language or the scholastic literature of Germany as he claimed.

These recurrent skirmishes with German scholars are rather surprising in a man who had many reasons for admiring Germany and the Germans. Perhaps one can see part, at least, of the reason for them in Mahaffy's meeting with the eminent Dutch scholar Cobet during the tercentenary celebrations of the University of Leyden in 1875.[52] Cobet, as noticed in an earlier chapter, impressed the young Mahaffy strongly and perhaps inspired him to emulation. Fourteen years later he wrote: 'One could not see his burly figure stalking through the quiet streets of Leyden without feeling that he walked there as a man un-challenged, intellectually head and shoulders above the rest, and speaking his mind with simple but dogmatic force.' (Madvig, the other famous protagonist at the celebrations, does not seem to have impressed Mahaffy so much.) In conversation Cobet told Mahaffy that 'the real combination for a scholar was English good sense with French taste', and that the only way to win respect from the Germans was to 'lash them well' – 'a task very congenial', Mahaffy adds, 'to his pugnacious and somewhat dictatorial manner'. The meeting seems to have left its mark on Mahaffy in more ways than one.

His *History of Classical Greek Literature,* apart from its polemics, suffered from another weakness. Mahaffy, unlike Tyrrell, had very little feeling for nuances of literary style. He relied mainly on epithets like 'exquisite' and excerpts quoted in the original Greek, in default of more subtle analysis. The reason is apparent. He was much more interested in authors as people and as commentators on life, than as literary artists. Yet as a whole the work was undeniably a notable achievement, and it remained a standard work for many years.

In 1881 he published a purely technical article that became a minor landmark in Greek studies – 'On the Authenticity of the Olympian Register'. [53] Mahaffy was in his element in this exercise in historical scepticism, finding good grounds for rejecting what had long been revered as basic evidence for early Greek chrono-logy. In the last years of his life he looked back with pride on this special achievement. Speaking of 'the deep satisfaction' of finding his conjectures 'established by subsequent researches' he remarks:

When I maintained, for example, that the so called Olympic Register – which Grote, and all the Greek historians after him up to 1870, had adopted as the sober starting-point of Greek history – was not genuine, but the compilation of a sophist, my Oxford friends said to me: 'How rash of you to publish these conjectures when the excavations at Olympia are just beginning, and the Register

itself may be found on some ancient inscribed stone!
Where will you be then?' I shall be in the wrong, was all I
answered. Since then my views on this Register have become
a commonplace, even in the most learned and stupid
German Histories of Greece. But had I waited till the
negative evidence at Olympia confirmed me, the pleasure
of dealing with attempted refutations would have been
wholly lost. [54]

Another publication in 1881 (significantly not mentioned in
his *Summary*) gave him less reason for satisfaction. In that year
Mahaffy's most celebrated pupil in ancient history, J. B. Bury,
later to be Regius Professor of Greek in Trinity and subsequently
Regius Professor of Modern History in Cambridge, was an
undergraduate. (Negotiations for his entry had occasioned a
characteristic Mahaffyism: Bury's father, a country rector from
Monaghan, had been dilating on his son's extraordinary intelligence: Mahaffy, reaching the limit of his never-very-extensive
patience, broke in to remark, 'What an exceptionally intelligent
person Mrs. Bury must be!') By his third year in College Bury
was looking for fresh worlds to conquer. He decided, with
Mahaffy's approval, to produce an edition of Euripides'
Hippolytus. Bury did most of the donkeywork of sifting the
material and composing the notes. Mahaffy wrote the general
introduction, finding space in its eight pages to include some
side-blows at English scholars who 'in philology, at least . . . are
thorough Tories' as well as at 'pedantic and foolish readers'. He
thought it opportune, too, to reflect on the dilemma of an
editor:

> There is no chance of his pleasing everybody. If he is
> conservative, he is called by that school safe – by his
> opponents dull and unsuggestive. If he is sceptical, he is
> called brilliant by one side – rash and reckless by the other.
> If he pursues an eclectic course, possibly he will incur the
> censure of both. But, on the whole, the conservatives are
> the most numerous, and perhaps the most intolerant. For
> they are supported by the herd of second-hand scholars,
> who are afraid or unable to think for themselves, or suggest
> anything new, and who naturally cry out against a sort of
> criticism which they dislike, if they do not envy it.

Unhappily for Mahaffy – but gleefully for Tories and pedants – the commentary contained a disastrous grammatical 'howler'.[55] An irregular verb was wrongly construed. The slip was adroitly amended in the second edition. But his enemies never allowed him to forget it,[56] though few scholars who publish voluminously have escaped occasional lapses of that kind. However, Mahaffy with his usual skill in salvaging useful material from any ship-wreck turned at least one line from the *Hippolytus* to good use in his conversation. Whenever the talk turned to Irish law courts he was apt to remark[57] that the best phrase he knew to describe the average Irish witness – and it should be hung up as a warning in every Irish jury-room – was the line spoken by the hero in that play,

'My tongue has sworn, but my mind has taken no oath.'

Perhaps it was through chagrin at his ill-starred collaboration with Bury in the *Hippolytus* that Mahaffy edited no more texts until he took up the Petrie papyri. He left it to his younger colleagues and successors, Tyrrell, Starkie, Palmer, Purser and (for a while) Bury, to work in that useful but restrictive field. In fact the *Hippolytus* was his last book dealing with the classical period of Greek literature and history. Soon, after brief excursions into *The Decay of Modern Preaching* in 1882 and *The Art of Conversation* in 1887, he entered less highly competitive areas.

Meanwhile, before his first book on the post-classical eras appeared, he had been fighting in two other academic controversies. The first was a gentlemanly skirmish in 1879 with F. A. Paley, once a household name for his conscientious editions of Greek authors.[58] Paley took exception in his mild way to some remarks by Mahaffy on his theories about Homeric poems. Mahaffy responded genially to Paley's 'courtesy and good temper' and apologized for some 'strong expressions' that he had used, confessing with unusual self-depreciation: 'It is, I suppose, partly a national but partly, I fear, a personal fault, that made me transgress the limits of perfect calmness, which he so strictly observes in his reply.'

Reading this the modest Paley may well have blushed with pride at having won so handsome a confession from the formidable Irishman. If so, he must have blenched a little as he read on: 'Nevertheless, I am bound to argue that his statements are

confused in themselves and unfair ... slovenly way of thinking...
arrant nonsense.' When he came to Mahaffy's distinctly derisive
ending, he might have sighed at the briefness of some people's
contrition. However, he let the controversy lapse.

The other conflict was more a civil war than a clash of
nationalities. In 1884 Professor Tyrrell, who had become a
fellow in 1868, four years after Mahaffy, and was now a strong
challenger for Mahaffy's title as the leading classical scholar of
Ireland, reviewed a new edition of Herodotus by Mahaffy's
friend A. H. Sayce. (Sayce had already in 1884 been fighting a
running battle in *The Academy* against Jebb's remarks on his
book, complete with *his* accusations of plagiarism.)[59] Tyrrell's
review appeared in *Hermathena*, the Trinity learned journal
founded in 1873 (Mahaffy and Tyrrell being among the four
original members of the editorial committee). Tyrrell was clearly
gibing at Mahaffy behind Sayce when he described Sayce as
having 'won a leading position in certain studies, which are by
some looked on as branches of the study of classics.' He claimed
that in nearly every instance where Sayce had commented on
the meaning or construction of a sentence his remarks were
either 'such as the grammar or dictionary would have readily
supplied' or else 'erroneous or misleading'. He listed many
examples. When Mahaffy saw the article he wrote to George
Macmillan:

> Tyrrell has assaulted Sayce's *Herodotus* on the lines of
> Verrall the Cambridge classical scholar, indeed copying him
> and has played Hell not with Sayce but with himself. I am
> going to have the lights out of him. . . . He knows neither
> Herodotus nor his commentators nor his Liddell and Scott.
> Very funny.[60]

Mahaffy's reply appeared in the same volume of *Hermathena*.
He alleged that Tyrrell had plagiarized from Verrall for most of
his examples, and that Tyrrell's own Greek was not as good as
he claimed, for there were errors in his allegations of error. Sayce
followed with a less excited, but hardly more convincing,
attempt to refute Tyrrell's strictures. Tyrrell's rejoinder
betrayed some personal animus:

> Now I should be sorry to accuse Mr Mahaffy of deliberate

falsification of a piece of evidence to screen himself and his friend. But, rejecting this alternative, we are forced to infer that Mr. Mahaffy misunderstood the German note. Yet I have always been led to believe that Mr. Mahaffy is so imbued with German that he finds it highly inconvenient to write correct English.

He went even further with his personal gibes, some trivial, some deeply wounding. Trivially – but not unjustly – he condemned Mahaffy's use of exclamation marks – like Queen Victoria's – to express emotional implications. Woundingly he affirmed: 'I may also point out that to Mr Mahaffy cannot be extended the privileges of inaccuracy which are claimed for Assyriology and Egyptology, for he is not an Assyriologist or an Egyptologist or even a Crocodilologist.' (The last Aristophanic epithet was presumably derived from a reference to the Egyptian town of Crocodilopolis in one of Mahaffy's books. It unexpectedly recoiled on Tyrrell, as will be noticed later.)

Sayce published a 'sur-rejoiner'. It failed to rebut Tyrrell's main linguistic criticisms, but it proved his loyalty to his friend by asserting that Mahaffy's eminence as a Greek scholar would 'relieve him from the necessity of noticing the uncourteous and inconclusive *"tu quoque"* of his Dublin colleague'. Mahaffy, who was then in Greece, took the implicit advice and did not reply – nor did he contribute again to *Hermathena* for five years. Tyrrell refrained from commenting on the matter further, but made a point of praising Jebb in the next issue. Relations between Tyrrell and Mahaffy remained uncongenial. (But when Tyrrell died in 1914 Mahaffy drafted a magnanimous epitaph: . . . *qui ut non alius in litteris humanioribus arbiter elegantiarum, fato functus inexorabili, socios, aequales, amicos, ingenium eius desiderantes vera paupertate afflixit.*)

Here once again, as in the Jebb controversy, the conflict was essentially between Mahaffy and a 'pure' scholar. As a grammarian, linguist and stylist, Tyrrell had the advantage. He knew the Greek language better: Mahaffy, essentially a social historian, knew the Greek people better. On the whole professional scholars in Britain preferred Tyrrell's work. As a result Tyrrell for a good while kept ahead of Mahaffy in the *cursus honorum*. He received honorary degrees from Cambridge, Edinburgh,

Belfast, Oxford, St Andrew's and Durham, and became a fellow of the British Academy. Mahaffy, presumably through Sayce's good offices, was made an honorary fellow of Queen's College, Oxford, in 1882 (and wrote to a friend, 'I go there and swagger as if I were at home in T.C.D.').[61] Later he became a D.C.L. of Oxford (1892), and LL.D. of St Andrews (side by side with Tyrrell) in 1906. Eventually Mahaffy's work on Hellenistic and papyrological material brought him wider honours – too late, he felt at times, for he told the same friend in 1895 when he became a corresponding member of the Vienna Academy, 'I believe it is a swell thing, but such do not affect me. . . . Even at my age I begin to despise them, whereas had they been conferred on me years ago they would have been both a pleasure and a profit.'[62]

chapter nine

A triumphant scholar

Shortly after his controversy with Tyrrell in 1884, Mahaffy entered a new phase in his published work, breaking away from the over-populated areas of pure classicism into less congested territories. In 1887 he produced his *Greek Life and Thought from the Death of Alexander to the Roman Conquest* and *Alexander's Empire* (in collaboration with A. Gilman). These were followed by *The Greek World under Roman Sway* in 1890 and *The Empire of the Ptolemies* in 1895, besides many articles on these post-classical periods. (He intended, in fact, to produce a continuous survey from Alexander's death to the Christianization of Greece with a volume on the epoch from Hadrian to Julian, but never completed it.)[1] His *History of Egypt under the Ptolemaic Dynasty* (1899) and his *Silver Age of the Greek World* (1906) were amplifications and revisions of these.

In exploring these post-classical eras as a social historian Mahaffy was a pioneer. A few others had already studied their political aspects, notably the German scholar Droysen who had published a history of Hellenism in 1877–8. But Mahaffy's social approach was a new departure. As he put it: 'I had no predecessor on this subject and was obliged to gather materials from many scattered sources.'[2] Also, it took courage for a classical scholar to enter this period at all, for the Hellenistic age had previously been despised by conservative scholars. Orthodoxy held that the glory had departed from Greek literature after the fourth century, except for some afterglow in a few authors like Theocritus and Plutarch. Prudent advisers, if Mahaffy had uncharacteristically consulted them, would probably have warned him that he would be wasting his time on that degenerate age and that – even more deplorably – he would probably corrupt the style of his classical Greek by reading the debased Greek of Hellenistic texts. But he dared to swim against the tide, and the wide popularity of his books soon refuted those who claimed that no writer could make post-classical Greece interesting.

Socially and scholastically Mahaffy was unusually well equipped for study of the Hellenistic kings and their kingdoms. As a child he had met royalty in Germany, and he was now meeting princes and viceroys again. As a teacher he had long been specially interested in Egypt and the Near East, and his earliest journey to the Eastern Mediterranean had been spent mostly in Egypt. Temperamentally he was particularly sympathetic towards an era when democracy had given way to monarchy, and when the rough-and-tumble of the agora had yielded to the protocol of royal courts and palaces, 'where', as he phrased it, 'stately ceremonial put a tight bridle on the rudeness of free speech, and taught men the importance of studied politeness'.[3] Its dynastic quarrels and agrarian troubles, its cosmopolitanism and stoicism, its opulence and magnificence in contrast with classical frugality and austerity,[4] all appealed to him as a nineteenth-century imperialist. He was stimulated, too, by his conviction that he was now a real pioneer. It gave him 'the intense interest of penetrating a country either unexplored or imperfectly described by former travellers'.

Though now superseded by the work of later scholars, these books still make vivid and profitable reading for students of the later Greek world.[5] One of Mahaffy's ablest successors, Edwyn Bevan, when revising Mahaffy's *History of Egypt under the Ptolemaic Dynasty*, commended Mahaffy's style and choice of material, and concluded: 'No one who works in this field can help feeling how much all scholars must owe today to the stimulus which a generation ago was given to the study of Hellenistic age by Mahaffy's vivid intelligence and large discursive erudition.'[6] Mahaffy's remarkable power of making plain sense from complicated social, moral and intellectual developments, of bringing latent problems into focus, of seeing the significance of the seemingly insignificant, and his ability to sift and evaluate scattered and disparate evidence both literary and documentary, were never better exercised than in these works of his maturity. His style, too, was at its best – buoyant, vigorous, fresh and lucid.

But there were always critics who disliked it, either on academic or on aesthetic grounds. Theodore Reinach[7] said that it sometimes gave the impression of *une causerie à batons rompus.* Others called it 'jaunty'.[8] George Moore[9] described it as 'the spring cart style', meaning that 'we jump in and away we go bowling along the broad road of cosmopolitan provincialism'. More mildly, others agreed that, though lively, lucid, and urbane, it was deficient in formal elegance, and not lapidary enough to conserve his ideas in their original words – hence his most original suggestions tended to be quickly absorbed into the common stock of accepted lore without any trace of their authorship. It lacked epigrammatic concinnity and he rarely used any touches of poetic colour, apart from a few lyrical passages in his book on Greece, as already illustrated. Perhaps his iron rule of writing five pages a day, whatever his mood, helped to make his style utilitarian rather than fine.

He admired Ruskin as 'a master of the long period' and as 'a greater stylist than all the Froudes and Newmans and Paters, who either use short sentences, or if they attempt the period, are neither melodious nor clear'. This suggests that in fact Mahaffy, though expert in logical directness, rapidity and clarity, had a poor ear for the subtleties of word-music and cadence that help to make prose memorable for its form as well as for its ideas. He occasionally tried his hand at poetry, but unfortunately no copy of his volume of verses entitled *Folia caduca,* written for his grand-children, has been traced by the present writers. However, a translation by him of Sappho's *Ode to Aphrodite* may be taken as characteristic:

> Venus, bright goddess of the skies,
> To whom unnumber'd temples rise,
> Jove's daughter fair, whose wily arts
> Delude fond lovers of their hearts;
> O! listen gracious to my prayer
> And free my mind from anxious care.[10]

This pastiche of Pope and *Hymns Ancient and Modern* – far removed from the fresh, heart-piercing style of Sappho – was

NM

published in 1895, the era of Tennyson, Browning, Morris and Swinburne. Two earlier contributions to *Kottabos* (1874), his *Epitaph on the books of a certain closed library*, and a translation of Goethe's lines on Gellert's monument (into Catullan hendec-asyllables) are equally derivative.

Mahaffy himself had no illusions about his merits as a stylist. In a footnote to his translation of Sappho's ode he admits that 'these verses lose all the transcendent beauty of expression in the original'. Finally in his *Summary* he commented:

> I will add here, once and for all, a word about what a good critic in those days [the eighteen-seventies] called 'the ungraceful graces of his style'. All through my College course, I had never been able to obtain any prize for English Essay or Composition, because the habit of having spoken French and German as infant tongues clung to me, and no doubt showed themselves plainly in various idioms to an examiner. But when I began to lecture as a Professor, and not merely as a Tutor teaching by question and answer, I adopted in writing my lectures the tone of easy conversation, so that those who read me in those days often said they heard me speaking from the page. I have never since (with rare exceptions) attempted anything else in my writings. There is not what men would call an eloquent page in any 500 pages of them. They are the simple and direct talk of a man who is telling what he knows. And the first object of all such writing, which is really teaching, is to be clear. My proudest boast would be that in all my writings there is not an obscure page. All my life I have protested against authors, such as my old friend Walter Pater, or as George Meredith, who seemed to cultivate obscurity, as if vagueness or difficulty of comprehension added a charm to their writings.

All in all, the testimony of Mahaffy's publications substan-tiates this assessment. He did achieve remarkable clarity and directness, like one of his examplars, Descartes, whom he specially praised for writing *clare et distincte*. But when he denies that there are many eloquent pages in his books, by some definitions of that word the denial hardly stands. In fact the characteristic feature that exasperated so many of his critics was his exaggerated rhetoric in advocating his personal views and his fondness for sweeping phrases like 'nothing can be more absurd than', 'any honest reader will see' and his reckless use of absolute words like 'all', 'always', 'the greatest', 'nobody', 'never'. His critics called it arrogant or over-confident, but in fact it was generally the result of zest and enthusiasm for the matter in hand.

Apart from matters of style, 'pedantic' reviewers of Mahaffy's books, even now in the eighteen-nineties when he was at the height of his powers, complained that he still suffered from *les défauts de ses qualités*, as Theodore Reinach called them. Inaccuracies still occurred: indeed one reviewer referred bluntly to 'all this wretched blundering'. His bold analogies still proliferated: several critics thought it misleading, for example, to present Greek rule in Egypt as similar to British rule in Ireland, or to call Aristotle 'a Liberal Conservative' and Polybius 'a busy politician for the Home Rule party of his day'. Whatever might be said in defence of analogies of that kind – and at least they served to give interest to a period that many scholars thought utterly arid – even Mahaffy's strongest supporters disliked his propagandist tone. How, for instance, could he justify devoting the last four pages of *Greek life and thought* to a homily on the virtues of imperialism and the faults of nationalism, with advice to the Poles and the Piedmontese to accept with gladness their absorption into Germany and Italy, and with strictures on Britain for encouraging nationalism on the continent? 'This book must make Grote turn in his grave,' a friendly reader exclaimed.[11]

But Mahaffy refused to abandon his determination to call in the modern world to illuminate the old, and persisted in asserting bold judgements and theories at the risk of being wrong. In another publication of that *annus mirabilis* of his (1892), *Problems in Greek History*, he defended his position as resolutely as ever:

> Above all, let us seek the truth with open minds, and speak out our convictions; and if we are wrong, instead of blaming us for appealing to the deeper interests and stirring the warmer emotions of man, let our errors be refuted. Let us save ancient history from its dreary fate in the hands of the

dry antiquarian, the narrow scholar; and while we utilize all his research and all his learning, let us make the acts and lives of older men speak across the chasm of centuries, and claim kindred with the men and the motives of today. For this, and this only, is to write history in the full and real sense, – this is to show that the great chain of centuries is forged of homogeneous metal, and joined with links that all bear the great Workman's unmistakeable design.[12]

The exhortation clearly illustrates what particularly exasperated some of his critics. On the one hand there is the preaching earnestness of 'let us seek the truth', and 'to show . . . the great Workman's unmistakeable design'. On the other there is the refusal to admit that any other academic *credo* could fully deserve respect – 'this, and this only, is to write history in the full and real sense'. His former pupil, Bury, for example, who had argued so strongly in his inaugural lecture at Cambridge that history should be a scientific study, would have emphatically contradicted it.

More provocatively still, Mahaffy, piqued by charges of inaccuracy, quite gratuitously attacked the reputation of other scholars of limited but precise scholarship. For example in eulogizing Grote, he asserted 'of course he occasionally missed the exact force of an optative, or the logic of a particle; he excited the fury of men like Shilleto to whom accuracy in Greek prose was the one perfection containing all the law and the prophets'.[13] This was unfair both to Shilleto (a Cambridge man) and unhelpful to Grote's reputation. But everyone knew who he was really defending, and readers familiar with Mahaffy's style would note the biblical reference as a mark of deeply felt emotion.

Antagonized by such assaults on precise scholarship, many classical scholars before 1891 might still have wondered whether Mahaffy was much more than a gifted popularizer, a versatile but self-opinionated man of letters. Unquestionably he had produced original and perhaps fruitful ideas on Greek social life and literature. But was he capable of sustained 'pure' scholarship? The popularity of his books proved nothing so far as strictly academic merit was concerned. Even friendlier critics withheld their complete approval. 'No living writer has done so much to justify Hellenic Studies in the popular eye as Professor Mahaffy', a notice in *The Classical Review* began,[14] but it went on to find his *Problems in Greek History* disappointing as a work of scholarship. And when his classical colleagues watched him spend his energies on books about the decay of preaching, the art of conversation, and a tour in the Netherlands; when they saw him writing copious and highly repetitive introductions to works by others and composing a 'drawing-room' illustrated volume on Greece (characteristically ending in a diatribe against the monks of the Orthodox Church), they may reasonably have wondered whether he could be a serious, dedicated scholar.

Fortunately, in 1890 Mahaffy had an opportunity to produce work that no fair-minded critic could refuse to accept as 'pure' scholarship of a high order.

In 1889 the British archaeologist Flinders Petrie discovered at Gurob in the Fayyûm district of Egypt a number of mummies dating from the Ptolemaic period, which were encased in layers of ancient papyrus documents. Petrie gave these papyri to A. W. Sayce of Queen's College, Oxford. Sayce invited Mahaffy to examine them with him. This was not simply an act of friendship. As Sayce knew, Mahaffy had long been interested in Egyptology and the Egyptian papyri. A letter of December 1870[15] from an official of the British Museum in reply to an inquiry by Mahaffy about papyri shows that Mahaffy's mind had been turned in that direction twenty years earlier; and in the following year he had used illustrations from the Turin satyric papyrus in his *Prolegomena*, a typical touch of originality and vision. Besides, Mahaffy's most recent book had been a study of the Ptolemaic kingdom. So he readily accepted Sayce's invitation and went to stay with him at Oxford in August 1890.

Sayce has described their excitement as they worked together on this treasure trove, as valuable in its way as the gold that Schliemann had unearthed at Troy and Mycenae:

The days passed quickly in which, as Mahaffy said, we lived over again the days of the Renaissance. Now, as then, lost fragments of classical literature were constantly coming to light along with copies of existing works centuries older than any manuscripts of them previously known. Day after day we pored over the precious texts in my College rooms until the dinner hour arrived, when we discussed our discoveries and hopes with other scholars over the dessert and wine of the Common Room. It was an ideal time but like all ideal times it came too soon to an end.[16]

Mahaffy was equally exhilarated. He wrote in the preface to the first volume of his *Flinders Petrie Papyri*:

Seldom has it fallen to the lot of modern scholars to spend such days as we spent together at Oxford in the Long Vacation of 1890: poring all day, while the sun shone [there speaks the open-air man, conscious of the sporting pleasures he was sacrificing], over these faint and fragmentary records, discussing in the evening the stray lights we had found and their possible significance.

In his autobiographical *Summary* he recalled this as 'a perfectly new and fascinating field of research whereon I used up much of my eyesight and long months of study'.

For the world at large the great question was whether there would be any fragments of the lost works of major Greek authors – a verse from Sappho, say, or part of a play by Sophocles – or would all be official documents and business records of narrower interest? First, a fragment of Plato's *Phaedo* was identified, valuable for its evidence on the early text of that dialogue, but not new literature. Then came a most spectacular discovery. As Sayce described it:

One of the first fragments which we attacked contained some three hundred lines of a tragedy, the style of which forcibly reminded us of Euripides. It was somewhat difficult to decipher, but at last the work was accomplished and Mahaffy and I began to puzzle over the nature of the plot. Suddenly he said to me: 'I have an inspiration: let us go to the library!' and to the library we went. In a few minutes he showed me a quotation from the lost Euripidean tragedy of *Antiope* which agreed exactly with one of the lines we had been copying. The fragment was identified, and a long-lost relic of the great Athenian poet was once more in our possession.[17]

Nothing else quite so spectacular emerged. But this new fragment from one of the great Attic tragedians (happily, too, Mahaffy's own favourite) was enough to excite the interest of the whole literary world. Mahaffy quickly published a transcription and commentary in *Hermathena*.[18] He could now smile at Tyrrell's gibe that he was not even a Crocodilologist, for these papyri from which he was soon to win so much honour and renown came, in fact, from near Crocodilopolis.

With amazing energy – especially when one recalls that 1892 was the year of the T.C.D. tercentenary ceremonies in which he was so active – Mahaffy published the first volume of his *Flinders Petrie Papyri* in 1891 and the second in 1893. (Most of the work for the third volume was done by his successor as a papyrologist, J. G. Smyly, a punctilious scholar who became Regius Professor of Greek in Trinity in 1915.) He also poured out articles and reports describing the latest discoveries and found time as well to publish his *Problems in Greek history*. The laborious work of decipherment and transcription of the tattered bits and pieces of papyrus must have sorely strained the patience of one so averse to academic drudgery. At times he must have felt like one of 'those musty grammarians who spent their lives among the bleak sandhills and dusty bookshelves of Alexandria'.[19] But he was sustained by a sense of absolute priority – no need here for embellishing an often told tale – and perhaps also he felt what W. B. Yeats was to call 'the fascination of what's difficult'. He has described his feelings:

> There are two moments in the deciphering of strange documents at which the explorer feels the high excitement of successful discovery, and on which he can look back with peculiar satisfaction. The first is when the general sense of a blurred and mutilated MS. suddenly flashes out upon him, as it were a guide to tell him the direction of his search . . . [and] when a happy moment of inspiration or the discussion of a problem with some kindred spirit, suddenly suggests the solution. This is the second moment of deep satisfaction, which indemnifies a scholar for long hours of apparently unsuccessful toil.[20]

These are the emotions of 'pure' scholarship, and they are likely to have appealed to many a scholar who had disliked the tone of Mahaffy's earlier prefaces. They showed that Mahaffy was not primarily a parson-politician or a facile popularizer masquerading as a classical historian, but, at his best, a scholar capable of dedicating himself to learning for learning's sake, a true initiate into the esoteric joys of pure research – *orgia quae frustra cupiunt audire profani.*

At the same time Mahaffy did not neglect his wider audience. He kept the general public well informed from month to month in a series of articles in the intellectual journals,[21] making society aware of the literary and historical value of the new discoveries. As he saw it, these rediscovered records of Greek civilization would give to classical literary and historical studies a fresh impetus, similar to what Schliemann's discoveries had given to archaeology. The old taunt of the moderns, that the material for classical literary criticism and history was worked out, could now be substantially refuted.

Mahaffy continued to produce notable contributions to papyrology until 1896, when he published his introduction to Grenfell's *Revenue Laws of Ptolemy Philadelphus.* Then, it seems, he began to feel satiated. Characteristically he annoyed fellow-workers by remarking about some official documents 'we almost think we have seen more than enough of them'.[22] But that came much later on. Now, in the mid 1890s, when the learned world had studied his two handsomely produced volumes, and when the world of polite letters had digested and discussed his lively articles, both acclaimed a capital achievement.[23] Though experts could point to serious errors in transcription[24] and interpretation as well as to editorial inadequacies – Gildersleeve, still sensitive to attacks on 'pedants', mocked him again[25] – yet the total effect of his work was undeniably impressive. His power of 'divination' (to use Bentley's term for that flash of inspiration which divines the true significance of a puzzling piece of evidence), his wide background knowledge, his ability to cope with fragments varying from high poetry to official archives, his zest and enthusiasm and his gift of conveying it to his readers, together with sheer industry – these were established beyond dispute. There had been good papyrologists before him – better, indeed, in technique and care – but none of those who had worked on literary papyri previously had been capable of doing what Mahaffy did in bringing out the full social and cultural significance of such material. One of his most eminent successors in papyrological work, A. S. Hunt of Queen's College, Oxford, called it in his obituary of Mahaffy a 'highly meritorious performance',[26] all the more remarkable because of Mahaffy's complete lack of previous experience in such work and his temperamental disability for the slow, laborious toil necessary for this kind of publication.

Mahaffy himself recognized that he owed his European reputation as a scholar mainly to his work on the Flinders Petrie Papyri. Academic honours soon came to him in plenty. He was elected an honorary member of the Academies of Vienna, Berlin, Munich, Utrecht, and Athens, the Lincei of Rome, and the Archaeological Society of Alexandria. The universities of Athens, Louvain, Oxford, and St Andrews gave him honorary degrees. The King of Greece raised him two grades in the Order of the Redeemer. America, dominated by Gildersleeve, offered him no academic laurels, but he received and accepted invitations to lecture at Boston, Chicago and Toronto, as well as to the Chautauquan reading circle. The Royal Irish Academy elected him president in 1911. By that time none of his academic rivals at home or abroad could claim to have completed a more illustrious *cursus honorum*, even though Cambridge and the British Academy continued to ignore him. He could now in fact claim to be what he had called a 'worldman'.

His last notable book on Greek history was his *Empire of the Ptolemies* in 1895, a worthy successor to his two earlier books on post-classical Hellenism, in which he made skilful use of the new papyrological material. Several other publications followed, but they were mostly amplifications of earlier theories and beliefs. They still make good reading, and provide some choice specimens of his polemics. He had not lost his power to produce striking ideas and judgements, comparing, for example, Orestes with Hamlet (an equation much exploited by later scholars); denouncing Brutus as a hypocritical scoundrel, and startling a pious American audience by a remark on Plato's eugenics that must have sounded quite outrageous in 1896:

> The human race will never improve as it ought till the
> physical conditions of the production of children are made
> a matter of scientific enquiry, till diseased or morally

worthless persons, if shown to be unsuitable parents, are
forbidden to undertake this all-important function: till the
march of public opinion makes it less repugnant to have the
conditions of parentage analyzed, and the secrets of
domestic life scrutinized, than to allow the breeding of the
most important of all animals to be carried on at mere
random. . . . Genius now appears sporadically, and
apparently from ordinary parents. If we once knew the law
of its production, even approximately, what strides in
advance the human race might make![27]

During the last twenty years or so of his life he was less
actively interested in classical themes than in the history and
politics of Ireland and Trinity, as his later publications show.
In these, too, he sometimes exhibited his impish humour. For
example he celebrated his seventy-ninth birthday in 1917 by
reading a paper to a crowded meeting of the Royal Irish
Academy, 'On the introduction of the ass as a beast of burden in
Ireland' – still widely remembered among less erudite Hibernians
as 'Mahaffy on the Ass in Ireland'. Indeed, by a caprice of fame
it alone of all his publications was remembered by a citizen of
his boyhood home-town Newbliss, when inquiries were being
made there in 1966.

Among his fellow scholars in Ireland Mahaffy's disinclination
to associate himself with a local classical enterprise brought him
some unpopularity. In 1908 a group of Irish teachers of the
classics decided to found an Irish Classical Association, independent of the recently founded Classical Association in England.[28]
Several of the younger dons of Trinity, notably Purser, Beare,
Alton and Goligher (who all became presidents later) joined with
colleagues in University College, Dublin, in promoting the new
foundation, but not Mahaffy or Tyrrell, though Tyrrell eventually agreed to become a vice-president. Eight years later Mahaffy
relaxed his opposition so far as to speak at the presidential
meeting in 1916, and he accepted an invitation to speak again
in 1918.[29] But his refusal to encourage or help the association in
its early years was resented. At least it was consistent with his
principle of preferring large political and cultural units to small,
the Hellenistic monarchies to the classical city states, the British
Empire to an independent Ireland.

At the beginning of his autobiographical *Summary*, which was completed a bare two months before his death, Mahaffy spoke of a 'life successfully accomplished'. Had he been challenged on this by a devil's advocate armed with sheaves of censorious reviews, he could have called many commanding witnesses in his defence – among them, the famous Heinrich Schliemann, Ulrich von Wilamowitz-Moellendorff, the greatest Greek scholar of the succeeding era, and Theodore Reinach, for a while supreme among the savants of Paris.[30] He could also have recited the long litany of his academic honours and distinctions. Soon his obituaries would acclaim his renown, some awarding him the guerdon of 'greatness'.

Even Gildersleeve – Mahaffy's most influential critic now that Jebb was dead – relented a little. Beginning by remarking that the world of letters had lost 'one of its most attractive personalities', he went on to describe his visit, related in an earlier chapter, to Mahaffy in Dublin in 1880. He ended:

> His wonderful versatility was paired with an equally wonderful capacity for lapses . . . Mahaffy lectured several times in America. His fame for errancy had preceded him. He was not invited to any of the great American universities, and his brilliant discourses were delivered to Chautauqua audiences. When I think of some of his misstatements and misinterpretations, I almost regret having called attention to them. . . . If Verrall's whimsies were forgiven by his students because 'he made all classics so gloriously alive', much may be forgiven Mahaffy by reason of his boyish frankness and undeniable charm. When I was in Greece in 1896, my guide, who had been Mahaffy's guide, spoke of him with admiration, emphasizing his readiness in the use of Modern Greek. His 'Rambles and Studies in Greece' is a delightful book, and when I talked to my classes on Sophocles' Oedipus at Colonus, I have never failed to quote his description of a spot sacred to the ill-fated hero and the fortunate poet.[31]

Others paid tribute to his talents as a lecturer, though here, too, he could be rather cavalier at times: later in life if he had a new set of proofs in hand for a book even remotely connected with a college course he would read them aloud to his classes, pausing when necessary to correct a misprint. He was at his best when acting as a guide or lecturer in Greece, where the sense of actuality moved him deeply. 'I have just delivered an oration in the Parthenon, on the Acropolis of Athens to the assembled Literati of Europe. What a momentous scene and how exciting,' he wrote when he was seventy-three.[32] At international conferences his mastery of continental languages combined with his superb self-confidence gave him moments of exhilarating triumph. A friend has described a scene at Athens:

> At one of the many meetings a German professor, using his native tongue, read a long paper on Pheidonian weights and measures. An important point of his argument was the untrustworthy character of the Olympic chronology. The lecturer was under the impression that he was here breaking fresh ground. When several speakers had felicitated the lecturer on his address, Dr. Mahaffy arose. He commended in generous terms the lecturer's hypotheses regarding the source of the Pheidonic standard. Then, with humorous pathos, he deplored the oblivion that is the fate of pioneers: he summarised his own researches into the source of the Olympic system of dating: he pointed out that more than twenty years previously he himself had advanced the views that now appeared so novel: he supplemented the lecturer's arguments by quotations from authorities that the lecturer had overlooked. The exposition of the chronological difficulties and the proposed solution was masterly: not less masterly was the speaker's command of idiomatic German. A famous German professor clutched my arm and whispered: '*Der Mahaffy ist ja ein grosser Mensch!*' In the roar of applause that followed the end of Dr. Mahaffy's speech, national differences were forgotten, and scholars paid homage to scholarship.[33]

One further aspect of Mahaffy's achievement as a Hellenist remains to be mentioned, though it cannot now be fully illustrated or re-created by anyone who does not remember the man at the height of his powers and has not directly felt that indefinable personal quality which made his greatness. Yet it is clear from the attempts that various contemporaries have made to describe the impact of his personality that the man himself was as much a part of his Hellenism as were his written and spoken words. Mahaffy was not satisfied simply to write and talk about the richness, variety and harmony of the Greek tradition: he was determined to embody it, 'always sculpturing his own statue' as the Greek philosopher had prescribed. His Attic wit, his Olympic skill in games and field sports, his Socratic influence on brilliant youths, his musicianship, his love of controversy – these combined to make him seem, to many young men of his time, a supreme embodiment of the Greek temperament, 'the last of the Olympians' as they called him. His well remembered remark when one day during a shooting expedition his hat was shot off his head by a careless companion – 'Two inches lower and you would have blown away half the Greek in Ireland'[34] – seemed fully justified to those under the spell of his personal Hellenism. And when someone reported in Dublin how at a banquet of classical scholars in Athens, when crowns of flowers were distributed for the guests to wear, Mahaffy alone had worn his with a graceful nonchalance, it was taken merely as further proof of his perfect *rapport* with the classical world.[35]

Finally, what emerges most vividly from a study of Mahaffy as a Hellenist and humanist, seen in the perspective of his long and tumultuous life, is not only an admiration for his zest, versatility, courage and energy, but also a sense of his deeper kinship with the spirit of classical Greece. He well knew that what the Greeks chiefly admired in a gifted man was not the brilliance of his several talents, but the balance and harmony of his personality as a whole, and, as their word 'harmony' implies, they habitually thought of this temperamental equipoise in terms of music, Mahaffy's favourite art. Perhaps, then, the best way of summing up what Mahaffy both embodied and taught will be to paraphrase a passage in the work that provided one of the more notable fragments in his Petrie papyri, the *Laches* of Plato:

Such a man is truly educated in music, the arts and literature, for he has attuned himself to the fairest harmony . . . and has achieved in his own life a true concord of words and deeds – not in the sophisticated Ionian mode, nor in the fanatical Phrygian, nor in the voluptuous Lydian, but in the well-proportioned, manly, Dorian mode, which is the only authentically Hellenic harmony.[36]

chapter ten

The final prize:
frustration and failure

In the first few years after his election to a fellowship in 1864 Mahaffy had no reason for complaining about lack of promotion. The board of the College, recognizing his unusual talents, created a new lectureship and then a professorship in ancient history for him. But the real plums of preferment, in terms of both academic power and of salary, were the seven senior fellowships and the provostship. A junior fellow holding a tutorship soon had, it is true, a competent salary and security of tenure for life (unless he incurred some heinous *culpa*); but he was not rich and he had no say whatever in the main government of the College. The attitude of the board – that is, the provost and the senior fellows – towards any junior who ventured to question their policy is well exemplified in a letter from the Registrar (John Kells Ingram) to the junior fellows in 1894:

> It would be impossible for the Board to get through their business if, after they had come to a decision with due deliberation, it was necessary for them to spend further time in discussing with irresponsible persons whether or not their decision had been the best and wisest. When, in due course, the responsibility of the care of the College devolves upon those who are now Junior Fellows . . .[1]

'In due course' might mean over forty years.

In speculating on his prospects of promotion Mahaffy did not rely on mere guesswork. As one of his notebooks shows, even as a third-year undergraduate in January 1858 he had consulted two sets of actuarial tables on the probability of vacancies for junior fellows in the coming years. He tabulated the ages of the provost and fellows with a set of figures entitled 'Rates of mortality according to the Carlisle and Equitable tables, containing the chance of death within a year at each age from 30 upwards.' Each risk was calculated to five places of decimals by both systems. The chance of the provost's death was ·05885 by one system and ·05645 by the other. The chance of a vacancy on the board by the death of the provost or one of the senior fellows was ·39618 or ·37028. In the matter that concerned him most as an undergraduate, namely, vacancies for junior fellows, he noted that, if one took into account the occasional resignations of fellows for a college living the likelihood of a vacancy was (in 1858–9) ·74602 or (by the less hopeful Equitable tables) ·74321. In fact this was a fairly accurate prediction, for in the six years and five months between these calculations and his own election there were five vacancies.

Mahaffy repeated these calculations from time to time in subsequent years. Unfortunately for him the speed of promotion to senior fellowship steadily decreased. In 1858 the age of the youngest of the senior fellows was fifty. Ten years later it was fifty-eight. By the time Mahaffy made his last entries on this topic – in 1897, two years before he became a senior fellow himself – it was seventy.

Long before then one could see his growing impatience with this 'gerontocracy', as he called it, in the many remarks on old age that he inserted into his *Social Life in Greece* published in 1874. In early Greece, he noted, 'worn-out men received scanty justice and little consideration'. He continued:

> . . . so in Greece, as in France, old age may have come to
> lack the dignity and that importance which it obtains in
> the British army, on our Governing Boards, and in
> Chinese society . . . the citizens could not brook the
> slowness and caution of old age, which often mistakes
> hesitation for deliberation, and brands prompt vigour as
> rashness.[2]

Later he emphasized the Greek 'horror and hatred of old age', and noted how in Greek society old men had to face 'a strong consciousness of the greater force and knowledge of youth'. In fact

> Old men had to contend with the rising generation upon even terms, and without those large allowances conceded to them by modern sentiment and modern good manners. . . . The most enlightened Greeks stood nearer, I fear, to savages of the present day, who regard without respect or affection any human being who has become useless in the race of life, or who even impedes the course of human affairs.

The deprecatory 'I fear' in the last paragraph shows a diffidence that evaporated by the time he came to write his later pages. Now with a clear note of regret he observes

> It was left for other nations, such as the Chinese and ourselves to tolerate, nay rather to honour governors who are long past their usefulness, to have great offices of trust filled by timid and hesitating old men, whose incapacity often ruins great interests and breaks the heart of the earnest workers who see their way clearly, but cannot lead or command till the same terrible disease has dimmed *their* vision, and made them in turn a burden and a drag on the progress of a younger generation.

Then, after mention of the Athenian law by which children could take legal action against old men who were considered incapable of managing their property, he continued:

> Such an attitude of public opinion would go far to explain the strange account given us of the old people in Ceos . . . who when they came to the age of sixty or upwards, and felt themselves growing useless, drank hemlock, and left the world in which they were becoming a mere incumbrance. How desirable would such a practice appear in some of our public services and institutions!

He added a footnote of positively Swiftian ferocity:

> In more barbarous nations, the same results are attained, despite of the want of public spirit in the old people, who put their relations to the trouble of deciding

the question of a rude but effective test. Waitz . . . tells us of tribes in Borneo, who when they think their elders have lived a reasonable time, and show signs of decay, put them up into trees, and then dance round the tree, shaking it violently, and singing a rude refrain: 'The fruit is ripe, the fruit is ripe, 'tis time for it to fall.' When the fruit does accordingly fall it is cooked and eaten. We are not informed what happens when it does not. Probably the old man has proved his further usefulness by his literal and not figurative tenacity of life.

Just at that time Mahaffy seems to have been considering some method of shaking the tree for himself. Writing to George Macmillan about his *Social life* he explained that the board had been 'disgracefully stingy' about subsidizing it, commenting: 'This is the way the old brutes behave often enough, but we will soon abolish them.' But he seems never to have gone beyond threats and denunciations. The years, a quarter of a century of them, went by, the old brutes grew older and older, the fruit riper and riper, before Mahaffy reached senior fellowship in 1899. Most frustratingly, when he recorded the ages of the board in his notebook for the last time, in 1897, the age of the provost with the senior fellows was a record for the whole history of the College. It was over seventy-six, in contrast with about thirty-five in 1700, forty-seven in 1800, and fifty-nine in 1850. One of the more recent fellows who has made a special study of the board's increasing longevity has commented:

This was not due to any preternaturally old man (the senior member Carson was only 82) as to the absence of any who by any stretch of the imagination be called young. It was this state of affairs which gave rise to much of the dissatisfaction which eventually found expression in the Royal Commission of 1906 and the reforms of 1911. 'The advanced age of the Senior Fellows', wrote Barlow . . ., 'has been noted as a crowning grievance against the present Board [in 1906] . . . I can speak from personal experiences, inasmuch as I am the senior member of the body. I am seventy-nine years of age . . . but I am still quite competent to discharge the duties of a Senior Fellow.'

Alas for human pride! It was only two years later that

the Provost [Traill] broke his leg and Barlow, as Vice-Provost, found the new duties thrust upon him beyond his powers; so that the Board had to be summoned out in a pair of cabs to receive his resignation.[3]

It was probably round about this most frustrating period in his life, when he was waiting just outside the threshold of preferment, that Mahaffy, according to a young contemporary, published a statement which cannnot have added to his popularity with his seniors:

> Writing an article for an English magazine, Mahaffy found that the combined ages of the seven [senior fellows] amounted to over 500 years, but, being in waggish mood, wrote 'amounted to half a millennium'. The printer, evidently taking the word to be 'million' and thinking this rather a tall story, which he must scale down a bit, proceeded to do so, for what appeared was 'the combined ages of the seven members of the Board of Trinity College, Dublin amount to a quarter of a million.'[4]

Mahaffy may have found it hard to convince his colleagues on the board how the error arose, especially in the light of his previously published remarks on old age.

Partly, no doubt, as a result of considering those frustrating vital statistics and partly because he was now in his sixtieth year, with the excitement of the tercentenary celebrations and his main papyrological work over and done with, Mahaffy showed an uncharacteristic mood of despondency in 1898. Preaching the memorial sermon in the College Chapel on Trinity Monday, the festival day when T.C.D. celebrates its foundation and achievements, he reminded his colleagues in the congregation that it was over forty years since some of them had begun their academic careers:

> While we look back it may be with pride it may be with disappointment, upon the share of success we have attained, [we] cannot but feel that the main chapters of *our* history are finished, that we have little more to hope for in this brief and treacherous life. Now, therefore, when our ambitions are either satisfied or stilled, when the main part of our work is over, and the autumn of our days with its

calm and chill is upon us; now is the time when we may
fairly review our career, and ask ourselves what we have
done for the College that shaped the course of our life.

He went on to exhort them (and himself) in their declining years
'when the frost of winter creeps upon us':

Now, therefore, while there is yet time, let us see that we
fall not short of our great traditions. This College is now
surrounded by rivals, threatened with external legislation,
accused of obsolete methods; and we are still, I trust,
striving to stem the tide of innovations in education, whose
advocates threaten to reduce all institutions, ancient and
modern, to the dead level of their own self-satisfied
mediocrity. In these evil days no reflections can be more
appropriate than those upon our ancient worthies, who, far
from regarding education a mere competition for prizes,
connected diligence with patience, knowledge with
humility, learning with religion. [5]

If he read this last passage again in the remaining twenty years
of his life he may have reflected how relative judgements of
contemporary history could be. 'These evil days' in 1898! Before
he died he would see events in Dublin and in France that would
make the last decade of the nineteenth century seem idyllic in
comparison.

In June 1899 one of the senior fellows died at a ripe seventy-
eight, and Mahaffy was co-opted as his successor. The promotion brought him loss as well as gain. The increase in power and
salary was enormous. But there was an automatic loss in
popularity to anyone who became one of the eight who controlled the College autocratically. As one of his colleagues wrote
in 1906, when the universities of Ireland were being critically
scrutinized:

The Board enjoys the privilege of being the most heartily
and universally abused body in Ireland. This is no peculiarity
of the present Board; unpopularity seems to be an
essential attribute of a Senior Fellow; my own personal
knowledge goes back as far as 1843, in which year I was a
Junior Freshman, and I have rarely heard the Board spoken
of without the prefix of some uncomplimentary adjective.

However, Mahaffy was now on the upper branches of the tree. But one further height remained to be climbed. In 1886 he had written to a friend about Provost Jellett, then only seventy-one:

> We are getting on badly in T.C.D. The Provost is getting all the vices of old age. He resents all reforms, is very rude and only thinks of maintaining the privileges of his rotten old Board. The place is sickening with bad government and everyone is discontented.[6]

Now in 1899 Jellett's successor, Salmon, was eighty, and good, as it turned out, for another five years. It was tantalizing for Mahaffy to watch him steadily outlast all the longest-lived provosts since 1592.

However, when Mahaffy contemplated the other possible contenders for the provostship he must have felt that he had more than an average chance of success. Ever since the appointment of vice-provost Murray in 1795, the provost (with one exception) had always been chosen from among the senior fellows. (The exception did not disprove the rule, because Salmon at the time of his appointment, would have been a senior fellow, if he had not resigned his fellowship twenty years earlier on being appointed Regius Professor of Divinity.) Here at the beginning of the twentieth century the seven senior fellows fell into two groups. Three, Barlow, Williamson and Abbot, were over seventy; four, Gray, Mahaffy himself, Traill and Tarleton were in their sixties. The members of the first group especially Williamson 'who never presented the appearance of a man who enjoyed very robust health'[7] (he died in 1916 at the age of eighty-nine) were presumably debarred by age, though Barlow might not have been very ready to concede this. Of the second group, Gray was a prime example of a senior fellow. A mathematician and a theologian, he had published nothing, though he had been a clear teacher and an outstanding junior dean – his interest in Napoleonic strategy being of help when it came to coping with trouble in Botany Bay. His stiff, upright figure garbed in clerical black relieved only by the old-fashioned white neck-tie symbolized his character – stern, fair, upright, and unyielding and unshakably conservative in national and academic politics. Tarleton, the most junior of the senior fellows, was also a mathematician who had published elegant work and was in addition a competent academic administrator. Brisk, pleasant and public spirited, an avowed conservative and protestant, he was scarcely of the calibre to compensate for his lack of seniority. Lastly there was Traill, and in no group of men could Traill be overlooked – he would see to that.[8]

Traill had entered college in the same year as Mahaffy, a fact he was to recall fifty years later at the unveiling of the Lecky statue, when in the words of *T.C.D.*, the college magazine, Traill 'described how four men who afterwards distinguished themselves, Lecky, himself, Lord Justice Fitzgibbon and Dr Mahaffy (with becoming modesty he placed himself second) had presented themselves at the entrance examination'.[9] As an undergraduate Traill not only showed himself to be a first class examinee, securing first class moderatorships in both mathematics and experimental science, but also won remarkable success in sport. He captained the first XI, he was a fine miler, he became the university racquets champion, and he shot at Wimbledon. Later he became a member of the Alpine club, climbing Monte Rosa on his wedding tour. When he ceased playing more strenuous games he took up golf, becoming the terror of the links as 'always on the run after every stroke, he never hesitated to push his way through the foursome in front'. In addition he was a forcible and frequent debater and a good chess player. When he graduated he read for the bar and after election to fellowship he took a medical degree. As a junior fellow he was an outstanding tutor, and, as Mahaffy pointed out in the obituary which he wrote on Traill, 'a vigorous lecturer of pass men'. He did not publish anything (pamphlets on political issues excepted). As a eulogist explained, in the scientific world Traill was best known 'as one of the originators of electric traction'. (In fact he and his brother were responsible for constructing the first electric tramway in the British Isles – from Portrush to the Giant's Causeway – which, with its noisy, romantically shaped cars, clattering along the coast, provided one of the great thrills of an Ulster childhood.) He was also a loyal supporter of the Church of Ireland, fighting hard against disestablishment, and, when the battle was lost, playing a leading part in reorganizing the finances of the disestablished church. As a landowner in three counties and a grand juror, connected by family ties with the close-knit Ulster landed world, he was a leader of the Irish landlords in testing times.

As this summary shows, Traill was a man of tremendous vitality, and considerable intellectual power. Admittedly his immense energy and understandable self-confidence led him to act on occasion with a direct naïvety which aroused amusement and inspired anecdotes. Of good family – even Mahaffy was constrained to admit that Traill was a gentleman – he had the manners of a Squire Western. A hearty trencherman, he could be brusque at table – on a famous occasion when lunching at the Portrush golf club 'his lobster proved refractory, so . . . he laid it on the wooden floor and jumped on it with his hobnailed boots. That foolish crustacean should have known better than to stand in the way of Anthony Traill.' Though in fact he was a generous man, his careful attention to minor items of expenditure (characteristic, it may be said, of his native province) was uncharitably interpreted as closeness. And his ebullient delight in his own doings was reflected in his frequently delivered lecture (with lantern slides) on his expedition to the Rocky Mountains in the early eighties. 'The Rocky mountains,' Mahaffy remarked, 'were worn out by Traill's constant climbing.'

This lecture was replaced in 1904 by one on his tours of South Africa. In his new lecture, as a candid critic wrote, Traill demonstrated such a grasp of strategic and economic factors that it was clear 'had the fates not deemed that Dr. Traill should guide the destinies of this University Lord Roberts might have found a formidable rival and the late Mr. Cecil Rhodes a worthy successor'. The lecture, which Traill delivered with gusto at every possible college gathering, ended – Traill was a fervent imperialist – with a flamboyant peroration on the Empire, 'on which the flowers of Spring ever bloom, the suns of Summer ever shine, the leaves of Autumn ever fall and the snows of Winter ever lie'. At last Mahaffy was persuaded to preside at a performance – 'he could only do justice to Dr. Traill in his own eloquent words, "You have heard a lecture on which the flowers of Spring ever bloom, the suns of Summer ever shine, etc. etc." The audience roared with delight, and Dr. Traill though looking rather puzzled, took it as a handsome tribute.'[10]

Mahaffy and Traill, almost exact contemporaries, working for years in the same close environment, were obviously very different men, almost bound to be incompatible. Mahaffy, with all his faults, was a scholar with far-ranging interests and a strong creative impulse. Traill was a brisk educationalist. Mahaffy had a conscious, possibly over-developed sense of ceremonial style. Traill cared only about getting things done, and was careless of form, ceremony, and the deliberate shaping of action and word. To accentuate their incompatibility, they were both in their very different ways, men of the world. If Mahaffy implied he was at home at royal and imperial courts, Traill was outstanding on a committee or a commission. Mahaffy, it was said, used to delight in upholding the Macedonian ideal of field sports when talking to the young men of the Kildare Street Club. 'He would,' one of his young admirers remembers, 'lay down the law incisively with a touch of well-bred arrogance, saying, "The Macedonians were very like the young men of our best county families: they could afford to neglect strict training, they ate and drank when they wanted, nay often they drank to excess but they worked off the evil effects by those field sports, hunting, fishing and shooting – which have always produced the finest type of man."' [11] Traill could hold the attention of young and middle-aged Irish landlords at least as effectively by explaining the details of the most recent land purchase scheme.

In 1901–2 Traill and Mahaffy were both given an opportunity of demonstrating in public their skill at coming to grips with a complex problem. They appeared as witnesses before a Royal Commission on University Education in Ireland. Mahaffy, before getting down to outlining his solution of the Irish university question, treated the commissioners to some reminiscences of his own undergraduate days, touched on the attitude of Hugh O'Neill to the problem in the sixteenth century, said something about the relations of church and state in Quebec, and reminded the commissioners of 'the mischief done by the University of Athens'. 'This University,' he explained at great length, gave free education 'to all clever people who like to attend. The result was that all sorts of adventurous poor came to the University from all parts of the Greek world, and lived as porters, and water carriers and as sweepers of streets. They could afford only one text book between three or four of them and one candle, and they used to read by turns during the night. . . . It was apparently a most delightful and pathetic thing to see the anxiety on the part of these persons for learning. But what was the result? The ordinary business of life was neglected, and those persons who had congregated together in Athens and obtained an education in the University devoted themselves to politics, became political agitators, wrote articles in the newspapers and magazines and ultimately became a most dangerous and turbulent element in Greek society.' When at last he came to deal directly with the Irish University problem he suggested that there should be a University of Dublin to which a number of colleges, including Trinity, might belong. Each college would be almost completely autonomous, controlling appointments to its staff and conducting its own examinations (including degree examinations). But degrees would be conferred by the University and there would be a small body of 'conservators' who would see that standards were maintained.[12]

Traill provided the commissioners in advance with a summary of his opinions and then gave his evidence with clarity and conviction. He criticized strongly the attitude of the Roman Catholic church to Irish educational problems, and argued that Trinity should be left alone (he had already written an article with the rousing title 'Hands off Trinity') and that if a university or college to meet the wishes of the catholic church was founded, it should not be established on a scale and with resources which would give it unfair advantages over Trinity when it came to competing for undergraduates.[13]

It is scarcely necessary to emphasize that as a witness before a commission, Traill, if less consciously entertaining, was considerably more effective than Mahaffy. His disciplined and documented replies and his outspoken but good-humoured pugnacity contrast forcibly and favourably with Mahaffy's condescending and digressory style. Mahaffy, however, had one advantage over Traill. His views on the Irish University question tended to coincide with those of some influential unionist politicians. Intelligent unionists had long favoured the policy termed 'killing home rule by kindness'. They believed that if specific Irish grievances were remedied the real driving force of Irish nationalism would disappear and the bulk of Irishmen settle down to enjoying their membership of the United Kingdom and contributing towards its development. George Wyndham, who had become chief secretary in 1900, was an eloquent advocate of this policy. Handsome, with a buoyant charm and a quick mind, a poet, a man of letters as well as a man of affairs, Wyndham saw politics in terms of bold and constructive achievement, and in 1903 he piloted through parliament a land act which constituted a substantial step towards a solution of what some would consider the outstanding Irish grievance. With the Wyndham act on the statute book Wyndham felt the moment propitious for settling the 'Catholic higher education question'. It was important, he wrote half seriously, 'to give the Irish something to think about and argue about if only to divert their undivided attention from the prices under the land act'.[14] He now considered catholic education to be the last subject of first class importance that remained to be dealt with. Moreover, the broad outlines of a scheme were available. In March 1903 the Royal Commission on Irish university education had reported in favour of setting up a federal university, comprising the three Queen's colleges and a new catholic college, to be founded in Dublin. At the beginning of January 1904 in a long letter to the press, Dunraven, a unionist who had helped to muster landlord support for Wyndham's land act, suggested that the University of Dublin should be extended to include not only T.C.D. but Queen's Belfast and 'King's College' (a new catholic college to be founded in Dublin).

A vigorous discussion of the Irish university question now began. At this critical moment Provost Salmon, after a very short illness, died on 22 January. The provostship was a crown appointment and one of those Irish appointments which were made on the advice of the Prime Minister, though naturally the lord lieutenant and the chief secretary might express their views on the matter. That Mahaffy highly approved of this method of appointment is suggested by a tantalizing fragment of a letter he wrote to Sidgwick just after the death of Salmon's predecessor, Jellet. 'You will have seen,' he wrote, 'the death of our provost, a leading public figure in Ireland. It is most fortunate that the government and not . . .'[15]

Wyndham, as far back as 1888, when he was staying at the chief secretary's lodge in Phoenix Park, had read Mahaffy's *Greek life and thought* and had been delighted by its bias in favour of oligarchies and imperial policies. After all, Wyndham wrote to a friend, 'this bias is no stronger than the usual one in the opposite direction, and it is just as fair to give the conservatives a pat on the back when extolling Ptolemy and to prod the Irish nationalists when dealing with revolts in Cyrene and Syria, as it is to praise radicals with Demosthenes and Ireland with Athens'.[16] Later Wyndham had become friendly with Mahaffy, and his trust in Mahaffy's judgement must have been strengthened by his attitude on the Irish University question – which to an impatient young politician in a hurry contrasted favourably with the intransigence of his colleagues. So it is scarcely surprising that Wyndham suggested to Balfour, the Prime Minister, that Mahaffy should be Salmon's successor.

But other names were being put forward. Less than a week after Salmon's death, Madden, the vice-chancellor of the university, a high court judge who had been a law officer when Balfour was chief secretary, after having a talk with the viceroy about the provostship, wrote to the Prime Minister. Four names, he said had been discussed, Mahaffy, Traill, Bernard and Bury. 'To speak quite frankly,' Madden wrote, 'Mahaffy is the advocate if not the author of a policy which involves the abolition of the existing University of Dublin' – a policy, Madden emphasized, which had been condemned by the university in general. 'No question of principle,' he went on to say, 'arises with regard to the other possible candidates, they are all loyal to the university.' Bury, Madden thought, would be 'an ornament to the college'. But he had not given proof that he had the administrative qualities which Bernard undoubtedly possessed. So Madden and the lord lieutenant had no hesitation in recommending Bernard, 'a man of proved tact and judgement, a broad-minded man'.[17]

A week later, the senior fellows, presumably being aware that Bernard's name was being canvassed, resolved that it would be injurious to the interests of the college to appoint as provost 'one who is distinguished solely as an ecclesiastic and a theologian and who holds a high ecclesiastical position in the Church of Ireland'.[18] About the same time a great majority of the fellows expressed what Madden termed 'a natural desire' that the provost should be chosen from among the fellows. And more significantly from Mahaffy's point of view a meeting of twenty-three fellows and professors, including at least three of the outstanding scholars in college, expressed 'the hope that the new provost may be an opponent of a certain policy condemned by the college'. In informing Balfour of this, Madden added that this resolution was 'frankly intended as a protest against an intended appointment', and that 'whatever the ultimate fate of the policy with which Dr. Mahaffy has identified himself and of which he is the reputed author, it is certain that he would not command the confidence of the university'.[19]

Balfour, on whom the final decision rested, knew Ireland and the academic world well. He had been chief secretary for four years and as a Trinity, Cambridge, man he had good contacts with the academic world. At the end of January he was suffering from a bad attack of bronchitis, so it was not until the end of February, when he was recuperating at Brighton, that he began to consider the Trinity appointment. He agreed with Wyndham that Gray, Traill and Tarleton were 'impossible'. About Mahaffy he was hesitant. Personally, Balfour was 'disposed to think that Mahaffy in some quarters is under-rated. Scholars attack the scholarship of his historical work; but it seems to me, nevertheless, to be on the whole excellent. His general knowledge and ability are beyond question. But he is not popular in or out of the college; and his unpopularity is not of that kind which is often combined with admitted worth. For people dislike him for certain qualities which arouse not merely antagonism but something near to contempt. I am afraid that, in addition to his personal unpopularity, there is the unpopularity to which you refer as resulting from his opinions on general Irish university policy. This is a fact which cannot be lost sight of, whether those who differ from Mahaffy be right or wrong.' Dudley, the lord lieutenant, was so strongly anti-Mahaffy that Balfour thought it wise to warn the impetuous Dudley not to commit himself on the subject 'in the heat of conversation'. Hesitantly the Prime Minister implied that the best choice in his opinion would be Bernard.[20] He as a young man had helped Mahaffy with his edition of Kant but had resigned his fellowship in 1902 on being appointed Dean of St Patrick's. Only forty-three, he had already produced work of value in philosophy and theology, and as an administrator was already displaying the qualities which made him an outstanding ecclesiastical statesman. Later he became archbishop of Dublin and finally was Mahaffy's successor as provost of Trinity.

A few days before the Prime Minister outlined his views to the chief secretary, the *Irish Times*, the newspaper which expressed moderate Southern Unionist opinion, in a leader on the provost-ship explained that the Prime Minister's task would be easy if there were an outstanding personality amongst the senior fellows. But, the *Irish Times* declared, 'there is only one of them who has what may be described as a European reputation and it may be doubted whether his talents great and varied as they are, include the qualities necessary for governing a large body of men'. If the Prime Minister could find in Trinity 'a man of learning, dignity and business capacity, who will command the respect, the loyalty and co-operation of his colleagues', then, in the opinion of the *Irish Times*, he need not look outside the college for a provost, but his choice should not be 'arbitrarily restricted'. This article may have hinted at the desirability of considering Bernard. It certainly ruled out Mahaffy. At the same time *T.C.D.*, an organ of undergraduate opinion, writing with an unwonted seriousness, emphasized that the new provost would have to resist the Wyndham-Dunraven surrender policy and suggested he should also be a clergyman (a combination of quali-fications which could have meant Bernard but not Mahaffy).[21]

Nevertheless, Wyndham seems to have continued to press the Prime Minister to appoint Mahaffy. Balfour's ability to see the many-sidedness of a problem often made him hesitant, but when he finally made up his mind he could display a steely determina-tion. At last in the middle of March he announced his decision in a lengthy letter to Wyndham. He began by saying that he had been 'more disturbed over Trinity College, Dublin, than over any of the not very easy questions on which I have lately had to take decisions' – a strong statement when tariff reform was splitting the unionist party. He then devoted most of his letter to marshalling the arguments against Mahaffy. He explained that he had come to the conclusion that it would be unwise to appoint Mahaffy without taking into account the difficulties which had arisen over the Irish university question.

> It is [he wrote] an opinion which I have held, with very little variance, during my many years of friendship with Mahaffy; and I think, indeed, it is an opinion at one time shared by yourself, long before recent complications made themselves felt.

It is not easy to put my reasons into words. I admit Mahaffy's ability, his learning, his wide interests, his alert and capable mind. Yet, somehow or another, these great qualities are not sufficient to counter-balance some defects of manner, and perhaps even of character, which seem to me to make him an unsatisfactory choice for the Crown to make.

I have, however, frankly to admit that, in the dearth of other eligible candidates, these somewhat indefinite defects might be forgotten, in the face of his undoubted and very definite merits, but for one thing, namely, that so far as I can judge, the great mass of graduate opinion in Trinity College, resident and non-resident, is distinctly, and even violently hostile.

I know that you hold that this hostility is chiefly due to the fact that Mahaffy has, in a casual and irresponsible way, advocated a scheme of university reform which you yourself hold to be the best, although you and Mahaffy both regard it as wholly outside the sphere of practical politics. I do not, however, take this view. His unpopularity may have been accentuated for the reason I have just given; but its origin, I am certain, lies deeper. Yet, even if I am wrong in this, I do not think we can leave out of account a sentiment, which, unless I am profoundly deceived, is much stronger, and more widespread, than you suppose. The greatest scholar whom England has ever produced was forced upon Trinity College, Cambridge, by the royal will, and Trinity College became, in consequence, a scene of indescribable Civil War for many years. Mahaffy is not Bentley, and if he has less scholarship, doubtless he has more tact. But it is impossible to believe that this particular exercise of the royal prerogative, if it produces a general outbreak, from Senior Fellows and Junior Fellows, from graduates and undergraduates, will not do harm to Trinity, and harm to the Government, which is rightly regarded as responsible for it.[22]

As on a far more famous occasion nineteen years later, Balfour, with cold public-spirited ruthlessness, destroyed the hopes of another ambitious, arrogant, able man.

With Mahaffy ruled out, the Prime Minister considered that the choice lay between Traill and Bernard. Bernard was the more distinguished man, but Balfour felt that Traill would be more acceptable to the fellows, 'partly for the unavowable reason that his appointment would produce collegiate promotion, partly for the avowable reason that he has taken an energetic and, I believe, very useful part in the business affairs of the college: also, he has money of his own'.

On 26 March the board was informed that Traill had been appointed provost, and since the vice-provost, the indomitable Barlow, had broken his leg, the senior fellows, with the exception of Mahaffy, went out to Barlow's house at Raheny, 'where they found the old man in a grey flannel night-shirt propped up in bed'. There Traill made the statutory declaration and was admitted by the vice-provost. At the end of the short ceremony, Barlow 'slammed the book together, saying, "And may God forgive me for what I am doing". Traill who was slightly deaf . . . pressed forward and shook him warmly by the hand, "Thank you, thank you my dear fellow" – and then in an aside, "I didn't quite catch what he was saying but I suppose it was something civil" '.[23]

It would be futile to attempt to describe Mahaffy's emotions at losing the prize which would have marked the apex of his college career. A few days before Traill's appointment was announced Mahaffy knew he had failed. He wrote to an old friend, 'Don't fret over what I am going to say. Wyndham writes that he has fought my battle for weeks and is defeated. He does not name the conqueror. To me it means liberty of speech and great ease, and I feel really relieved.'[24] And the public comment attributed to him was a jesting quotation from the psalms – 'Promotion cometh neither from the east nor from the west nor yet from the south.'[25] But the depth of his resentment was shown when he first met Balfour after the event at Clouds, George Wyndham's home. Then he 'cut' Balfour with an emphasis long remembered.[26]

Mahaffy must have felt profound disappointment mingled with shocked surprise. As his historical work shows, he was very conscious of how outstanding provosts had influenced the development of the college and he must have looked forward to seeing Trinity, with Mahaffy as provost, advancing in renown.

Gifted as a host and with a zest for scholarly gatherings, he could reasonably have hoped to make the provost's house a centre of good living, high thinking and sparkling conversation where, under his genial presidency, the worlds of learning and power would intermingle. His ambitions were not only abruptly dashed, but he was defeated by a contemporary whom he could not have considered to be a rival. Mahaffy bore his disappointment with Spartan courage. But his restraint sometimes broke when he referred to Traill. In private correspondence he wrote of him as 'a rotten bigot of a provost' and as 'a beastly fool of a provost'. Once, too, Birrell, when dining on the Trinity high table, was startled when Mahaffy in the course of conversation spoke of the provost as 'a beast'. Noticing Birrell's warning glance at Traill who was presiding, Mahaffy immediately added, 'But fortunately a deaf beast.' All the same Mahaffy was constrained in justice to admit that Traill made an excellent chairman of the board.[27]

Traill himself was clearly undisturbed by doubts about the wisdom of his appointment. Quickly settling down in the saddle, he proved himself to be a vigorous, practical and decisive provost in trying times. His tenure was marked by stress and argument in Trinity as the college strove to adapt itself to the requirements of the twentieth century. Two years after he became provost further debate began over the reorganization of Irish university education – a debate in which Mahaffy found himself separated from the mainstream of college opinion at a time of crisis. In 1905 the new Liberal government decided to try to solve the Irish university problem. Then towards the end of March 1906 Bryce, the chief secretary, announced that the government intended to set up a commission to inquire into the administration of Trinity College and to consider the position Trinity should occupy in Irish higher education. Before this announcement was made, Traill, straightforward and shrewd, had taken steps to put what he considered to be the Trinity attitude on these questions before the government. Early in March, in the course of a long talk with Sir Anthony MacDonnell, the Under Secretary, Traill admitted that 'the Trinity College system of learning is antiquated and not up-to-date and said he would be glad of modernisation'. He also admitted that an inquiry into Trinity could not exclude a consideration of the catholic demand for university facilities, but he emphasized that by internal reform Trinity could meet all reasonable demands. Two months later, in a short letter to MacDonnell, Traill summed up the Trinity attitude by saying that the College would welcome any solution which while solving the larger question 'will preserve our individuality as the university of Trinity College, Dublin'.[28]

At this time Mahaffy was also in touch with the government. MacDonnell, when they met at dinner, asked him if he could recommend anyone to act as secretary to the commission. Mahaffy at once suggested the name of Harold Murphy, an able young graduate, then lecturing in history at Trinity, whose 'sympathies were known to be for reform and national aspirations'. When pressing Murphy's claims on MacDonnell, Mahaffy took the opportunity to 'insist that you won't find out the whole truth without some men from inside on the committee'. And he proposed as a suitable member Brougham Leech, his old travelling companion of forty years before. Leech, Mahaffy pointed out, was an acute lawyer and 'no friend to the present powers and likely to cease his connection with us in a couple of years – such a man could not only suggest the right questions but disclose the reticences and prevarications which will certainly mislead any commission of outsiders'.[29]

Leech, a doctrinaire academic radical who wanted sweeping changes in Trinity, would certainly have been *persona non grata* to an influential section of the college. The government avoided the invidious task of picking a representative and acceptable Trinity don by asking the board to nominate a member of the college staff for membership of the commission. The board discussed the question on 13 and 14 May – Mahaffy being absent in London. The first day was spent in discussing whether to nominate a junior or senior fellow and it was decided by five votes to two (Traill being in the minority) to nominate a junior fellow. The next day two junior fellows were considered, Beare and Kelleher. J. I. Beare, the professor of Greek, was an academic conservative, Stephen Kelleher, a mathematician who had graduated in the Royal University of Ireland and Trinity, was the only catholic fellow. In the event Kelleher was chosen by the provost's casting vote – Cathcart, the most senior of the junior fellows, who had been called up to replace Mahaffy, voting for Beare. Traill was extremely pleased. Kelleher, he told

PM

Bryce, 'is a most independent Roman Catholic layman, not afraid to express his opinion and most loyal to this place. Besides that, he is not an irreligious Roman Catholic and therefore could not be unacceptable to the bishops of their church.'

By asking the college to submit a name, the government had accepted Mahaffy's suggestion that there should be a Trinity representative on the commission. But Mahaffy did not share Traill's satisfaction with the board's decision. A week after the decisive vote Sir Anthony MacDonnell informed the Chief Secretary:

> I had a visit today from Mahaffy who tells me that 'all that is good' in T.C.D. is furious with Traill over the Kelleher incident. Mahaffy was away from Dublin during the board meeting. Traill, he says, had intrigued to find a protestant and a catholic who would be his reflex on the committee – and having found them placed these two names before the board to choose from. There was an even division, and Traill cast his vote for Kelleher hoping, as Mahaffy says, to gain credit with the catholic interest for ulterior purposes. This is just as we thought. Mahaffy says Kelleher is a 'mere peasant' and will be a 'negligible quantity' in the commission. It is all very squalid.[30]

The Royal commission on Trinity, under the chairmanship of Sir Edward Fry, started hearing evidence in 1906, and in due course Mahaffy appeared as a witness before it. As might be expected, he was fluent and flamboyant, displaying a magnificent vagueness about college statistics which as senior lecturer he should have had at his finger-tips (fortunately he was helpfully prompted by Kelleher). His evidence as a whole made clear that on major issues of college politics he was a moderate if pessimistic progressive and on minor matters a somewhat complacent conservative.

When asked his opinion on the composition of the board Mahaffy spoke with less assurance than usual. About twelve years earlier when he was still a junior fellow, writing about college in the seventeenth century, he had pointed out that 'the concentration of power into the hands of a small and irremovable body sets temptations before its members to look after their own interests . . . and cumulate upon themselves office and emolument to the damage of the corporation'. But when the Fry commission invited him to comment on the composition of the board he gave an irritable and unhelpful answer: 'If anybody will show me a reformed system which is likely to be as good – I will not say better – I should be willing to adopt it, but all the proposals appear to me to be so perfectly rotten that they had better be left alone.'

Questioned on matters of relatively minor detail he stoutly defended current Trinity standards and practices. Asked if the matriculation standard was not somewhat low, he replied that he 'could quote a number of cases of boys who came up with bad promise and turned out satisfactory afterwards'. He praised the pass course as giving an excellent general education, quoting as a practical instance of its value the experience of his son who, when he went out to the South Seas, had to learn to navigate a sailing boat and found that 'the knowledge of astronomy he had got with his degree enabled him to do it in a day'. When it was put to him that the rule allowing senior junior fellows to give pass lectures only, leaving honours lecturing to their juniors, was 'a curious arrangement' Mahaffy at once replied that it was an excellent idea: 'there is,' he remarked, 'no lecturer so patient with an ignorant boy as an elderly man'. He even defended an aspect of college administration which did not fall within the senior lecturer's sphere. When asked were the sanitary arrangements in college not very defective, he both pointed out that the arrangements at Queen's, Oxford – where he was an honorary fellow – were much more primitive and that 'one of the real causes why we have never had an epidemic is that there has never been a system of water-closets throughout the college'.[31]

The Fry commission produced an inconclusive report and early in 1907 it was announced that the government intended to deal with the Irish university problem by constituting an enlarged university of Dublin which would include not only Trinity, but the Queen's colleges in Belfast and Cork and a new college in Dublin acceptable to catholic opinion. The Trinity reaction to this proposal was energetically expressed. It was vehemently argued that the new university would contain institutions based on different principles – Trinity standing for intellectual liberty, the new college bound to defer to ecclesiastical authority. A 'Defence of Trinity committee' was set up which produced pungent pamphlets, great meetings of the senate and graduates addressed by an impressive array of eminent Trinity men were convened and addresses in support of the college's autonomy were secured from a number of learned bodies. In the event the government yielded and the Irish Universities Act of 1908 established the National University of three colleges (Dublin, Cork and Galway) and the Queen's University of Belfast. All this, it must be said at once, is of strictly negative relevance in an account of Mahaffy's career. Already committed to a policy which involved an enlarged University of Dublin, alone amongst the great Trinity figures of his day he was conspicuous by his absence from the defence movement.

Mahaffy suffered a most severe blow in 1908 when his wife, to whom he was so deeply attached, died. 'It is indeed impossible,' he wrote to a young friend, 'for a youth like you to know what the rupture of a close intimacy of love and respect lasting nearly 43 years is to a man of declining years. I feel that in the deepest sense I have lost my home, and am henceforth a mere lodger in my own house. She was so sound in sense, tender in heart, large in sympathy. Many people loved her, all respected her.'[32]

Out of his family of four children only his two daughters now remained with him in Ireland. His sons were pursuing careers in England and abroad. Robert, the elder, a barrister and author, was in London. Arthur, the younger, a wayward boy of great charm, after an academic career at Oxford and Trinity in which he had attained distinction as an oarsman, had entered the colonial service in which he finally rose to being administrator of Dominica. Mahaffy's two daughters, Elsie, whom he found rather difficult, and Rachel, who cherished him most affectionately, stayed at home after their mother's death and managed his house for him.

chapter eleven

'Sir Provost'

Mahaffy did not allow himself in these years of academic frustration to be crippled by self-pity. Though after 1895 he did not produce any major work of classical scholarship, he moved in a completely new field, even more dangerously strewn with controversial issues – Irish history. In 1892 the board of Trinity college, as part of the tercentenary celebrations, had published the *Book of Trinity College*, which contained a substantial section on college history. Mahaffy wrote four chapters covering the history of Trinity from its foundation to 1800. He had to work quickly since the production of the book was delayed by 'jealousies and opposition', but he had as a basis the work of one of the senior fellows, John Stubbs, who had recently published his *History of the university of Dublin from its foundation until the end of the eighteenth century*. In Mahaffy's opinion it was unfortunate that Stubbs, who had an unrivalled store of college anecdotage, had not begun his work at 1800. His own chapters in the *Book of Trinity College* certainly give a more coloured and coherent account of the first two centuries of college history than that presented by Stubbs. When he had finished editing his papyri Mahaffy started to work intensively on the early history of the Trinity, though he was bitterly aware that he belonged to a college which 'is singularly incurious about its own history, and where is found but little gratitude to the scholar who labours to recover its past from oblivion'.[1] He produced two works of considerable value on Trinity history, an edition of the *Particular book*, the oldest extant college record, and *An epoch in Irish history: Trinity college, Dublin 1591–1660*. The *Epoch* is the work of an able historian with forty years of academic administration behind him. Aspects of the college's development – its finances, its buildings, the shaping of the curriculum, undergraduate life, the personalities of the more outstanding dons, the relation of the college to the government and the community at large are skilfully balanced, and a bold attempt is made to place Trinity in its historic setting. The foundation and early fortunes of the college, were, as Mahaffy emphasizes in his introductory chapter, decisively influenced by two movements, the efforts of the English crown to establish its power over the whole of Ireland and the great European conflict between protestantism and the counter-reformation.

Next, two of Mahaffy's early interests, art and social history, together with sheer curiosity about the historical background of his own environment, impelled him to tackle another important Irish historical problem, the architectural history of Dublin. At the beginning of the twentieth century, Dublin, or at least its centre, the wide area straddling the Liffey and bounded by the great canals, was to an extraordinary extent a Georgian city with classical public buildings, streets and squares of well-proportioned, flat-façaded, brick houses, many of them urban mansions. When Mahaffy was a young man eighteenth-century architecture was not highly regarded. He himself recalled that in his youth nobody thought of admiring the great west front of Trinity (according to Mahaffy, 'probably the finest academic front in Europe') and apparently Mahaffy himself in his early years shared the general indifference. After reading Ruskin he had commented that if anyone was 'to set about the revival of a healthy school of architecture in England' it would first be necessary to 'cast out utterly whatever is connected with Greek, Roman and Renaissance architecture in principle or in form'.[2] By a curious chance Mahaffy as a boy had been brought into close contact with Ruskin's architectural ideals. During the early eighteen-fifties the board of T.C.D. decided to employ the architect Benjamin Woodward to design their new Museum Building. The result was in the very latest style, a Venetian *palazzo* which Ruskin described in his lecture delivered in Dublin in 1868 as 'the beautiful building . . . which was the first realization I had the joy to see, of the principles I had, until then, been endeavouring to teach!' Mahaffy had watched the gifted Irish stone-carvers, the O'Shea brothers (who afterwards employed their skill and Celtic imagination on the Kildare Street Club, Dublin, and the Oxford museum) as they carved the rich floral patterns of the capitals and string course of the new building, using freshly gathered flowers as their models.[3] As he admired their work the young boy little guessed how much trouble and obloquy their fellow-craftsman's son, Patrick Pearse, would cause him in later life.

But the maturer Mahaffy, influenced by devotion to classical antiquity, and by pride in the identity and achievements of the Anglo-Irish, turned to a severer style. At some stage he began to explore the decayed Georgian grandeur of the Dublin slums, paying 'domiciliary visits' to admire the staircases and stucco work, always cordially greeted by the tenement dwellers, many of whom 'were surprised and delighted to find they were living in a beautiful house'. Understandably, then, he played a leading part in the inauguration of a society, the Irish Georgian Society, which had as its object 'recording examples of eighteenth century architecture and decoration in Dublin'. The society was founded in February 1908 at a meeting in the Royal Irish Academy, attended by a number of ladies and gentlemen, including the vicereine, the Countess of Aberdeen, 'who on her way to another meeting showed her interest in the proceedings by paying a short visit'.[4]

Mahaffy was in the chair and, in proposing that the society should be founded, he provided a vivid compressed survey of eighteenth-century Dublin architecture, the work 'of Irish genius and Irish workmen'. Having drawn attention to three eighteenth-century styles which could be seen in Dublin, the panelled, the Palladian, and the Adam, he tried to answer the question why, after an age of great creative achievement, should there be a marked decline in taste. It was largely due, he suggested, to the evangelical revival. From about 1815 onwards 'the pious and respectable gentry who inhabited Dublin were not only inartistic but anti-artistic . . . cupids and such like ornaments were hateful to them'.[5] And, some time later, he again emphasized how the growing seriousness which marked the early nineteenth century had detrimentally affected the decorative arts. 'Who cares,' he wrote, 'about the adorning of the ceiling with stucco and the particular curve of his sofa's back when Napoleon is threatening to land upon the coast, and when the insurgent peasants are actually burning down his neighbour's mansion in the country? . . . Who, above all, that is thinking of a house made without hands, eternal in the heavens, will spend time and care adorning his earthly tabernacle?'[6]

Mahaffy proved a dynamic president of the society. He not only encouraged the younger men who were responsible for the production of six volumes of records (four relating to Dublin and two dealing with country houses) which appeared between 1909 and 1915, but he himself when travelling about Ireland worked hard, collecting information and making architectural sketches (some of which, unpublished as yet, remain as a useful record of a past era). He also contributed to the third volume on society in eighteenth-century Dublin, a lively digressory survey of many aspects of Dublin and Irish life. To Mahaffy the ruling world of eighteenth-century Ireland seemed to be a self-contented society, lacking in depth but with sound standards of taste.

Mahaffy also had academic duties to perform which occupied and interested him. He was now a member of the board, and he was registrar, 1899–1902, and senior lecturer, 1902–7, and again from 1910 until 1913 when he became vice-provost. As an academic administrator he was competent without being outstanding. In keeping the senior lecturer's book he reverted to the custom which had been abandoned about half a century earlier of entering the Christian names of the candidates and their fathers' occupations in Latin, an affected archaism rendered all the more tiresome by his handwriting. He rationalized the system by which entrance rewards were made, and, having an easy-going sympathy with the passmen, he permitted those who had failed in only one subject in a pass examination to present themselves in that subject a month later at a re-examination (which became known as a *post mortem*). Eager to encourage research, he attacked the principle on which prizes at graduation were awarded. During the nineteenth century Trinity, by giving generous prizes – studentships and money awards to the better first class men, had encouraged and awarded undergraduate endeavour. Mahaffy's aim was to use these prizes to promote postgraduate work.

In 1908 he tried in an able memorandum to persuade the board to make it obligatory for the holder of a studentship either to lecture in Trinity or to go and study at another university. 'The use of foreign languages,' Mahaffy emphasized, 'and foreign thinking would prevent them continuing in a mere provincial groove and ignoring what the rest of Europe is doing for their respective studies.' Characteristically he ended his memorandum by a plea for archaeology, which had received as yet no consideration 'while the insatiable claims of modern science are absorbing thousands every year'. He failed, and the changes he advocated were not made until the twenties. He also urged that the substantial money grants to the better firsts should be made on condition that the recipient undertook research. After discussion the board accepted Traill's compromise that the grants should be given at the discretion of the board to students who appeared deserving for 'the purposes of research or otherwise'.

There was one important issue on which Mahaffy clashed with Traill as provost and won a partial victory. When the Home Rule Bill of 1912 was at the committee stage, Campbell, a leading southern Irish unionist and one of the Trinity M.P.s, proposed an amendment the effect of which would have been to exempt Trinity from the jurisdiction of the Irish parliament. The government refused to accept the amendment but Birrell promised to add 'some words to meet the case' on the report stage. Inquiries the following day at Trinity elicited that Campbell's amendment had not been officially sponsored by the college, but Traill explained that it represented his own views (and it is reasonable to suppose that Campbell had been inspired by him). Mahaffy at once made his opinion clear. In a letter to *The Times* he pointed out that Campbell's amendment had not been sanctioned by the board, the junior fellows or the professors and there was in college 'at least a strong minority' which regarded 'exemption from Irish control as a great danger in the future to Trinity College'. He himself, he added, objected to the amendment because he believed that 'the exemption will alienate Trinity college from Ireland and create a feeling amongst the people that Trinity is not an Irish institution'.

On 26 October Traill brought the question before the board, which by nine votes to two, Gray and Mahaffy forming the minority, resolved that it approved of the Campbell amendment.

The fact that Gray, 'a unionist of the most unrelenting type', opposed the amendment shows that unionists were divided over the value and expediency of the suggested safeguard. As the *Irish Times* emphasized, if Trinity were exempted from Irish control, 'the very presence of the college buildings would be a permanent eyesore to the members of the Irish parliament' who obviously would be in a position to injure the college indirectly in a number of ways even if they were unable to legislate expressly for it. On 11 November a meeting of the fellows and professors by 24 votes to 13 resolved that if an Irish parliament were to be set up they did not wish the college to be excluded from its jurisdiction but that they wanted a guarantee that the *status quo* concerning the Irish university question established by the Irish Universities Act of 1908 should be maintained. Such a guarantee, they suggested, could be provided by inserting in the Home Rule Bill a proviso restraining the Irish parliament from altering the status of Dublin university save with the consent of the board, of the majority of the fellows, and of the university council. The government naturally enough decided to try to conciliate Trinity opinion by adopting this suggestion. In fact they improved on it by proposing an amendment which specifically stated that no act of the Irish parliament altering the constitution or diverting the property of Dublin University or Trinity College should be valid unless approved by a majority of the following bodies, the board, the junior fellows and professors, the university council, and the senate.

At this point university politics intruded. A strong section in Trinity which included Mahaffy was alarmed that the elaborate machinery which was being devised to protect the college against Irish parliamentary action might be used to obstruct internal reform, and as a result Birrell, in his own words, 'spent a very troublesome Christmas' because every post brought him letters and printed documents from groups and individuals in Trinity. Besides writing to Birrell, Mahaffy lobbied Redmond, the leader of the Irish parliamentary party, asking him to support an amendment sponsored by a Trinity graduate, C. B. Harmsworth, which provided that the constitution and status of Dublin university and Trinity college could not be altered by an act of the Irish parliament, save with the consent of the majority of those present at a joint meeting of the board, fellows and professors and the council. 'You will be doing T.C.D. a far greater benefit than it deserves,' Mahaffy told Redmond, 'if you would promote Mr. Harmsworth's amendment requiring only a general consent on our part to give the Irish parliament a right to help us in obtaining reforms. . . . I and all my friends repudiate strongly the exhibition of distrust shown by requiring four independent consents as in the chief secretary's amendment. It will make all reform impossible. Would that my outcry would reach the Irish members of the house.'[7]

In 1912 Mahaffy was a leading member of a committee which produced for the board a set of conditions for governing future elections to fellowship. These would have permitted the board at intervals to fill a fellowship without examination but solely on published work, as well as widening the range of subjects for the fellowship examination. At a first glance these proposals might be regarded as 'non-political', because after all even strong college conservatives had been willing to consider alternative methods of election to fellowship and the addition of new subjects to the examination. However, once the problem of fellowship was under discussion the ultra-conservative Gray and his staunch ally Cathcart were to be found as usual in opposition. They were often joined by Tarleton and by Burnside, another mathematician, who it was rumoured sometimes lectured wearing hunting clothes under his gown and is said to have been the last man habitually to ride on horseback into Trinity.

From the beginning of 1914 Mahaffy as vice-provost had to guide the board in its deliberations, because Traill, long noted for his robust energy, after a serious illness in the winter of 1912, began to decline rapidly and was continuously absent from board meetings. During Traill's illness Mahaffy frequently called at the provost's house to inquire how he was progressing. His calls were probably inspired by kindness, but his solicitude aroused satirical comment.

Traill's absence from the board naturally delayed the discussion on fellowship. Eventually in June Mahaffy suggested the board should resume consideration of the subject. Gray insisted that since the provost, the '*caput societatis*', was ill and absent, all consideration of the fellowship system should be postponed. He was overruled by seven votes to four, the proposals were then accepted in principle by six votes to five, and at the end of June the board finally approved of the scheme. Just before adjourning for the Long Vacation on 30 June the board concluded its labours for the Trinity term of 1914 by voting – Gray, Cathcart, Tarleton and Burnside dissenting – a grant towards the expenses of a new games pavilion in the college park. It was the last decision of pre-war Trinity, a care-free gesture, a few weeks before an epoch ended with the beginning of the great European conflict.

Mahaffy summoned an emergency meeting of the board for 12 August. Before it met he had already given permission to the National Volunteers (the section of the volunteers which under Redmond's leadership supported the war effort) to practise signalling in the college park, on condition they abstained from doing so on Sundays. The board approved his decision and resolved that steps would be taken to ensure that no student 'should suffer any check in his college career' in consequence of volunteering for the forces. But it firmly turned down an application from a pugnacious tutor who requested that one of his pupils, who had failed his degree examination, should be granted a degree on the grounds he had just joined the Con-naught Rangers. On 29 August the board arranged for the bursar's duties to be carried on in the absence of Cathcart, interned at Hamburg, and on the same day a special com-mencements was held for the purpose of conferring degrees on students who had qualified and volunteered for the forces. Early in September an encampment of forty bell tents sprang up in the college park to accommodate members of the O.T.C. who were taking an intensive course of training before being commissioned in the special reserve of Kitchener's army. When undergraduates returned at the beginning of Michaelmas term, they were conscious that 'the hustle and bustle of military effort that has invaded our academic torpor makes us feel ill at ease in college and begets in us the desire to get away from an environment which we have so long associated with careless peace'. And at the beginning of November the name of the first Trinity man to be killed in action was published.[8]

Shortly before the long vacation ended Mahaffy had another tiresome tussle with the ultra-conservatives on the board. Tyrrell died on 19 September, and a few days later Mahaffy suggested that the board should proceed to co-opt Purser, the senior junior fellow, and sanction some consequent changes, including the appointment of a new tutor. Gray strongly opposed these moves, arguing that nothing should be done until the beginning of term. Considering Mahaffy's procedure illegal, he refused to attend at board meetings. This did not mean an absence of obstruction, because he arranged that his views should be expounded by Cathcart, recently released and returned. After two strenuous meetings Mahaffy prevailed. But within a fortnight he was involved in a short, sharp controversy with a group of students who proved as unyielding as some of the senior fellows.

The college Gaelic society had been founded in 1907 with the aim of promoting the study of the language, the literature, the archaeology, art and economics of Ireland. The society decided to begin the academic year 1914–15 by holding on 17 November a meeting to commemorate the birth of Thomas Davis, a Trinity graduate who had made an outstanding contribution to the Irish nationalist tradition. The meeting was to be addressed by W. B. Yeats, Francis Bigger, an Ulster antiquarian and an enthusiastic nationalist, and by Patrick Pearse, the founder and headmaster of Saint Enda's, a school inspired by Irish nationalist ideals. Pearse was one of the leaders of the section of the National Volunteers which had repudiated Redmond's policy of participation in the war. On 10 November Mahaffy wrote to the society saying he had been informed that 'a man called Pearse' who 'was a supporter of the anti-recruiting agitation' was to be one of the society's speakers, and could not permit him to address a meeting in college. 'Why,' he asked, 'do you place me in this unpleasant necessity?' A brisk interchange of letters followed, Mahaffy insisted that he would not allow Pearse, 'a speaker with these to me traitorous views' to address a meeting in college, unless he assured Mahaffy through the society, that 'he said nothing against enlisting in the imperial army'. The committee of the society pointed out that Pearse had been secured as a speaker some time back, that they were prepared to relieve Mahaffy 'of any embarrassment, by not pressing on you their invitation to take the chair'. They also emphasized that the speakers would not make any references irrelevant to the subject under discussion, so that 'the matter of the present European war could not be introduced'. When

A caricature of Mahaffy after the Davis Centenary incident in 1914
(from *A Book of Caricatures* by V. L. O'Connor: published by Tempest, Dundalk)

Mahaffy proved obdurate, the committee expressed its regret that 'the teaching of Thomas Davis which at least represented the gospel of free speech and liberty of conscience should have borne no fruit in Trinity college'.

The society released the correspondence to the press, omitting, as Mahaffy was quick to point out, a sentence expressing the hope that the vice-provost would explain to ladies and gentlemen who had accepted the society's invitation why the meeting was not being held – an omission which, the *Irish Times* observed, was 'more creditable to their good taste than good faith'. The board, having approved Mahaffy's action in forbidding the meeting in college, suppressed the society but abstained from action against the students concerned. The meeting was held on the advertised evening in the Antient Concert Rooms but was not reported in the major Dublin newspapers. The *Irish Times* contrasted Mahaffy's decision to prevent the meeting in Trinity very favourably with the attitude of the Irish executive and the military authorities who were refusing to take any notice of the anti-recruiting campaign. Mahaffy also had the support of *TCD*, traditionally critical of authority. It was 'highly amused . . . by the splash which the drowning of the remnants of the Gaelic society caused in the calm pool of lecture term'.[9]

A few days later, on 20 November, about ten in the morning, Mahaffy received a telegram from the Lord Lieutenant informing him that on the previous day the Prime Minister had received the King's approval of his appointment as provost. When the members of the board assembled later in the morning, Mahaffy laid the telegram and confirmatory letters which had followed it before them. He was accepted as provost, and as it was the duty of the vice-provost to hear the new provost's declaration, he immediately proposed Tarleton as his successor as vice-provost. Cathcart at once proposed another candidate, Williamson (aged eighty-seven). Tarleton was elected, but Mahaffy had been sharply and soon reminded that he had not attained *otium cum dignitate*.

Mahaffy must have felt a deep sense of satisfaction on becoming provost. At last he had attained the position that his personality and prestige merited. At the board he was now something more than *primus inter pares*. He now received those outward marks of deference, the doffing of caps, the escort of a mace bearer, so pleasing to a proud man, very conscious of tradition. He took up residence in the great eighteenth-century mansion, the history of which he had traced with such devoted care and which he enjoyed restoring to 'a condition worthy of its dignity and beauty', remodelling the fireplace in the drawing room 'formerly the ugliest in Dublin' and calling in Sir Hugh Lane to advise on the cleaning of the pictures. He could reflect that his name was now listed in the long line of provosts whose achievements he had had recorded and assessed.

But we know that his satisfaction was strongly tinged with melancholy. He believed that the great majority of the fellows only welcomed his appointment 'because (1) the promotion of a senior fellow gave it to all his juniors, and (2) they disliked the appointment of someone else more than they did mine'. And to congratulations he replied 'Ten years too late'. Though robust, mentally alert, and at times provocative, he was seventy-five. His creative days were passed and he found himself head of a college at a time when its vitality was ebbing fast. Many of the younger members of the academic staff left to join the forces or take part in war work. The number of men undergraduates on the college books fell by fifty per cent. Academic routine continued, but the clubs and societies languished, and student life was continuously overshadowed by an awareness of the war. 'The best men are away,' *TCD* declared, 'and the hearts of the rest of us cannot be wholly in our college life.'[10] The cheerful energy and exuberance of undergraduate youth was clouded to an unusual degree by seriousness and sadness. The spirit of the time is reflected in some lines from a poem by an undergraduate entitled 'April 1915' which begins:

There's a magic in the moorland, there's a magic in the rain
Sweeping onward grey and gusty o'er the stretching midland
    plain,
There's a magic in the mountains climbing rugged to the sky,
And a thousand little magics in the dripping peewits' cry.

and ends with the lines

But the south wind, sighing softly, holds a distant cry of pain,
And borne upon its eddies drift the spirits of the slain,

Who marvel at the springtime, for mid gun and sword and
     lance,
The spring has never broken on the battle fields of France.[11]

Mahaffy symbolized the continuity of college life in those
poignant and uncertain times. Upright in spite of his age,
massive and slow, he moved across the college squares, halting
from time to time to survey his demesne. Throughout the world
Trinity men had been glad and 'curiously satisfied' at hearing
the news that at last Mahaffy was provost.[12] His superb self-
confidence, which in happier days had often been a source of
amusement, was now reassuring. An impression of the invigorat-
ing confidence and geniality (not overdiluted with tact) that
Mahaffy could diffuse is conveyed by the memories of a conversation he had with a young officer in the Royal Army Medical
Corps on leave from France after the dreadful winter of 1914–15.

I visited the college and met the provost in the Front Square.
He was in a very genial mood and one of his first questions
to me was, 'Are any of the generals any d—— good?', to
which I replied that we all thought French had done a great
job but that Hubert Gough was one of the younger ones
with a great future. Mahaffy said, 'Gough. Let me see, he
must be a grandson of my old friend the Field Marshal of
the Sikh war. So you think well of French – very interesting,
for he was once a pupil of mine – and I see that Crozier,
another pupil, has been made primate. Both poor second
rates or good third rates and still they've done well – that
should be some consolation to you.'

A few months later on being told in a letter from this young
doctor about the tremendous number of rats which plagued the
trenches and the dressing stations, Mahaffy wrote back, 'I regard
your rats as a good omen for it is well known how they desert
a sinking ship'.[13]

Although from August 1914 life flagged, the board, under
Mahaffy's guidance, was busy. The process of adapting the
Trinity system to the twentieth century continued. The number
of subjects in which scholarship could be taken was increased:
the ordinance of 1916 'boldly broke through the accustomed
mode of electing fellows only through examination' and steps

were taken to improve the workings of the tutorial system. One problem which arose directly from the war proved time-consuming and contentious. The fall in the number of students led immediately to a fall in fees, and this affected a very important group in college, the tutor-fellows, who received a large proportion of their incomes from a special fund formed by fees. It was naturally suggested that they should receive assistance from 'the common chest' of the college, and whether relief should be given and, if it was, on what terms it should be granted, offered to an academic body, such as the board, a wide field for discussion. Gray and Cathcart were critical of the relief measures which were drafted and in the words of an indignant tutor-fellow 'proceeded to block their application by an insolent employment of various methods of obstruction'. Finally, on 18 March 1916 Mahaffy announced that if the matter were not finally settled at the next board meeting, he would hold a meeting every morning and afternoon until a decision was reached – a threat which broke the opposition.[14] It may be added that in the event the long and acrimonious discussions over the terms on which loans might be made to members of the staff turned out to be unnecessary. When the war ended, the treasury made a grant to Trinity which wiped out the debts incurred.

Six weeks after Mahaffy so dramatically overbore the conservative opposition on the board he was faced with a far more serious emergency.[15] The morning of Easter Monday 1916 was bright, if a little cool, and the provost's household – his two daughters, three men and six women servants – was in a holiday mood as the Misses Mahaffy planned 'outgoings' for servants, including a visit to the Zoo for two of the maids. Shortly after twelve the news reached the front gate 'that the Sinn Feiners had risen and were in possession of the Post Office and College Green'. The porters on duty locked the gate and one of them went along to the provost's house to give the news and suggest that the shutters should be closed. Holiday plans were cancelled, to the dismay of the maids, and the shutters covering the windows of the large salon were fastened. While this was being done, Swift MacNeill, the nationalist M.P., whom Mahaffy had examined fifty years back, arrived. He had been with Dillon, the nationalist leader, in North Great George's Street, and was able to confirm that the insurgents were in possession of the Post

Office. Later he recalled how the provost took him for a stroll in his garden and discussed the situation 'with perfect quietude of manner'.[16] After MacNeill left, the provost and his daughters sat down to lunch with a guest, who, every time a shot was heard, tried to console his hosts by saying 'we are making history'. At tea-time another guest arrived, 'a foolhardy lady' from the south side, who, with a determination to see what was happening which characterized many respectable Dubliners during this terrible week, had been walking all over the city centre. As she said herself, 'I shall never see another revolution'. After tea, Mahaffy let her out by the back gate and then surveyed the force available for the protection of the College.

By the late afternoon some members of the O.T.C. had managed to slip into College and they had been joined by a few soldiers including a group of Anzacs who were excellent shots. The whole force (forty-four strong) was commanded by Alton, a fellow in classics, who had accompanied Mahaffy on a tour of Greece and was later celebrated as an authority on Ovid. Alton's ebullient enthusiasm was always an inspiration to those who knew him, and he had experienced advice from another junior fellow on leave from France. Such a small force obviously could not effectively man the whole perimeter of College. So it was decided to mount a guard at the front gate, to place a strong detachment at the O.T.C. headquarters at the east end of College, and to post sentries.

One of the sentries patrolling the east end of College was Joly, the eminent geologist, celebrated for his work on radio-activity and colour photography. A man of almost sixty, who had always had 'a strong dose of that native curiosity which is one of the requisites of a first class scientist', Joly during the afternoon let himself out through a side gate with his College key and walked down to Sackville Street, 'to ascertain if possible the magnitude of the movement and to get some idea of the numbers engaged in it'. Having a good look at the Post Office and the 'huge green banner' floating above it, he returned to College and secured some instruction from a cadet in the use of a service rifle. With the precise judgement of an able scientist, he decided 'that to rank as a good shot with a rifle to which one was unaccustomed, under conditions when probably the sights could not be seen, was of course out of the question'. But, he added, 'On the other hand, there was the comforting reflection that if attacked, the fighting must necessarily be at close quarters and accurate shooting would not be required.'

When darkness fell on Monday, a long, anxious night began. All the usual street sounds – the footsteps, and the beat of the cab-horses' hoofs – were missing. From time to time stray shots or volleys of rifle fire were heard, breaking the strange silence. The Trinity sentries peering out from their cover saw or sensed menacing movements. Figures, insurgents possibly, were seen on the railway embankment above the college Rugby ground. Near dawn, a car full of men was seen creeping down the lane that runs along the north wall of College. A sentry signalled a warning to the O.T.C. headquarters, and the garrison braced itself. Meanwhile, the car had turned and left. As the grey dawn slowly broke, the sentries were relieved, and Joly after steadily patrolling for hours stretched himself out on a hard store room floor. Just before he dropped to sleep, he realized that he was now a more contented man than he had been for weeks: 'The life of action is perhaps, after all, the happiest. I have been making a great mistake all along. That boyish instinct for the navy was perhaps the truest wisdom. But now it is too late a day. The present episode can only be a late farewell to what might have been. But let me sleep while I may.'

On Tuesday morning the garrison, which was growing in numbers, began to learn that war is largely a matter of waiting. It was decided to evacuate the O.T.C. headquarters and concentrate on the squares, and the stores were removed in carts. Riflemen placed on the west front covered the Bank of Ireland and Grafton Street and exchanged shots with insurgent snipers. The college kitchen started to function, the French chef producing tea and bully beef. A medical unit, staffed by members of the R.A.M.C., students, and teachers from the medical school, was established in Number 6 (later when it was felt that the sight of the wounded would affect the morale of the troops camping in college it was moved to Number 15). Throughout the week, stretcher bearers went out, frequently under fire, collecting casualties from the streets round college and carrying them to the dressing station for treatment. Their first call came early on Tuesday morning, when a Sinn Fein despatch rider was shot in the neighbourhood of the college. When the stretcher bearers went out he was found to be dead, and the provost's household was roused when the body was carried in and laid down in the hall. Later, Joly saw the body, and 'in no irreverent spirit lifted the face cloth. He looked quite young; one might almost call him a boy. The handsome waxen face was on one side concealed in blood. Poor boy, what crime was his?' Joly went on to deplore 'the insane wickedness and folly', as he saw it, which had caused this young Irishman's death.

At eleven o'clock the *Irish Times* reached the provost's house. It was not very informative. A column was devoted to Goldsmith and Ireland. The only Irish news given at length was the opening day of the Spring Show. And the viceregal proclamation printed in deep black, calling on 'loyal and law-abiding citizens' 'to abstain from any acts which might interfere with the action of the executive government' was only exasperating to unionists standing to arms (the same day a subsequent proclamation struck a more resounding note, calling on loyal subjects 'to aid in upholding and maintaining the peace of the realm').

Two important events were due to take place in Trinity on Tuesday morning, the nomination of candidates at a bye-election for the University constituency and the beginning of junior sophister term examinations. Campbell, one of the M.P.s for Trinity, as a result of sustained unionist pressure, had been appointed in April attorney-general for Ireland and of course had to submit himself for re-election. The date, 25 April, had been fixed as nomination day. At 11 a.m. Mahaffy, as returning officer, entered the Examination Theatre. Beare, the senior proctor, read the writ. Campbell was proposed by Louis Claude Purser and Sir William Moore, a distinguished Dublin medical man. There were no other candidates, the provost declared Campbell elected, and the successful candidate made a very brief speech of thanks. Mahaffy's historic sense must have been stirred to see the royal writ (executed by himself) running in such close proximity to rebellion. Meanwhile, at the dining hall a small group of junior sophisters, including four young women, who had dared flying bullets to get into college, were mustering for their examination. Mahaffy, finding no examiner present, took the examination himself and asked the women candidates to lunch. One of them who sat beside the provost, recalled that he 'told me about the flowers he had brought from Greece, made a few remarks about the people of the Northern Capital (Belfast) and bade me feed the dog who was looking appealingly at my piece of mutton'.

From morning the firing grew in volume as the military began to work towards the city centre. Shortly after midday the third reserve cavalry brigade (dismounted), which was establishing a line of posts from Kingsbridge, along Dame Street to College Green, made contact with Trinity. But it was not until the close of the afternoon that the inmates of the provost's house (by then including a honeymoon couple caught in the line of fire on their way home from Fairyhouse) heard the reassuring tramp of regulars on the march, and soon khaki-clad men were pouring through the front gate, and the Trinity garrison, though still responsible for posting sentries, could relax.

From then on for a week or so Trinity, bathed in brilliant spring weather, presented an extraordinary blend of a college and a camp. Masses of troops were based on the college. A battery of eighteen-pounders clattered over the cobbles, and on Thursday, when two of them began to shell Sackville Street, the provost's house shook to its solid foundations. Horses grazed in the college park, young soldiers exhausted by marching sprawled on the grass plots in the squares and to the shocked surprise of one observer even played football on the tennis courts. On Sunday, for the first time since at the latest the days of James II, mass was said in Trinity in a room in Mahaffy's old quarters, Number 1. The college servants gazed with awe at a turbaned Indian batman kindling his charcoal stove; the 'co-op', the college shop, did a roaring trade, but since, in the absence of its manager, it was run by the O.T.C., its accounts were soon in hopeless confusion. Dr Gwynn, the regius professor of Divinity, handsome and bearded, a patriarchal figure who remembered well '48 and '67 (and who was once mistaken for John O'Leary, the Fenian), 'took on a new lease of life' as he made his way amongst the skittish mules; Joly talked about life with the 'Tommies' and was delighted by their unaffectedness and their essential decency, and 'thanks to the plucky exertions of a messenger from the Junior Army and Navy stores in D'Olier Street', the high table was not reduced to 'ships' biscuit and bully beef, the universal ration elsewhere. The provost's house was a scene of continuous coming and going. Mahaffy entertained a succession of army officers to luncheon and dinner; Dr Gwynn, cut off from his home in Clontarf, and Professor Pope, a bachelor (long commemorated by a small flower bed in New Square, known as the Vatican Garden), came into meals. By Thursday, though fighting was still going on at different points in the city, the provost gave his usual Thursday 'undress dinner party'.

Undoubtedly many Dublin Unionists must have felt a touch of exhilaration at the close of the week. After all, they had shown they could rise to an emergency and stand fire for their principles. Those who, like Mahaffy, had a son in the fighting forces, must have felt a touch of comradeship with the men at the front. But they displayed little or no exultation. As Sir John Maxwell, who had been sent over during the rising to take command in Ireland, told the Trinity O.T.C. when he inspected it in May, there was 'no more distasteful thing to men than to be called on to quell civil disturbances'. *TCD* in an able editorial used almost the same words. 'To be called upon,' the editor wrote, 'to defend our university against the attack of Irishmen, to be forced in self-defence to shoot down our countrymen – these are things which even the knowledge of duty well fulfilled cannot render anything but sad and distasteful.' He went on to declare that 'it was a mere freak of circumstances that the defence of Trinity had such a bearing upon the safety of the rest of the city. It is rather to the deeds of her sons in Flanders and the Dardanelles that Trinity looks for enduring honour.' Mahaffy's similar views have already been quoted in chapter six.

Next year Mahaffy re-entered politics in a way which must have appealed to him, as a member of an assembly which it was hoped would manage to solve the Irish question, largely by discursive discussion. In the spring of 1917, with tension increasing in Ireland, the government summoned a convention of representative Irishmen, which it was hoped would arrive at a settlement between nationalists and unionists. The convention, which had a membership of about a hundred, included representatives of the northern unionists, the southern unionists, the Irish parliamentary party, the churches, the Irish peers, labour, the chambers of commerce, and local authorities. There were also fifteen members nominated by the government, and in this group of well-known Irishmen of widely varying views Mahaffy was included.[17]

The convention met in Trinity in the Regent House, a large room over the front gate, noted for its fine plaster work and bad acoustics. (The provost was pleased to have the expenses of its much-needed restoration borne by the British exchequer.) Mahaffy's voluminous convention notes, summaries of speeches interspersed with pungent comments scrawled in his bold hand, show that at eighty he took a conscientious and lively interest in the proceedings. Indeed, though he was probably the oldest member, he soon acquired the reputation of an *enfant terrible*. When he spoke for the first time on 25 August, he began by explaining that having been for most of his life a unionist, he had during the last twenty years 'quietly and silently . . . drifted over towards home rule'. This outline of his political progress was bound to annoy unionists. Nor could the grounds he gave for his gradual conversion have gratified the nationalists. He had, he explained, been driven towards accepting home rule by the culpable weakness of British politicians. Birrell, while drawing a large salary as chief secretary, had seen Ireland drifting into rebellion without raising a finger; his successor, Duke, had let loose on the country, ' a pack of condemned criminals' (the Sinn Feiners arrested after the rebellion) 'to begin again their nefarious practices'. Near the close of his speech, speaking as an historian, he issued an impressive warning. Referring to the view that all bodies of men were dominated by their own interests, he solemnly emphasized, 'there is another terrible factor in history – passion – which often has, and often will again dominate men in spite of their interests'. This warning he tried to reinforce with an epigram. 'Patriotism,' he remarked, 'has many curious analogies to alcohol. If taken neat it is a deadly poison.'

About a week later when the convention was about to hold a series of meetings in Belfast Mahaffy let it be known that he intended to introduce a plan for the future government of Ireland. On hearing this a leading northern unionist remarked to the chairman, 'For God's sake keep him till the last day, for it would play the mischief if it got out we were not serious on the first or second day.'[18] Mahaffy in fact expounded his solution for the Irish question on the third day. Ireland, he argued, should have a constitution on the Swiss model. There should be four provincial assemblies and a central parliament to which they would send representatives. The imperial government should, he thought, retain control of defence and to a great extent of taxation. Switzerland, he emphatically declared, was a good place to copy constitutionally. 'None of you,' he said, 'could deny that I am a genuine Irishman doing my best, and I venture to say not without some success, for the good of my country. Well, like the constitution I recommend you, I too was born in Switzerland and received there the beginnings of my education.'

Mahaffy continuously and emphatically dwelt on one feature of the situation, the necessity of providing the Irish protestants with adequate and reassuring safeguards. 'As long as Roman catholics and protestants exist in Ireland,' he explained, 'it marks and emphasises the contrast not only of two creeds, but two breeds, of two ways of thinking, of two ways of looking at all the most vital interests of men. The whole temper of the two is totally at variance – the one based on authority, the other on the right of private judgement.' If a man claimed to be able to separate his religion from his politics, it meant that 'his political aims will not stand the pure light of the moral law or the contrast of a holy life brought to bear on it'. Mahaffy frankly admitted that when the protestants were in the ascendancy they treated the catholics unfairly, and that what they now dreaded was the 'tit for tat policy', this 'so-called redressing of the balance which generally means to make good one injustice by doing another'. As an example of what the protestants were afraid of he referred to 'the making of the dying and impracticable Irish language or rather a smattering of it, of no value to anyone, a condition of County Council scholarships. Do you imagine it was done really from patriotism? Not a bit of it. It was done to exclude the protestant schools of the country from competition.'

To illustrate the strength of sectarian feeling Mahaffy told a couple of anecdotes.

A poor man in County Monaghan, an Orangeman, who was an old friend of mine, when I revisited him after a lapse of some years, seemed in very low spirits, and I asked him why. 'Oh the country has gone to the devil. Sure there are the papists beating drums on the hills [an old Orange privilege] and you daren't make them quit it.' 'Why not,' said I. 'Don't you know Sir, that if you shot a papist now, you'd be tried for it.'

On the other side, when Mahaffy remarked to a Roman catholic professor from Maynooth, who came from Clones in County Monaghan, 'There are many fine protestants in the town of Clones,' the Maynooth man replied, 'Out of hell you would not meet the like.' A fellow-member of the convention, Stephen Gwynn, a liberal-minded Irish protestant nationalist, was afraid Mahaffy's outspokenness might offend some of the catholics in his audience. Gwynn was reassured, however, by the comment, 'Sure it's only the provost, and nobody minds him.'[19]

In December 1917 Lord Midleton, the leader of the southern unionists, suggested as the basis of an agreed settlement a moderate home rule scheme, under which the control of customs duties would be reserved to the imperial parliament. Mahaffy strongly supported him. Replying to the argument that if Ireland were allowed to frame its own tariff policy it would be against its interests to injure Great Britain, he bluntly pointed out that to a nation intoxicated with patriotism every serious violation of their money interests is possible, 'even if it were to satisfy some utterly silly sentiment'. A couple of months later Mahaffy came to the fore by making a decisive, if in the opinion of some an inopportune, move. He had become convinced that the government's efforts to create an atmosphere in the country favourable to the convention by refraining from interference with the extreme nationalists was arousing 'anxiety and alarm among the loyal minority' and 'jubilation among the herd of disloyal and rebellious people'. It seemed clear to Mahaffy that 'between confident ignorance, over-scrupulous indecision, silly indolence and placid acquiescence' they were sliding towards a precipice, and that it was urgently necessary that a new Irish administration, determined to restore law and order, should be appointed.

On 26 February, just before the convention embarked on a momentous discussion of a letter from the Prime Minister suggesting terms on which an agreement might be based, the provost rose and proposed a motion to the effect that the convention would not consider the Prime Minister's proposals until it received an assurance from the government that effective steps would be taken to restore law and order. An animated debate followed. In the end Mahaffy was defeated by 50 to 33. It was the first division that had been taken during the convention's proceedings, and it was noted that the convention divided on party lines, the unionists forming the minority. Mahaffy and the thirty-two who supported him transmitted to the Prime Minister a memorial on the state of the country. Lloyd George in reply assured Mahaffy that the government was determined to take all the necessary steps for dealing with disorder in Ireland and that, in his opinion, 'neither the task of the government nor that of the convention would be made easier by the publication of the memorial at the present time'.[20]

Until the close of the convention Mahaffy remained an unabashed independent. On the whole he supported in detail the very limited home rule scheme which the centre bloc in the convention carried by a narrow majority against the opposition of the more extreme constitutional nationalists and the Ulster unionists. He was more sympathetic than the southern unionists to the Ulster claim to authority; on the other hand he did not agree with the Ulster unionists' demand that their province should be excluded from the jurisdiction of the Irish parliament. And unlike the nationalists he believed that large powers ought to be reserved to the imperial parliament. At the very end of the convention's labours, Mahaffy and the Church of Ireland Archbishop of Armagh added to its report a short note in which they suggested the solution of the Irish problem was to be found in a federal scheme on the Swiss or Canadian model. They could not, they declared in sentences which bear Mahaffy's hall mark, vote for the scheme accepted by the majority of the convention, because it involved 'either of two alternatives. The coercion of Ulster, which is unthinkable, or the partition of Ireland, which would be disastrous.'

Mahaffy was undoubtedly an outstanding member of the convention, conspicuous for his oratorical powers, his intellectual audacity and his geniality together with the sheer force of his presence. Nevertheless, it must be said that his individualism and idiosyncrasies prevented him from possessing the weight equivalent to his abilities. However, he himself was highly satisfied with his achievements. 'The dragons' teeth I sowed in the convention are bearing fruit,' he wrote in November 1918. 'Stephen Gwynn is an acknowledged convert to me and the Swiss system, and Carson writes in a letter to the papers that it was my conduct at the convention that mainly determined him to abandon his seat here. So after all my *vox clamantis in deserto* is still not dead, in spite of my being in my second childhood.'[21]

Gwynn had just stated in his election address to the Trinity constituency that he had been 'driven by the logic of facts' to adopt the policy proposed by the provost. Carson had also acknowledged the provost's influence on his outlook. He had decided not to stand for Trinity, which he had represented for twenty-six years, at the general election of December 1918, on the grounds that since the convention had brought to the surface 'differences between northern and southern unionist', it was better that the university should be represented by a member not so closely identified with the Ulster standpoint. Mahaffy was annoyed by Carson's decision, which precipitated a contest in the university constituency, and complained that Carson had given insufficient notice of his intention. Carson in his reply asserted that the provost's behaviour in the convention was one of the 'chief elements' which impelled him to withdraw from Trinity. Mahaffy reserved his reply until, as polling officer, he announced the result of the Trinity contest. Having complimented all the candidates and having paid a tribute to Clements, an eighteenth-century M.P. for the university who had secured for Trinity lavish building grants, he went on to admit that he was accused of marring the convention. He protested that if he had been guilty of any misconduct it was of being fast asleep during a long part of the discussions, and that when he did intervene his aim was 'to keep the convention in good humour and to prevent the various parties from falling into each other's wools'. And he regretted that Carson had 'bartered his high and important seat as representative of this great university for a very new constituency in the slums of Belfast'.[22]

At the general election of 1918 Mahaffy was not only returning officer for Trinity, but as high sheriff of County Monaghan, he was the returning officer for that county. A deputation of Sinn Feiners from Monaghan called on him in Dublin and requested that he should allow the Sinn Feiners to mount guard over the ballot boxes, 'because they mistrusted the police'. Mahaffy thanked the deputation for making its request in an orderly way and told them 'that the court house was my property for the year and that I was quite content with the police whom I trusted and could get soldiers to reinforce them'. When the deputation pointed out that in other counties similar requests had been granted, Mahaffy retorted that 'it was not his business to criticise the conduct of other high sheriffs. It was his business to govern his own county as well as he could.' 'Luckily,' he reflected when writing to an old friend, 'I am not on the spot but issue my orders from this safe place. After all Ireland is a place really worth living in. There is always some new villainy cropping up.'[23]

Early in 1918 Mahaffy had entered into his eightieth year, but as his political activities show he was still remarkably vigorous, intellectually and physically. In June he received an honour which greatly gratified him, the Grand Cross of the newly-founded Order of the British Empire. Mahaffy believed that his friend Lord French, the recently appointed viceroy, had recommended that he should be given the O.M., but that the King himself had preferred the Grand Cross. So on 8 September at the viceregal lodge, before dinner, in the midst of a small circle, the lord lieutenant, 'conferred the honour of knighthood on the Rev. John Mahaffy . . . and invested him with the insignia of a Knight Grand Cross of the Most Excellent Order of the British Empire'. This formal official announcement is somewhat startling because it has always been held that a man in holy orders cannot be dubbed a knight. But French was a bluff soldier and Mahaffy an unclerical clergyman, and between them, carelessly or deliberately, they broke with tradition. Certainly Mahaffy was extremely pleased with his new status, explaining to a friend that 'I won't be called Sir John but Sir Provost of Trinity.'[24]

Some months later at the end of the year he published his last book, a work on the college plate, in which he displays his life-long readiness to grapple with a new and intricate subject. The book is based on a catalogue of the plate, compiled by Dudley Westropp, an assistant keeper in the National Museum. Though Mahaffy acknowledges that Westropp was 'a seasoned expert', he trenchantly corrects what he considers mistakes in the catalogue and boldly advances an ingenious theory (which Westropp summarily dismissed) to explain discrepancies between the hallmark and the date of certain pieces.

As 1918 drew towards its tumultuous close with peace now restored he was able to look forward to a revival of college life.

He entertained the lord lieutenant to dinner, and French declared he had seen nothing like it since before the war.[25] Early in 1919 he set to work to push through the board a reform of the tutorial system and he began to consider plans for a war memorial worthy of the college – what he had in mind was to erect in the front square a replica of the Nike of Samothrace.[26] And he set to work to write for his family a summary of his life.

In this terse but revealing document, which he finished at the end of February 1919, Mahaffy surveys his career with remarkable detachment. Always interested in the relations of the individual to his environment, he comments in passing on the influence of a number of factors – his family, evangelicalism, class consciousness, the university, literary ambition. Taking his life as a whole, he sees himself as a successful and to a great extent a fortunate man. His happiness is only seriously qualified in one respect: his feelings towards the college in which he had spent over sixty years are clearly ambivalent. He is proud of the great foundation of which he had become a most distinguished member. But in Trinity he had met with snubs and setbacks. As an undergraduate he had been disappointed by the teaching; as a don he had found his colleagues unappreciative. Significantly enough he does not refer to his failure to attain the provostship in 1904. But in other ways life had treated him well. Parents, wife and children had given him in abundant measure the family care and affection he always craved for. From boyhood he had been intellectually active and ambitious, and his ambitions had been realized. Even his detractors would have to admit his achievement. He had travelled, seen men and cities, made many good friends, and thoroughly enjoyed the sports in which he excelled.

His good fortune continued to the end. He was spared a long irksome decline. On 17 April he had a stroke. He lingered for only a fortnight and on the morning of 30 April, quietly and painlessly, he died. His funeral, conducted with full academic ceremonial, was attended by a vast crowd drawn from many sections of Irish life. One of the first telegrams of condolence was from Windsor, expressing the King's sympathy. By Mahaffy's express desire the college chapel was not draped in black. After the service, at which some of his own music was played, the long *cortège* followed the road that he himself had so often travelled between his country home and his college. He was laid to rest in a grave beside his wife's in the ancient churchyard of St Fintan, where the Hill of Howth slopes westwards towards Ireland's unquiet metropolis and the distant mountains.

Notes and references

Chapter one

1 A. B. Granville, *The spas of Germany*, 1837, pp. 282–307; *Murray's Handbook for Travellers in Southern Germany*, 1843, pp. 78–80.
2 A. B. Granville, *Kissingen: its sources and resources*, 1846, pp. 151, 155–6.
3 *Annual Register 1848*, p. 359.
4 G. F. Black, *The surnames of Scotland*, New York, 1946.
5 *The Parliamentary Gazetteer of Ireland*, Dublin, 1845, ii, 796.
6 Salmon to Bernard, 22 July 1902 (Salmon letters).
7 E. Somerville and M. Ross, *The real Charlotte*, London, 1894, chapter I.
8 *Correspondence relative to the Warden of St. Columba's College*, 2nd edition, 1853.
9 R. Whately, *Miscellaneous essays and reviews*, London, 1861, pp. 85–6.
10 W. E. H. Lecky, *Historical and political essays*, London, 1908, p. 93.
11 M. D. Petre, *Autobiography and life of George Tyrrell*, London, 1912, i, 97–8.
12 *Hibbert Journal*, i, 198.
13 *Irish Digest*, July 1939; *T.C.D.*, 18 March 1914.
14 *Irish Times*, 18 February 1896.
15 J. G. Swift MacNeill, *What I have seen and heard*, London, 1925, p. 61.
16 *Daily Express*, 19 December 1887.
17 W. E. H. Lecky, *Historical and political essays*, London, 1908, pp. 82–94; 'Early recollections of Mr. Lecky', by a college friend, in *National Review*, xliii, 108–22.
18 *The idler in college, or the student's guide*, Dublin, 1850, pp. 36–7.
19 *Freeman's Journal*, 22 November 1895.
20 *Saunders News Letter*, 24 November 1858.
21 Memorandum for the Board, 1907.

22 *Royal commission on the civil service, second appendix to fourth report, minutes of evidence*, p. 254, H.C. 1914 Cd (7340), xvi.
23 J. Ross, *The Years of my pilgrimage*, London, 1924, p. 185.

Chapter two

1 *Dublin university commission: report . . . with minutes of evidence . . .* , p. 37, H.C. 1878 [c. 2045], xxix.
2 *Ibid.*, p. 32.
3 J. P. Mahaffy to A. Macmillan [1886], [1876], II Ap 1882 'Add. MS. 55118.'
4 J. G. Swift MacNeill, *What I have seen and heard*, London, 1925, p. 57.
5 *Royal commission Trinity College, Dublin and the University of Dublin . . . appendix to the final report:* minutes of evidence; p. 173, H.C. 1907 Cd. (3312), xii.
6 'The tercentenary festival at Leyden' in *MM*, xxxi, 516–21.
7 *Letters of John Richard Green*, ed. L. Stephen, London, 1901, pp. 414, 416.
8 *The Letters of Oscar Wilde*, ed. R. Hart-Davis, 1962, pp. 7–10.
9 *A survey of Greek civilization*, p. 147, and *What have the Greeks done for modern civilization?* p. 109.
10 For this visit to Greece see *Rambles and Studies in Greece*, 1876. See additional note below.
11 *Greek pictures*, 1890, p. 70
12 Hart-Davis, op. cit., pp. 23, 25.
13 *Ibid.*, pp. 34–5.
14 Letters from Mahaffy to Mrs Mahaffy in Leslie papers.
15 Hart-Davies, op. cit. in note 8 above, p. 36.
16 Salmon to Bernard 1899, 15 July 1899 (Salmon papers).
17 *American Journal of Philology*, xl, 446–8.
18 J. P. Mahaffy to John Bright, 7 December 1880 (with Mahaffy memoir).
19 *Dublin Evening Mail*, 4, 17, 18 November 1868.
20 *Irish Times*, 12 May 1882.
21 Mahaffy's report is printed in *Endowed Schools, Ireland, Commission report*, Vol. I, p. 62, H. C. 1881 [c. 2831].
22 Mahaffy expressed his views on education in articles in *MM*, I, 355–62, and *NC*, xxxiii, 19–35, and xxxiv, 212–29.
23 *Royal Commission on the Civil service, second appendix to fourth report, minutes of evidence*, p. 253, H.C. 1914, Cd. 7340.
24 For the tercentenary celebrations see *Records of the tercentarian festival of the university of Dublin held 5th to 8th July 1892*, Dublin, 1894.
25 *The Dublin Figaro*, 27 February 1892, p. 20.

Additional note: We are grateful to the Royal Greek Embassy, London, for confirming that the Golden Cross of the royal Order of the

Redeemer was conferred on Mahaffy on 15 February 1877, 'for his philhellenic feelings'.

Chapter three

1   Leslie papers. There is a letter from C. V. Stanford (5 April 1917) in the T.C.D. papers replying forcefully to a criticism by Mahaffy. There are also letters to Mahaffy in the same collection from Prout, Richter and Oakley.

2   The T.C.D. papers contain a letter from R. W. Church, Dean of St Paul's (28 January 1876) congratulating Mahaffy on his setting of these canticles as sung in St Paul's on St Paul's day. The Dublin University Choral Society has a copy of the orchestral setting of Mahaffy's quartet; the library of the College Chapel, copies of his *Amen*; and the Professor of Music copies of his Grace (which is still sometimes sung at College dinners).

3   The whole incident is well documented in the minutes of the D.U. Choral Society.

4   Professor J. R. H. Weaver in the Leslie papers.

5   *What have the Greeks . . . ?*, p. 142.

6   Starkie, *Scholars*, p. 56.

7   Starkie, *Scholars*, p. 63. Mahaffy gave a lecture on 'The immorality of music' in Newcastle upon Tyne in 1888 (Mahaffy to G. Macmillan, 1888). See also *What have the Greeks . . . ?*, pp. 133–46.

8   Quoted by Lord Rathconnell, *Memories of a long life*, London, 1931, p. 47.

9   Mahaffy to Wilson King, 13 September 1882.

10 Hone, *Cricket*, to which we are indebted for much of the material used in the paragraphs on Mahaffy as a cricketer.

11 See Lord Frederic Hamilton, *The days before yesterday*, London, 1920, p. 120: other versions in Hone, *Cricket*, p. 54; Starkie, *Scholars*, pp. 98.

Chapter four

1   Frank Harris, *Oscar Wilde*, London, 1938, p. 29.

2   Gogarty, *Tumbling*, p. 220.

3   *Twelve lectures*, p. 2.

4   Flinders Petrie, *Seventy years in archaeology*, London, 1931, p. 144.

5   Quoted by H. H. Henson, *Retrospect of an unimportant life*, Oxford, 1943, ii, 346.

6   *Art of conversation*, p. 95.

7   Gogarty, *Tumbling*, p. 200.

8   Starkie, *Scholars*, p. 101.

9   Augustus John, *Chiaroscuro*, London, 1952, p. 101

10 Rogers, p. 514.

11 *H.*, xlii, 1920, p. vii.

12 R. M. Gwynn, F.T.C.D.
13 According to Gogarty (*As I . . .*, p. 32, and *Intimations*, p. 49) Mahaffy used deliberately to practise *eutrapelia*, which Aristotle (*Rhetoric* 2, 12, 16) defined as 'educated arrogance'.
14 Cited by A. S. Hunt in his obituary of Mahaffy, *Aegyptus*, i, 2, 1920, 217–21.
15 Leslie papers. A similar remark is attributed to Father Healy.
16 Leslie papers.
17 G. B. Grundy, *Fifty years at Oxford*, London, 1945, p. 202.
18 Leslie papers.
19 Leslie papers. See *Epoch 13* for the source of the story.
20 Ramsey Colles, *In castle and court house*, London, 1911, pp. 85–6.
21 *Art of Conversation*, p. 148.
22 The titular bishop of Canea at that time was Dr Nicholas Donnelly.
23 Goligher gives a different version in which the lunatic thought that she, not Mahaffy, was God.
24 See, e.g. Gogarty, *Intimations*, pp. 49ff.; Starkie, *Scholars*, p. 101.
25 *Social Life*, p. 329.
26 Hart-Davis, *The Letters of Oscar Wilde*, p. 187.
27 T.C.D. papers.
28 Hart-Davis, *The Letters of Oscar Wilde*, p. 338, thinks the play in question was *A woman of no importance*.
29 *Ibid.*
30 Leslie papers.
31 See also *The Speaker*, 4 March 1905, p. 543, and Tyrrell's introduction to Calverley's translation of *The Idylls of Theocritus*.
32 J. H. Shaw, then assistant registrar in T.C.D.
33 See report in *The Times*, 2 October 1897, and the letters in the issues for 6, 9, 12 October 1897.
34 Gerald Griffin, *The wild geese*, p. 68 (see also note 15 to Chap. 6). The remark sounds more like Tyrrell than Mahaffy.
35 Frank Harris, *Oscar Wilde*, p. 29.

Chapter five

1 Hesketh Pearson, *Life of Oscar Wilde*, 1960 edn., p. 30.
2 *Progress*, p. 54.
3 See *Retrospect* by the Marchioness of Londonderry, London, 1938, p. 191.
4 See letters from Wolseley and Saxe-Weimar on the T.C.D. papers, for this and the following paragraph.
5 Leslie papers.
6 T.C.D. papers.
7 *Greek world*, p. 251.
8 *What have the Greeks . . . ?*, p. 111.
9 Letter to Wilson King, 15 December 1886 (Leslie papers).
10 Mahaffy to G. Macmillan, 18 July 1894.

11   Mahaffy to G. Macmillan, 2 November 1910.
12   *T.C.D.*, 14 February 1903.
13   Starkie, *Scholars*, pp. 98–9.
14   MacNeill, *What I* . . . , p. 57.
15   Letter, 30 June 1887 in T.C.D. papers.
16   Letter from Mahaffy, 27 August 1918: see *The Times*, 6, 8, 9 May 1919.
17   Leslie papers: other versions in Leslie, *Doomsland*, p. 146, Starkie, *Scholars*, p. 99 and oral tradition. The original remark about the uses of the languages mentioned is attributed to the Emperor Charles V.
18   Sayce, *Reminiscences*, pp. 157–8. Some further glimpses of Mahaffy in Dublin society during the 1890s may be found in *Irish Life*, Dublin, from 20 February 1892 (title changed to *The Dublin Figaro*, 27 February 1892), e.g. vol. i, 20, 40, 130, 337.
19   Personal information from Mrs G. Waterhouse.
20   Starkie, *Scholars*, p. 100; George Moore in *The Leader*, 20 July 1901.
21   Leslie papers.
22   Personal information from the late Mr Duffy of Dalkey.
23   Harold Nicholson, *Good behaviour*, London, 1955, pp. 281–3.
24   *Art of conversation*, pp. 123–29.

Chapter six

1   Quoted by Dominic O'Riordan in *The Irish Times*, 27 May 1967.
2   *Appendix to the final report of the Intermediate education (Ireland) commission*, 1899, part 1, pp. 31–43. Douglas Hyde's reply is in the same volume.
3   'Education in Hungary', *Ath.*, 1882.
4   'Recent fuss . . .', *NC*, 1899.
5   Quoted by George Russell (AE) in *Ideals in Ireland*, edited by Lady Gregory, London, 1901.
6   Gogarty, *As I* . . . , p. 31.
7   George Russell as cited in note 5 above.
8   *New Ireland Review*, xii, 1899, 196ff.
9   See further in David Greene, 'Robert Atkinson and Irish studies', *H.*, cii, 1966, 6–15.
10   'The modern Babel', *NC*, 1896.
11   'How to circumvent . . .', *NC*, 1898.
12   'Recent fuss . . .', *NC*, 1899.
13   See Diarmid O Cobhthaigh, *Douglas Hyde*, Dublin, 1917, pp. 113–14.
14   *The Leader*, Dublin, 20 July 1901; cf. letter of W. B. Yeats of 16 July 1901 in *The letters of W. B. Yeats*, ed. Allan Wade, London, 1954.
15   So far as we can find Gerald Griffin's *The wild geese*, London, 1938, p. 23, is the only source for the alleged remark by Mahaffy, 'Joyce and Moore have one thing in common—a flair for latrine humour. Thank God they have both cleared out of Dublin, but not before they had squirted stink like a pair of skunks on all decent people with whom they came in contact. It's an ill bird that fouls its own nest. James

Joyce is a living argument that it was a mistake to establish a separate university for the aborigines of this island—for the corner-boys who spit in the Liffey.' We doubt the authenticity of this because we have not seen other examples of similarly phrased vituperation from Mahaffy, nor have we seen evidence that Mahaffy was interested at all in James Joyce (who was little known outside a small circle in Dublin until after Mahaffy's death). Further, Joyce in fact, was not a student of the National University whose foundation Mahaffy opposed. Also, the term 'latrine humour' is scarcely apt as a description of Moore's work (as distinct from Joyce with his early *Chamber music*). Griffin has also a good deal to say about Mahaffy in his fanciful study of Irishmen, *The dead march past*, London, 1937, but nothing that adds significantly to previously known information about him.

16 'Recent fuss . . .', *NC*, 1899.
17 Op. cit. in note 13 above, p. 114.
18 See Hyde's autobiographical *Mise agus an Connradh*, Dublin, 1937, on the pages cited at *Mahaffy* in the index.
19 Gwynn, *Saints*, p. 144.
20 *Salve*, p. 83. According to the *Life of George Moore*, London, 1936, by J. M. Hone (a cousin of Mahaffy's), p. 23, when Moore was told (quite unreliably) that his attack on Mahaffy may have injured Mahaffy's chance of being elected provost of T.C.D. he was 'filled with horror'. Hone thinks that Moore originally met Mahaffy at Gosse's house in London.
21 Berg collection, New York Public Library (by permission).
22 Starkie, *Scholars*, p. 121.
23 See Philip Edwards, 'Yeats and the Trinity chair', *H.*, i, 1965, 5–11.
24 *Letters*, ed. Wade, 1954, p. 560.
25 See the foreword to *A tribute to Thomas Davis* by W. B. Yeats, ed. by Denis Gwynn, Oxford, 1947. Cf. the caricature facing p. 225 above.
26 See *The Irish Times*, 27 May 1867 and 28 May 1867.
27 *Rambles*, p. 114.
28 *Social Life*, pp. 90–1.
29 'The humanity of the Greeks'.
30 Recent fuss . . .', *NC*, 1899.
31 *Social life*, p. 351.
32 *Epoch*, p. ix.
33 *Social life*, p. 109.
34 'Irish landlords', *Cont.R.*, 1882.
35 John Butler Yeats, *Early memories*, Dublin, 1923, p. 88.
36 *Epoch*, p. 323.
37 *Twelve lectures*, p. 9.
38 Report in *Ath.*, 5 December 1914.
39 Introduction by Mahaffy (p. xv) to Murray's *Revolutionary Ireland*.
40 'What is a nation?', 1893, p. 361.
41 Leslie papers. Cf. Mary Colum, *Life and the dream*, p. 286.
42 Quoted by Ulick O'Connor, *Gogarty*, p. 206.
43 Leslie papers.

Chapter seven

1   Gogarty, *Tumbling*, p. 203; Starkie, *Scholars*, p. 97.
2   Matthias Bodkin, *The port of tears: the life of Father John Sullivan, S.J.*, Dublin, 1954, p. 20.
3   T. P. O'Connor, *Daily Telegraph*, 2 May 1919.
4   Goligher memoir.
5   Starkie, *Scholars*, p. 97.
6   Leslie papers.
7   *Prolegomena*, pp. 416–17.
8   *Social life*, p. 8.
9   Mahaffy to G. Macmillan, 19 November 1881.
10 Gogarty, *Intimations*, p. 49. N. J. D. White, in *Some recollections of Trinity College, Dublin*, Dublin, 1935, pp. 22–3, refers to a sermon in the College Chapel which was 'in effect a public recantation' but gives no date. He says that in this sermon Mahaffy warned any sceptics that might be in his audience 'not to nail their false colours to the mast'.
11 *Decay*, pp. 24–5. This book was based on lectures given to the Midland Institute of Birmingham on 17 and 24 March 1882.
12 Leslie papers.
13 Arthur Barton's memoir in the Leslie papers.
14 *Plate*, pp. 47–8.
15 *Report of the Commission on Irish University Education*, 1901, i, 215.
16 *What have the Greeks . . . ?*, p. 20.
17 *The Chautauquan*, 1889, ix, 384.
18 *Epoch*, p. 44.
19 *Epoch*, p. 47.
20 Mahaffy to Wilson King, 15 December 1886. There are four letters from Archbishop Walsh to Mahaffy in the T.C.D. papers.
21 Mahaffy to John Bright, 17 December 1897.
22 Leslie papers. Cf. Augustus Hare, *The story of my life*, London, 1896, ii, 233.
23 Mahaffy to John Knott, 5 February 1913, in the Leslie papers. Cf. Mahaffy's introduction to Landor's *Imaginary conversations*.
24 Mahaffy to Lady Leslie, 6 January 1916, the Leslie papers.
25 *Ad clerum*, pp. 178–85.
26 Mahaffy to Lady Woods from a transcript supplied by her daughter, Mrs Gilbert Waterhouse.
27 In the Leslie papers.
28 Arnold Harvey, *The Irish Times*, 9 June 1961.
29 Information supplied to the authors by Bishop de Pauley.
30 MacNeill, *What I . . .* , p. 56.
31 Letter from Jane Barlow in the T.C.D. papers. Mahaffy's ghost was reputed to haunt Earlscliff (information from Mrs Sheelagh Harbison).
32 *Survey*, p. iv.
33 *Social Life*, p. 342.

Additional notes: some further views of Mahaffy on religion will be found in his review of *John Inglesant* in *Hibernia*, 1 April 1882. For a defence of Mahaffy's religious sincerity and of his motives in becoming ordained see the letter of his junior colleague, the Rev. R. M. Gwynn, F.T.C.D., in the *Evening Mail*, Dublin, 25 January 1956, in reply to an anonymous attack on Mahaffy in the same newspaper, 23 January.

Chapter eight

1   Preface to *Greek life*, 2nd edn. Cf. *MM* 1876 for an earlier self-defence.
2   *AJP*, ix, 1888, 255. Gildersleeve, the rising star of American classical scholarship, may have been piqued by Mahaffy's rather cavalier treatment of him as a visitor to Dublin (as described in chap. three) and by Mahaffy's disparagements of Pindar (a favourite of Gildersleeve's) in his *History of Greek literature*: see *AJP*, xxvii, 1906, 483.
3   *Ac.*, 16 January 1875.
4   *Summary*, cf. *Plate*, p. vi.
5   Mahaffy to George Macmillan, 1874.
6   *Problems*, p. 13: censured by a reviewer in *CR*, vi, 1892, 361.
7   *Survey*, p. iii.
8   *CR*, v, 1891, 186.
9   Evidence for Mahaffy's care in correcting mistakes can be seen in his master-copy of the first edition of his *History of Greek literature*. He has corrected over 40 slips in the Greek and has moderated many sweeping statements (e.g. by substituting 'in many respects' for 'the whole tone of', and 'excels' for 'far exceeds'). He has also reduced the frequency of 'I' by substituting phrases like 'it seems' and 'no doubt' for 'I think' (thereby at times making the assertions in fact more absolute).
10   Mahaffy to G. Macmillan, 1887.
11   Letter from Acton, 14 March 1897, in T.C.D. papers. Mahaffy agreed to supply the required 'purple patch', but after Acton's death (a record of the agreement was found among Acton's papers) he was asked by the succeeding editors to release them from the commitment, and did so (according to his son, R. P. Mahaffy, cited in the Leslie papers).
12   Humphrey Ward, *A history of the Athenaeum 1824–1925*, London, 1926, pp. 87, 271–2.
13   Cited by Gwynn, *Saints*, p. 142.
14   *Ac.*, 29 September 1896, cf. *Ath.*, 15 July 1911.
15   *Problems*, pp. 140–1.
16   Preface to *Greek life*, 2nd edn., 1896.
17   T. P. O'Connor in *Daily Telegraph*, 2 May 1919.
18   Obituary in *Irish Times*, 2 May 1919: 'He was not merely indifferent to public opinion: a streak of impishness made him, perhaps, too fond of challenging it.'
19   *AJP*, xiii, 1892, 383.
20   *Rambles*, 2nd edn., p. 192, note I.
21   *History of Greek Literature*, 5th edn., 1916, ii, I, p. 176.
22   *Greek world*, p. xii.
23   *Rambles*, 5th edn., p. ix.

24 'Finlay's love of large principles and his dislike of long and minute difficulties . . . made him somewhat careless of smaller points . . .': Mahaffy in *Cont.R.*, 1878.
25 Review of *Rambles* in *The Nation*, 19 April 1877.
26 *History of Greek literature*, 1908 edn., p. ix.
27 T. P. O'Connor in *Daily Telegraph*, 2 May 1919.
28 Goligher.
29 Mill to Mahaffy, 26 October 1867, T.C.D. papers. For fairly favourable reviews of Mahaffy's books on Kant see *Ac.*, 15 September 1872 (Henry Sidgwick) and *Ac.*, 18 July 1874 (Edward Caird). Mahaffy wrote to thank Sidgwick for the former on 18 September 1872, adding, 'I am just going off to shoot partridges and have no time to weigh your criticisms and emendations . . .' (Sidgwick papers).
30 The work was continued in collaboration with his young colleague J. H. Bernard (then a fellow of T.C.D., later Archbishop of Dublin and Provost of T.C.D.) in 1889 (*Kant's critical philosophy for English readers*, 2 vols).
31 *Plate*, p. 48.
32 *Prolegomena*, p. 25.
33 *Ac.*, 15 December 1871.
34 Sayce, *Reminiscences*, p. 126.
35 *Spectator*, 3 April 1874.
36 Mahaffy to Wilson King, 8 September 1885.
37 Leslie says that J. E. C. Bodley commented on Wilde's 'chaffable innocence' when he came to Oxford. Cf. Leslie's Memoir of *J. E. C. Bodley*, London, 1930, p. 18. Cf. p. 39 of the present work.
38 For the biographical references to Jebb here and in what follows see Caroline Jebb's *Life and letters of Sir Richard Claverhouse Jebb*, Cambridge, 1907, pp. 8ff., 14, 196–8; and Mary Reed Bobbitt, *With dearest love to all: the life and letters of Lady Jebb*, London, 1960, p. 104.
39 Mahaffy to George Macmillan, 4 May 1886.
40 For the correspondence between Jebb and Alexander Macmillan see *Letters to Macmillan* by Simon Nowell-Smith, London, 1967; and the Macmillan papers in the British Museum.
41 Mahaffy to Grove (Macmillan papers).
42 For the continuation of the Mahaffy-Jebb controversy see *JHS*, ii-iv, 1881–3 (Jebb, Mahaffy and Sayce); *Ac.*, 1882, 5 August (Monro); 21 October (Mahaffy); 18 November (Sayce); 9 December (Goodwin); 16 December (Mahaffy on Monro's *Homeric grammar*); 23 December (Monro's reply). See also *Ath.*, 4 and 11 September 1880.
43 Mahaffy to Wilson King, 8 September 1885.
44 Letter in Library of Trinity College, Cambridge.
45 Ward (as cited in note 12 above), p. 87.
46 Cited by R. St John Parry, *Henry Jackson: a memoir*, Cambridge, 1926, p. 168. Parry quotes Jackson as saying, 'I am heretical: I like and believe in Mahaffy. At Cambridge I dare not say so . . . '
47 *English Illustrated*, 1884.
48 Mahaffy to Wilson King, 19 November 1881.

49 Mahaffy to Wilson King, 31 May 1880.
50 Mahaffy to Grove, 30 November 1878 (Macmillan papers). For Browning's consent see *Letters of Robert Browning*, ed. Thurman L. Hood, London, 1933, p. 198.
51 Karl Sittl, *Berliner philologische Wochenschrift*, 24 January 1891, pp. 113–14. For other reviews of works by Mahaffy in that journal see the issues for 6 June 1891, 24 April 1897, 22 June 1906.
52 *Ath.*, 9 November 1889. For Mahaffy's account of the Leyden celebrations see p. 30 above.
53 On the value of Mahaffy's article on the Olympic register see, e.g., Bursian's *Jahresbericht*, 172, p. 67.
54 *Plate*, p. vi.
55 In the note on *Hippolytus*, 291, the aorist of a Greek verb meaning 'to follow' is misconstrued as if from a verb meaning 'to say', (εἰπόμην as if from λέγω).
56 E.g. Gildersleeve in *AJP*, xi, 1890, 520.
57 Leslie papers.
58 For the Paley controversy see *MM*, xxxix, 1879, 314–25, 411–18, 524–9, and F. A. Paley, *Remarks on Prof. Mahaffy's account of the rise and progress of epic poetry*, London, 1881.
59 For Sayce *versus* Jebb see *Ac.*, xxv, 1884, 315, 331–2, 351–2, 368, 387, 404.
60 Mahaffy to George Macmillan, 6 February 1884.
61 Mahaffy to Wilson King, 13 September 1882.
62 Mahaffy to Wilson King, 15 December 1895.

Chapter nine

1 The pre-title page of *Greek life* (2nd edn.) has the heading 'The Social life of the Greeks II': see also preface to that edn.
2 *Greek life*, 2nd edn., p. ix.
3 Preface to *Empire of the Ptolemies*.
4 Evidence for Mahaffy's lack of sympathy with the frugality of the Periclean era is found in his emendation to change the remark in the Funeral Speech (Thucydides 2, 40) from 'we are lovers of beauty with frugality (μετ'εὐτελείας), to '. . . with good repute (μετ'εὐκλείας). Cf. *Plate*, p. vi.
5 In the following assessment of Mahaffy as a Hellenistic historian the authors are indebted to Mr Peter Fraser for advice.
6 Edwyn Bevan, *History of Egypt under the Ptolemaic Dynasty*, London, 1927, pp. vii–viii.
7 *REG*, v, 1892, 138. Cf. *REG* ix, 1896, 243.
8 *CR*, x, 1906, 472.
9 See p. 111 above.
10 *Survey*, pp. 91–92.
11 Letter of George Wyndham, 20 January 1888, cited in the Leslie papers.

12   *Problems*, p. 197.

13   Introduction to Duruy's *History of Greece*, i, 8–9. This introduction contains a trenchant critique by Mahaffy of his historical predecessors, ancient and modern, and some vigorous reaffirmations of his own favourite opinions.

14   R. W. Macan, *CR*, vi, 1892, 361–3.

15   T.C.D. papers.

16   Sayce, *Reminiscences*, p. 279.

17   Sayce, *Reminiscences*, p. 279. Mahaffy's usual good luck had already prepared him for this recognition of the *Antiope* fragment: he had studied the pre-existing fragments for the second edn. of his *Rambles*, and also in 1885 Charles Graves (Bishop of Limerick, formerly a fellow of T.C.D.) had discussed the name *Antiope* in an article on two fragments of papyri, bought by him at Luxor, in *H.*, xi, 243. Sir J. Gardner Wilkinson had presented a copy of his *Fragments of the hieratic papyrus at Turin* to the T.C.D. library in 1852.

18   *H.*, xvii, 1891, 38–51. In this article Mahaffy acknowledged help from the German scholar Weil, and two of his younger colleagues in T.C.D., J. B. Bury and W. J. M. Starkie. In a following article (*ibid.*, pp. 310–21) he also mentions Gomperz, Blass and Diels. In vol. i of *The Flinders Petrie papyri* he adds Wilamowitz, R. Ellis and G. Rutherford.

19   *MM*, xxxix, 1879.

20   *Flinders Petrie papyri*, ii, 1. Cf. Wilamowitz as cited in note 30 below.

21   See Bibliography C for 1890–8.

22   Cited by A. S. Hunt in his obituary of Mahaffy, *Aegyptus*, i, 2, 1920, 217–21.

23   The authors are indebted to Professor E. G. Turner for advice on the value of Mahaffy's work as a papyrologist.

24   See, e.g., Hermann Usener in *Nachrichten v.d. K. Gesellschaft der Wissenschaften . . . zu Göttingen*, 1892, pp. 25ff.

25   *AJP*, xiii, 1892, 383.

26   *Loc. cit.* in note 22 above.

27   *Survey*, pp. 178–9.

28   See *A page of Irish history: Story of University College, Dublin*, compiled by Fathers of the Society of Jesus, Dublin, 1930, pp. 198–203.

29   See Bibliography C for 1916, 1917.

30   Schliemann's opinion is expressed in the letter of his wife Sophia to Mahaffy (28 February 1884) in the T.C.D. papers: 'Dr Schliemann speaks daily of you with admiration.' (He invited Mahaffy to contribute an appendix to his *Ilios*.) On Wilamowitz's respect for Mahaffy see his *Recollections* (English edn.), pp. 266–7 and 272 (so, too, in his letter to Mahaffy, 5 November 1909, in the T.C.D. papers); for Reinach's praise see note 7. The T.C.D. papers also contain letters to Mahaffy from the following scholars: Acton, Blass, Bywater, Diels, Dörpfeld, Arthur Evans, Gomperz, Jowett, Lumbroso, Maspero, Flinders Petrie, Ridgeway, Wilcken, Wissowa.

31   *AJP*, xl, 1919, 446–8.

32   Mahaffy to Leslie, 21 April 1912.

33 *Irish Times*, 2 May 1919.
34 Variously phrased versions by T. P. O'Connor (*Daily Telegraph*, 2 May 1919), Gogarty (*It isn't . . .* , p. 51), Leslie (*Doomsland*, pp. 72–3).
35 Information from Miss Olive Purser.
36 Plato, *Laches*, 188d (adapted).

Chapter ten

1 Quoted by K. C. Bailey, *A history of Trinity College, Dublin, 1892–1945*, Dublin, 1947, p. 75.
2 *Social life*, p. 34.
3 D. A. Webb, 'The age of the board', in *TCD: An anthology, 1895–1945*, 1945, pp. 16–19.
4 *Irish Times*, 9 June 1961.
5 *Peplographia Dublinensis*, pp. 95–8.
6 Mahaffy to Wilson King, 15 December 1886.
7 *Irish Times*, 5 January 1916.
8 For accounts of Traill see *TCD*, 14 May 1904, and by R. M. Gwynn in Webb, *Of one company*, pp. 81–4.
9 *TCD*, 12 May 1906.
10 *TCD*, 17 February 1906, and *Of one company*, p. 84.
11 *Of one Company*, p. 96.
12 *Royal commission on university education in Ireland, appendix to the third report, minutes of evidences*, pp. 200–10, H.C. 1902, Cd. 1229, xxxii.
13 *Royal commission on university education in Ireland, appendix to the second report, minutes of evidence*, pp. 215–19, H.C. 1902, Cd. 900.
14 J. W. Mackail and G. Wyndham, *Life and Letters of George Wyndham*, London, 1925, ii, 467–8.
15 Mahaffy to Sidgwick, 22 February 1888, Trinity College, Cambridge MS., 44100.
16 J. W. Mackail and G. Wyndham, *Life and letters of George Wyndham*, i., 216–17.
17 Madden to Balfour, 28 January 1904 (Add. MS. 49815).
18 Board Companion (T.C.D.).
19 Madden to Balfour, 18 February 1904 (Add. MS. 49815).
20 Balfour to Wyndham, 26 February 1904 (Add. MS. 49804). This letter of Balfour's and another on the same subject are printed in 'Two letters relating to the appointment of Anthony Traill to the provostship of Trinity College, Dublin' by R. B. McDowell in *H.*, xcvi, 31–7.
21 *Irish Times*, 23 February 1904; *TCD*, 20 February 1904.
22 Balfour to Wyndham, 16 March 1904 (Add. MS. 49804).
23 Gwynn, *Dublin new and old*, Dublin, 1938 pp. 124–5.
24 J. P. Mahaffy to Wilson King, 19 March 1904 (Leslie papers).
25 It was said that Traill's promotion to the provostship was the result of pressure exercised by the Ulster unionists on the government. We have found no evidence that this was so.
26 C. Asquith, *Diaries 1915–1918*, London, 1968, p. 217.

27　J. P. Mahaffy to Macmillan, 14 February, 18 July 1907 (Add. MS. 55118) Leslie papers; S. Gwynn, *Dublin old and new*, p. 125.

28　MacDonnell to Bryce, 8 March, and Traill to MacDonnell, 24 April 1906 (N.L.I.MS. 11012).

29　MacDonnell to Bryce, 30 April, and Mahaffy to MacDonnell, 30 April 1906 (N.L.I.MS. 11012).

30　Traill to Bryce, 13 May 1906, MacDonnell to Bryce, 21 May 1906 (N.L.I.MS. 11012).

31　*Royal commission Trinity College, Dublin . . . Final report . . . minutes of evidence*, H.C. 1907, Cd 3312, pp. 171–7, xli.

32　Mahaffy to Leslie, 11 March 1908 (Leslie papers).

Chapter eleven

1　*Particular book of Trinity College, Dublin*, 1904, preface, v.

2　*H.*, xxxv, 309; xxxvii, 288.

3　Leslie papers.

4　*Irish Times*, 22 February 1908.

5　*Ibid.*

6　*Georgian Society Records*, iii, 49–50.

7　*The Times*, 22 October 1912; *Irish Times*, 20, 23, 28, 29, 30 October, 12 November 1912; *Hansard*, series xlii, 1763–93; xlvi, 121–3; Mahaffy to Redmond, Thursday, 26 December 1912 (Redmond papers).

8　*TCD*, 11 November 1914; *Irish Times*, 16 September 1914.

9　*Irish Times*, 16 September 1914; *TCD*, 18 November 1914.

10　*TCD*, 10 November 1915.

11　*TCD*, 26 May 1915.

12　*TCD*, 14 May 1919.

13　Information supplied by Dr J. H. Grove-White.

14　W. A. Goligher, Address to University Philosophical Society.

15　Accounts of events in Trinity College during the rising of 1916 are given in Elsie Mahaffy's 'Ireland in 1916: an account of the Dublin rising'; J. Joly, *Reminiscences and anticipation*, 1920, pp. 218–64; and *TCD*, 19 June 1916.

16　J. G. Swift MacNeill, *What I have seen and heard*, 1925, p. 58.

17　Mahaffy privately printed his speeches of 6 September and 19 December 1917 and 15 March 1918 (Irish Convention papers, Box 1).

18　Plunkett to Redmond, 1 September 1917 (Plunkett papers).

19　S. Gwynn, *Dublin old and new*, 1939, pp. 125–6.

20　Lloyd George to Mahaffy, 28 February 1918 (Autograph letters, T.C.D.).

21　Mahaffy to Macmillan, 28 November 1918 (Add. MS. 55118); *Irish Times*, 17 December 1918.

22　*Irish Times*, 23 December 1918.

23　*Dublin Gazette*, 10 September 1918; Mahaffy to A. Macmillan, 24 January 1919 (Add. MS. 55118).

24　Mahaffy to Macmillan, 24 January 1919 (Add. MS. 55118).

25　*Ibid.*

26　*TCD*, 14 May 1919.

Bibliography A

List of books and other separate publications

An address delivered at the opening of the session 1858–9 before the undergraduate Philosophical Society of the University of Dublin, Browne and Nolan, Dublin, 1859.

A commentary on E. Kant's Critick of the pure reason: translated from the History of Modern Philosophy by Prof. K. Fischer, with an Introduction, Longmans, Green, London, 1866.

Twelve lectures on primitive civilizations and their physical conditions, Longmans, Green, London, 1869.

Prolegomena to ancient history, containing Part 1 – The interpretation of legends and inscriptions. Part 2 – A survey of old Egyptian literature, Longmans, Green, London, 1871.

Kant's critical philosophy for English readers, Vols. 1 and 3, Longmans, London, 1872–4. (Vol. 2 not published in this edition.) New edn. (with J. H. Bernard), 2 vols, Macmillan, London, 1889.

Social life in Greece from Homer to Menander, Macmillan, London, 1874; 7th edn., 1890 (with four reprints, 1894–1907).

Rambles and studies in Greece, Macmillan, London, 1876; 7th edn., 1913.

Reply to the 'Remarks' of R. C. Jebb, Esq., M.A., on a review in the 'Academy', Longmans, Green, London, 1876.

Old Greek life, Macmillan, London, 1876. Spanish translation by J. J. Martí, New York, 1884. French translations, Paris (with a supplementary 150 pp.) and Oran, 1889. Mahaffy in his *Summary* refers to Russian and Hungarian translations. See *Greek antiquities* (1889).

Euripides, Macmillan, London, 1879.

Descartes, Blackwood, Edinburgh and London, 1880.

A History of classical Greek literature, Longmans, Green, London, 1880; 5th edn., Macmillan, London, 1910. Russian translation of vol. 1 by A. Wesselowski, Moscow, 1882.

Old Greek education, Kegan Paul, London, 1881.

Über den Ursprung der homerischen Gedichte (with A. W. Sayce, *Über die Sprache der homerischen Gedichte*), Hanover, 1881. Translations of parts of vol. 1 of *A History* etc. above.

The Hippolytus, edited (with J. B. Bury), Macmillan, London, 1881; 2nd edn. 1889.

The decay of modern preaching. An essay, Macmillan, London, 1882.

Victor Duruy's history of Rome edited with an introduction and occasional footnotes, 6 vols., Kelly, London, 1883–6.

Greek life and thought: from the death of Alexander to the Roman Conquest, Macmillan, London, 1887; 2nd edn., 1896.

Alexander's empire (with A. Gilman), T. Fisher Unwin, London, 1887.

The principles of the art of conversation, Macmillan, London, 1887; 2nd edn., 1888.

Greek antiquities (a reprint of *Old Greek Life*, 1876), Macmillan, London, 1889.

Sketches from a tour through Holland and Germany (with J. E. Rogers), Macmillan, London, 1889.

Greek pictures, Religious Tract Society, London, 1890.

The Greek world under Roman sway, Macmillan, London, 1890.

The Flinders Petrie papyri with transcriptions commentaries and index, University Press, Dublin (vol. 1, 1891; Vol. 2, 1893; Vol. 3 (with Gilbart Smyly), 1905).

Problems in Greek history, Macmillan, London, 1892.

The empire of the Ptolemies, Macmillan, London, 1895.

A survey of Greek civilization, Chautauqua Century Press, Meadville, Penna., 1896; Macmillan, London, 1897.

A history of Egypt under the Ptolemaic dynasty, Methuen, London, 1899. (Vol. IV of the Flinders Petrie *History of Egypt*.)

An epoch in Irish history: Trinity College, Dublin, its foundation and early fortunes, 1591–1660, T. Fisher Unwin, London, 1903.

The Particular Book of Trinity College, Dublin, T. Fisher Unwin, London, 1904.

The progress of Hellenism in Alexander's empire, University Press, Chicago, and T. Fisher Unwin, London, 1905.

The silver age of the Greek world, Chicago University Press and T. Fisher Unwin, London, 1906. (An amplified version of *The Greek world under Roman sway*, 1890.)

What have the Greeks done for modern civilisation? (The Lowell Lectures for 1908–9), G. P. Putnam's Sons, New York and London, 1909. Italian translation, Palermo, 1925.

John Stearne: an address delivered in Trinity College at the bicentenary celebrations of the medical school, Dublin, 1912.

The plate in Trinity College, Dublin. A history and a catalogue, Macmillan, London, 1918.

Bibliography B

Introductions to works by other authors

Introduction to Victor Duruy's *History of Greece*, London, 1892 (almost identical with his *Problems in Greek history*).

Introduction to B. P. Grenfell's *Revenue laws of Ptolemy Philadelphus*, Oxford, 1896.

Introduction to *Imaginary conversations by Walter Savage Landor* (selected by Mahaffy), London, 1909, reprinted 1925.

Introduction to *Revolutionary Ireland and its settlement* by Robert H. Murray, London, 1911.

Introduction to *Chronicles of three free cities*, by Wilson King, London, 1914.

Bibliography C

Articles and addresses on classical, modern Greek and Egyptological topics

Unsigned articles, reprints and second publications of articles are not listed. Mahaffy, in his *Summary*, refers in general terms to unsigned articles in *Ath.*, which, he says, contained some of his best work, especially his obituary notices of famous Irishmen during a period of twenty years.

1869

'Three epochs in the social development of the ancient Greeks', in *The afternoon lectures in literature and art*, fifth series, 1867–8, Dublin and London, 1869.

1873

'Notes' (on Aristophanes, *Knights*, 258–65; Euripides, *Medea*, 68; Tacitus, *Annals* II, 29), *H.*, i, 237–42.

1874

'The degradation of Ulysses in Greek literature', *H.*, ii, 265–75.

1875

'The Olympic games at Athens in 1875', *MM*, xxxii, 324–7.
'Archaeological notes from Greece', *Ac.*, 26 June, 662.
'The lion of Chaeronea', *Ac.*, 6 November, 481.
'The museums of Athens', *Ac.*, 11 December, 604–5.

1876

'The humanity of the Greeks', *MM*, xxxiii, 355–67.
'Theseus or Hermes?', *Ac.*, 1 January, 12.
'The lion of Chaeronea', *Ac.*, 11 March, 242.
Review of R. C. Jebb's *Attic Orators* etc., *Ac.*, 1 April, 314–16.
'The cats in ancient Greece', *Ac.*, September, 291.
'Studies in Greek literature: Hesiod', *H.*, iv, 297–330.

1877

'Old Greek athletics', *MM*, xxxvi, 61–9.
'Modern excavations', *Cont. R.*, xxix, 888–900.

1878

'Schliemann's Mycenae', *MM*, xxxvii, 214–30.
'Recent Homeric studies: Gladstone, Geddes, Jebb', *MM*, xxxviii,
    405–16. 'Modern Greece' (a review article on Finlay's *History of
    Greece*), *Cont. R.*, xxxi, 728–44.

1879

'The Age of Homer. II. Mr Paley's recent criticism', *MM*, xxxix,
    314–25. 'Recent Homeric criticism – Mr Paley's defence', *MM*,
    xxxix, 524–9. 'On the date of the capture of Mycenae by the Argives',
    H., v, 60–66. 'Supplemental note on the destruction of Mycenae by
    the Argives', *H.*, v, 277–8.
'Notes' (on Thucydides, Plato and Demosthenes), *H.*, vi, 458–64.

1880

Review of Kock's *Comicorum Atticorum Fragmenta*, *Ac.*, 11 December,
    426–7.
'On the relation of Novum Ilium to the Ilios of Homer', Appen-
    dix 2 to *Ilios* by Henry Schliemann.

1881

'Notes' (on Euripides, Plato, Herodotus, and Thucydides), *H.*,
    vii, 82–9.
Kock's *Greek Comic Fragments*, *Ac.*, 12 February, 120.
'On the authenticity of the Olympian Register', *JHS*, ii, 164–78.
    Sᴍ

1882

'The site and antiquity of the Hellenic Ilion', *JHS*, iii, 69–80.
'Brentano on the site of Troy', *Ac.*, 21 October, 300–1.
Review of Monro's *Homeric Grammar, Ac.*, 16 December, 436–7.

1883

'Contemporary records: Greek classics and archaeology', *Cont. R.*,
xliv, 936–9.

1884

'Greece in 1884', *The English Illustrated Magazine*, i, 772–6.
'Three books on the Greek drama', *Ac.*, 2 February, 81–2.
'Mr Tyrrell on Mr Sayce's "Herodotus": a reply', *H.*, x, 98–105.
'Contemporary records: Classical philology', *Cont. R.*, xlv, 901–5.

1888

Review of *Athos, or the mountain of the monks* by A. Riley, *The Church
Quarterly Review*, xxvi, 222–8.
'Monasteries and religion in modern Greece', *The Chautauquan*, ix,
1–3.
'Greek history', *ib.*, 65–7.
'Greek history', *ib.*, 127–29.

1889

'The new constitution of Greece', *ib.*, 191–3.
'Features of the country: the Morea', *ib.*, 255–8.
'Alps and plains of Greece', *ib.*, 319–21.
'Present condition and prospects of Greece', *ib.*, 383–5.
'The theatre of Dionysus at Athens', *Ac.*, 4 May, 313.
'The work of Mago on agriculture', *H.*, xv, 29–35.
'Notes from Mount Athos', *Ath.*, 18 May, 631.
'Carolus Gabriel Cobet', *Ath.*, 9 November, 635.
'Mount Athos in 1889', *Murray's Magazine*, v, 782–94.

1890

'The Petrie papyri. Acts of a Greek probate court in the Fayoum',
Ath., 25 October, 547–8.

'The Petrie papyri II. The classical fragments', *Ath.*, 6 December, 777.
'The slave wars against Rome', *H.*, xvi, 167–82.

1891

'New fragments of the Antiope of Euripides', *H.*, xvii, 38–51.
'The Petrie papyri III', *Ath.*, 25 April, 536–7.
'The Petrie papyri IV', *Ath.*, 11 July, 63.
'The Petrie papyri V', *Ath.*, 7 November, 617–18.
Translation of a Ptolemaic will in W. M. F. Petrie's *Illahun, Kahun and Gurob 1889–90*, London, 46–7.

1892

'The Petrie papyri VI', *Ath.*, 30 July, 160.
'The Petrie papyri VII. The *Laches* of Plato', *Ath.*, 29 October, 591.
'The Petrie papyri VIII. A new historical document', *Ath.*, 10 December, 818.
'The Petrie papyri', *New Review*, vii, 549–61.

1893

'An ancient payprus fragment of the *Laches* of Plato', *H.*, xix, 310–21.
'Further gleanings from the papyri', *New Review*, ix, 526–35.
'On the Antiope fragment', *CR*, v, 186–7.
'Su i papiri greci e demotici trovati nel Fayum dal sign. Petrie', *Rendiconti della reale Accademia dei Lincei, Classe di sc. morale etc.*, ser. v, ii, 3, 4, 199–203.

1894

'Notes from Nubia', *Ath.*, 17 February, 219.
'Notes from Nubia II', *Ath.*, 17 March, 353.
'Notes from Nubia III', *Ath.*, 7 April, 451.
'Notes from Nubia IV', *Ath.*, 28 May, 546–7.
'Documents égyptiens', *Bulletin de correspondance hellénique*, xviii, 145–54.
'The Flinders Petrie papyri Part II', *Ath.*, 21 April, 511.
'Recent archaeology', *NC*, xxxv, 845–62.
'The proposed Nile reservoir. The devastation of Nubia', *NC*, xxxv, 1013–18.
'Recent archaeology', *NC*, xxxvi, 268–78.

'A new Greek papyrus', *Ath.*, 21 July, 98.
'The present position of Egyptology', *NC*, xxxvi, 268–78.

1895

'Pauly's Real-Encyclopaedie', *H.*, xxi, 155–9.
'On two inscriptions from Dimeh (Fayyûm)', *H.*, xxi, 160–4.
'A new inscription from the Fayyûm', *H.*, xxi, 243–7.
'British Museum papyrus cccci', *H.*, xxi, 251–4.
'Forms of politeness in Greek letters', *Ath.*, 13 July, 67.
'Greek papyri', *The Chautauquan*, xvi, 413.

1896

'The new inscription at Philae', *Ath.*, 21 March, 388.
'A stele from Aswân in the British Museum', *H.*, xxii, 273–90.
'The royalty of Pergamum', *H.*, xxii, 389–405.
'The laws of succession among the Ptolemies', *Ath.*, 1 August, 164.

1897

'Pompey's pillar at Alexandria', *Ath.*, 27 February, 285–6.
'Pompey's pillar at Alexandria' (a reply to criticisms of the previous
    article by Flinders Petrie), *Ath.*, 17 April, 516.
'Greek inscriptions at Clandeboye', *Ath.*, 22 May, 688–9.
'New papyri', *Ath.*, 27 November, 750.
'About Alexandria', *NC*, xli, 437–45.
'Papiro greco inedito', *Rendiconti della reale Accademia dei Lincei*,
    Classe di sc. morale etc., ser. v, vi, 91–6.
Review of Jannaris' *Historical Greek Grammar*, *Annual of the British
    School at Athens*, iii, 215–20.
'Pompey's pillar', *Cosmopolis*, vi, 39–47.

1898

'On new papyrus fragments from the Ashmolean Museum at Oxford',
    Transactions of the Royal Irish Academy, 31, 197–208.
'The army of Ptolemy IV at Raphia', *H.*, xxiv, 140–52.

1900

'On Antigonus' letter to Scepsis', *CR*, xiv, 54.

'The ancient name of Smith', *Ath.*, 14 March, 465.
'Les deux Ptolemées IV et IX', *Atti del Congresso Internationale di Scienze Storiche*, ii, iii.
'Greek inscriptions at Didlington Hall, Norfolk', *Ath.*, 20 November, 517.

1901

'A second edition of some Petrie papyri with additions and corrections', *Archiv für Papyrusforschung*, i, 285–90.

1905

'The Jews in Egypt', *Mélanges Nicole*, Geneva, 1905, 659–62.

1908

'Magdola-papyri xxxvii and xi', *Archiv für Papyrusforschung*, iv, 56–9.
'A new inscription', *Archiv für Papyrusforschung*, iv, 167–8.

1909

'On a passage in Euripides' *Hypsipyle*', *H.*, xxxv, 347–52.

1910

Contributions to Herbert Spencer's *Descriptive sociology*, no. 10, division 2, London, 1910. Further contributions to no. 12, division 2, London, 1928, were completed by W. A. Goligher.

1911

'The decay of papyrus culture in Egypt', *H.*, xxxvii, 237–41.

1912

'Pauly-Wissowa's Encylopaedie vol. vii', *H.*, xxxviii, 174–5.
Review of Lesquier's *Les institutions militaires de l'Egypte sous les Lagides*, *H.*, xxxviii, 179.

1913

Review of Walker's *Hellenica Oxyrhynchia, H.*, xxxix, 427–9.
'The arithmetical figures used by Greek writers during the classical
  period', *Essays and studies presented to William Ridgeway*, Cambridge, 1913, 195–7.

1915

'Cleopatra VI', *Journal of Egyptian Archaeology*, ii, 1–4.

1916

Summary of a speech on 'Plato and Poetry' (delivered 28 January
  1916), *Proceedings of the Classical Association of Ireland for 1915–
  16*, 77–81.

1918

Summary of a speech on 'Alexandria and its literary influence'
  (communicated 25 January 1918), *Proceedings of the Classical
  Association of Ireland for 1917–18*, 60–3.

Bibliography D

Articles and addresses on other topics

1867

'The Duke of Argyll and the reign of law', *Cont. R.*, v, 68–84.

1869

'Trinity College, Dublin', *MM*, xx, 463–72.

1871

'Life in Trinity College, Dublin', *The Dark Blue*, i, 487–93.

1875

'The tercentenary festival at Leyden', *MM*, xxxi, 516–21.

1878

'Dr William Stokes of Dublin, a personal sketch', *MM*, xxxvii, 299–303.

1882

'The Irish landlords', *Cont. R.*, 160–76.
'John Inglesant', *Hibernia*, 1 April, 53.
'Education in Saxony', *Ath.*, 12 August, 208.
'The education in Hungary', *Ath.*, 7 October, 82, 464–5, and *Ath.*, 14 October, 496.

1884

'Untrodden Italy–the Sila forest', *Cont. R.*, xlvi, 87–96.
'The decay of genius', *MM*, 1, 355–62.

1890

'Higher education in America', *Ath.*, 11 October, 482.
'Country life in Ireland', *Review of Reviews*, ii, 155.

1892

'The tercentenary of Trinity College, Dublin', *NC*, xxxii, 77–96.
Four chapters on the history of T.C.D. from the foundation to the
   close of the 18th century and one on the College plate, in *The book
   of Trinity College, Dublin*, Belfast, Ward, 1892.

1893

'Sham education', *NC*, xxxiii, 19–35. (See also *Spectator*, 21 January,
   'Lord Justice Bowen on the professor'.)
'The future of education', *NC*, xxxiv, 212–29.
'What is a nation?', *New Review*, viii, 349–62.

1895

'Provincial patriotism', *NC*, xxxvii, 1027–35.

1896

International jealousy', *NC*, xxxix, 529–43.
'The modern Babel', *NC*, xl, 782–96.

1897

'Modern education', *NC*, xlii, 703–18.

1898

'How to circumvent "cramming" in Irish secondary education',
   NC, xliv, 867–80. Also, see under 1902 below.

1899

'Recent fuss about the Irish language', *NC*, xlvi, 213–22. (Also in
   Living Age, 110 ff., 223; *Ecclesiastical Magazine*, 133, 880 ff.)

1900

'Attachment against Sir James Carroll', *H.*, xxvi, 122–5.

1901

'The Romanisation of Ireland', *NC*, 1, 31–43.

1902

'Sermon on Bishop John Stearn', preached in 1898, published in *Peplographia Dublinensis*, ed. by J. H. Bernard, London, 1902, 85–98.

1903

'The library of Trinity College, Dublin: the growth of a legend', *H.*, xxviii, 68–78.
'The drifting of doctrine', *Hibbert Journal*, i, 498–509.

1905

'On the history of sizarship in Trinity College', *H.*, xxxi, 315–18.

1906

'Irishtown near Dublin', *H.*, xxxii, 165–7.

1907

'Elizabethan Ireland' (a lecture to the Royal Dublin Society), *Church of Ireland Gazette*, 22, 30 March, 5, 12 April, 225, 249–50, 277, 301.

1909

'Notes on the architectural history of Trinity College', *H.*, xxxv, 303–10.

1910

'Notes on the architectural history of Trinity College', *H.*, xxxvi, 11–18.

1911

'Letters about the Georgian Society', *Ath.*, 18 March and 9 September.
'About the front of Trinity College', *H.*, xxxvii, 288–90.

    TM

1912

'Two notes on Trinity College', *H.*, xxxviii, 177.

'Memorandum on trout fishing', *Report of the departmental committee on Irish inland fisheries*, Dublin, 1912, 15–21.

'What is nationality?', *Blackwood's Mag.*, cxci, 155–61.

'Will home rule be Rome rule?', *Blackwood's Mag.*, cxcii, 153–9.

'The furnishings of Georgian houses in Dublin in the early part of the century', *Georgian Society Records*, iv, 1–10.

'John Stearn: an address delivered to Trinity College at the bicentenary celebration of the medical school', 5–7 July 1916.

1913

'On the origins of learned academies in modern Europe', *Proc. R.I.A.*, xxx, C, 429–44.

'Introduction' (on Irish country houses), *Georgian Society Records*, v, 1–22.

'Mount Ievers', *ib.*, v, 23–9, 35–42.

'Bellamont Forest' (Co. Cavan), v, 35–42.

1914

'Two early tours in Ireland', *H.*, xl, 1–16.

1917

'On the introduction of the ass as a beast of burden into Ireland', *Proc. R.I.A.*, xxxiii, C, 530–8.

'The post-assaying found on dated pieces of plate in the collection of Trinity College, Dublin', *Proc. R.I.A.*, xxxiv, C, 33–46.

1918

'The ethics of retaliation', *Ad clerum: lectures delivered in the Regent House, Trinity College, Dublin, July 8th to 13th, 1918*, ed. A. J. Johnston, A. Lockett Ford, and J. G. F. Day, Dublin, 1918, 178–85.

1919

'The origin and growth of pensioners in the colleges of Cambridge and in Dublin', *H.*, xli, 175–83.

'Students' fees and tutorial duties', *H.*, xli, 184–203.

Bibliography E

Poems and classical compositions

Aere perennius, a version in sixteenth Latin hendecasyllables of Goethe's lines on a monument to Gellert, *Kottabos*, i. 1869, 29.

Epitaph on the books of a certain closed library, 8 lines of English heroic couplets, *Kottabos*, iii, 2, 1870, 24.

Translation into Latin of two lines from the Greek Anthology (on Niobe), *Kottabos*, v, 1870, 127.

Folia caduca: verses to three grandchildren, printed for private circulation, 1893. No copy has been traced. The sole printed reference to this is in the short bibliography of Mahaffy's works in the *Irish Book Lover*, x, 1919, 112.

Dedicatory epigram (6 Greek iambic trimeters), in *Mélanges Nicole*, Geneva, 1905.

Epitaph suggested for R. Y. Tyrrell, see *H.*, xlii, viii (and p. 175 above).

Bibliography F

Letters to *The Times*

On the Irish University Bill, 25 February 1873.

On the Irish University Bill, 21 May 1879.

On Toronto musical degrees, 27 May 1890.

On Dublin graduates tercentenary memorial, 14 March 1892 and 11 February 1896.

On education, 9 October 1897.

On Victoria university, 23, 24, 28 March 1898.

On accession oath, 4 July 1910.

On position of Trinity College, Dublin, under the Home Rule Bill, 23 October and 14 November 1912.

On exclusion of Ulster, 24 February 1914.

On the destruction of Louvain, 1 September 1914.

On position of Trinity College, Dublin, 4 September 1914.

On inclusion of Trinity College, Dublin, in the Universities Financial Relief Bill, 3 March 1915.

On Sinn Fein revolt, 16 May 1916.

On reconstruction proposals, 27 June 1916.

On exchange of British and German prisoners, 20 November 1916.

On German proposal to retain the *status quo*, 20 August 1917.

On the administration of Ireland, 24 November 1917.

List of sources

Manuscript sources

London
    British Museum
        Balfour papers
        Macmillan papers

    Plunkett House
        Plunkett papers

Cambridge
    Trinity College Library
        Sidgwick papers

Dublin
    National Library
        Bryce papers
        Redmond Papers

    Trinity College, manuscript room
        Mahaffy autographs
        Mahaffy notebooks
        Salmon papers

    Trinity College, muniment room
        Leslie papers
        Mahaffy correspondence

In the private possession of Mr Rupert Mahaffy
    'Brief summary of the principal stages of my life . . .', composed in
    1919 by J. P. Mahaffy.

Printed sources

FEARON, W. R. F.: 'Gentlemen, the Provost', *The Irish Digest*, July 1939, 73–6.

GOGARTY, OLIVER ST JOHN: *It isn't this time of year at all*, London, 1952.

Tumbling in the hay, London, 1939.

GOLIGHER, W. A.: Address to the Dublin University Philosophical Society (unpublished).

GWYNN, STEPHEN: *Saints and Scholars*, London, 1929.

HART-DAVIS, R.: *The letters of Oscar Wilde*, London, 1962.

HONE, W. P.: *Cricket in Ireland*, Tralee, 1956.

LESLIE, SHANE: *Doomsland*, London, 1923.

LYONS, F. S. L: 'John Pentland Mahaffy and the "Phil." ', *University Philosophical Society: centenary review*, Dublin, 1953, 40–3.

O'CONNOR, ULICK: *Oliver St John Gogarty*, London, 1964.

ROGERS, ROGER WILLIAM: 'Sir John Pentland Mahaffy', *Methodist Review*, July, 1919, 507–17.

SAYCE, A. H.: *Reminiscences*, London, 1923.

STARKIE, WALTER F.: 'Sir John Pentland Mahaffy', *Of one company*, ed. D. A. Webb, Dublin, 1951, 89–100.

Scholars and gypsies, London, 1963.

WEBB, D. A., ed., *Of one company*, Dublin, 1951.

Select index of names